Vocabulary for Achievement

FIRST COURSE

Margaret Ann Richek

Arlin T. McRae

Susan K. Weiler

GREAT SOURCE
WILMINGTON, MA

AUTHORS

Margaret Ann Richek
Professor of Education, Northeastern Illinois University; consultant in reading and vocabulary study; author of The World of Words *(Houghton Mifflin)*

Arlin T. McRae
Supervisor of English, Evansville-Vanderburgh School Corporation, Evansville, Indiana; Adjunct Instructor in English, University of Evansville

Susan K. Weiler
Instructor of Art History at John Carroll University in Cleveland, Ohio; former teacher of Latin, Beaumont School for Girls, Cleveland Heights, Ohio

CONSULTANT

Larry S. Krieger
Social Studies Supervisor, Montgomery Township Public Schools, New Jersey; author of World History *and* U.S. History *(D.C. Heath), co-author of* Mastering the Verbal SAT 1/PSAT *(Great Source)*

CLASSROOM CONSULTANTS

Jack Pelletier
Teacher of English, Mira Loma High School, Sacramento, California

Valerie M. Webster
Teacher of English, Walnut Hill School, Natick, Massachusetts

ACKNOWLEDGMENTS

Definitions for the three hundred words taught in this textbook are based on Houghton Mifflin dictionaries—in particular, the *Houghton Mifflin Student Dictionary*—but have been abbreviated and adapted for instructional purposes. The dictionary entries in the skill lessons on pages 19–20 and 39–40 are from the *Houghton Mifflin Student Dictionary*, copyright © 1986; those on pages 59–60 are from the *Houghton Mifflin College Dictionary*, copyright © 1986. The pronunciation key on the inside front cover is adapted from *The American Heritage Dictionary of the English Language, Third Edition*, copyright © 1992.

CREDITS

Production: PC&F, Inc.

Illustrations: Dick Cole: pages 31, 191; Simon Galkin: pages 111, 131; Sal Murdocca: page 97; Charles Scogins: pages 17, 25, 57, 65, 105; Valerie Winemiller: pages 45, 77

Printed in the United States of America

ISBN: 0-669-46477-5

10 HS 04

CONTENTS

COMPLETE WORD LIST

Even though you have probably used dictionaries many times, you may not be aware of all the kinds of information they contain. Besides providing definitions and pronunciations of words, some dictionaries also give information about word origin, tips about how to use words correctly, facts about geography, and short biographies of well-known people. Certain dictionaries even provide illustrations and photographs that add to the information given in definitions. In this lesson you will learn words that describe the parts of a dictionary and the task of making a dictionary. In addition, you will read an article on how dictionaries were developed.

WORD LIST

abridge
browse
citation
compendium
etymology
gazetteer
glossary
lexicography
phonetics
syllabication

DEFINITIONS

After you have studied the definitions and example for each word, write the vocabulary word on the line to the right.

1. **abridge** (ə-brĭj′) *verb* To shorten a piece of written material, such as a dictionary. (From the Latin word *abbreviare,* meaning "to shorten")

   Related Word **abridgment** *noun*
   Example The president of the company asked the secretary to *abridge* the report.

   1. _____
   MEMORY CUE: *Abridge* and *abbreviate* have the same Latin root—*brevis,* "short."

2. **browse** (brouz) *verb* **a.** To read here and there in a book or other piece of written material. **b.** To look in a casual manner.

   Example While I was *browsing* through the dictionary, I noticed an interesting word origin.

   2. _____
   USAGE NOTE: *Browse* can also mean "to feed on young shoots and other vegetation." When you browse through a book, you "nibble" from the text.

3. **citation** (sī-tā′shən) *noun* **a.** A quotation or reference from a source that has a reputation for accuracy. **b.** A summons that calls for an appearance in court. (From the Latin word *citare,* meaning "to summon")

   Related Word **cite** *verb*
   Example Dictionary entries sometimes contain *citations* showing how a word is used.

   3. _____

4. **compendium** (kəm-pĕn′dē-əm) *noun* A short but complete summary of information on a topic. (From the Latin word *compendere,* meaning "to weigh together")

   Example The baseball team's annual magazine was a *compendium* of the highlights of that season.

   4. _____

5. **etymology** (ĕt′ə-mŏl′ə-jē) *noun*   **a.** The study of the origin and history of words.   **b.** The origin and history of a particular word. (From the Greek word *etymon*, meaning "true sense of a word")

   Related Words   etymological *adjective;* etymologist *noun*
   Example   By reading the *etymology,* Paul learned that the word *panel* comes from *pannus,* the Latin word for *cloth.*

   5. _____

6. **gazetteer** (găz′ĭ-tîr′) *noun*   A dictionary or a section of a dictionary that contains the names of places and information about those places.

   Example   The *gazetteer* says that Casablanca is in Morocco.

   6. _____

7. **glossary** (glô′sə-rē) *noun*   A list of terms and their definitions, often placed at the back of a book. (From the Latin word *glossa,* meaning "an unfamiliar word")

   Example   Larry found the definition of *glucose* in the *glossary* of his science textbook.

   7. _____

8. **lexicography** (lĕk′sĭ-kŏg′rə-fē) *noun*   The process of writing or of compiling a dictionary. (From the Greek words *lexis,* meaning "word," and *graphein,* meaning "to write")

   Related Word   lexicographer *noun*
   Example   Because James had always been interested in words, he prepared for a career in *lexicography.*

   8. _____

9. **phonetics** (fə-nĕt′ĭks) *noun*   The study of the sounds of language. (From the Greek word *phōnein,* meaning "to speak")

   Related Words   phonetic *adjective;* phonetically *adverb*
   Example   *Phonetics* is a fascinating area of language study.

   9. _____
   USAGE NOTE: You must use a singular verb with the word *phonetics:* "*Phonetics* is interesting."

10. **syllabication** (sĭ-lăb′ə-kā′shən) *noun*   The process of dividing words into units of sound called *syllables.*

    Related Words   syllabicate *verb;* syllable *noun*
    Example   The *syllabication* of the word *division* is *di vi sion.*

    10. _____

EXERCISE 1 COMPLETING DEFINITIONS

On the answer line, write the word from the vocabulary list that best completes each definition.

1. When you look casually through a book, you _____.

2. A word's origin and history are known as its _____.

3. If you shorten a piece of writing, you _____ it.

4. Dividing words into units of sound is known as _____.

5. A list of difficult words and their meanings in the back of a book is a _____.

6. A quotation from a reliable source is a _____.

7. A short but complete summary is a _____.

8. When you study the sounds of language, you study _____.

9. A person who writes or compiles a dictionary is involved in _____.

10. A reference book that lists the names of places is a _____.

1. _____

2. _____

3. _____

4. _____

5. _____

6. _____

7. _____

8. _____

9. _____

10. _____

EXERCISE 2 USING WORDS CORRECTLY

Each of the following questions contains an italicized vocabulary word. Decide the answer to the question, and write *Yes* or *No* on the answer line.

1. Would you look in an *etymology* for information about Dallas, Texas?

2. If you *abridge* your class report, do you shorten it?

3. Might the *syllabication* of a word help you to pronounce it?

4. Would a *glossary* be useful if you were reading a textbook on an unfamiliar subject?

5. Does a *gazetteer* list verbs and pronouns?

6. Would the study of *phonetics* help you to understand the sounds of language?

7. When you quote a passage from an encyclopedia, are you making a *citation*?

8. Is *lexicography* the study of land formations?

9. Is a definition in a dictionary also known as a *compendium*?

10. If you are to study a textbook chapter carefully, should you *browse*?

1. _____

2. _____

3. _____

4. _____

5. _____

6. _____

7. _____

8. _____

9. _____

10. _____

EXERCISE 3 CHOOSING THE BEST WORD

Decide which vocabulary word or related form best expresses the meaning of the italicized word or phrase in the sentence. On the answer line, write the letter of that word.

1. Barney was unable to read his art history book without looking at the *list of difficult words and their definitions.*
   a. glossary   **b.** etymology   **c.** compendium   **d.** citations

   1. _____

2. The word *prim* has an uncertain *history and origin.*
   a. phonetic   **b.** etymology   **c.** syllabication   **d.** abridgment

   2. _____

3. Through *the study of the sounds of language,* experts have developed symbols for pronouncing words.
   a. phonetics   **b.** lexicography   **c.** syllabication   **d.** browsing

   3. _____

4. *Dividing a word* can help a person to pronounce the word.
   a. Citation   **b.** Browsing   **c.** Lexicography   **d.** Syllabication

   4. _____

5. Ramona became a dictionary editor because of her interest in *the writing and compilation of dictionaries.*
   a. abridgments   **b.** browsing   **c.** citations   **d.** lexicography

   5. _____

6. Many people read the *shortened* version of the novel *Don Quixote.*
   a. browsed   **b.** phonetic   **c.** abridged   **d.** etymological

   6. _____

7. Jacques liked to *read bits and pieces of* the books in the library's mystery section.
   a. gloss   **b.** syllabicate   **c.** browse through   **d.** cite

   7. _____

8. Mary used a *quotation* from a medical journal.
   a. glossary   **b.** citation   **c.** syllabication   **d.** compendium

   8. _____

9. Our classroom has a *short but complete summary* of William Shakespeare's plays.
   a. gazetteer   **b.** lexicon   **c.** compendium   **d.** syllable

   9. _____

10. To find out where Timbuktu is, look in a book with a *list of place names.*
    a. etymology   **b.** browse   **c.** syllable   **d.** gazetteer

    10. _____

EXERCISE 4 USING DIFFERENT FORMS OF WORDS

Decide which form of the vocabulary word in parentheses best completes the sentence. The form given may be correct. Write your answer on the answer line.

1. The teacher prepared a _____ of the students' reports. (*compendium*)

   1. _____

2. An _____ is a person who studies the origin and history of words. (*etymology*)

   2. _____

3. Ben's ambition is to be a _____. (*lexicography*)

   3. _____

4. The newspapers printed an _____ of the speech. (*abridge*)

   4. _____

5. Lorraine had to look through three _____ before finding the information. (*gazetteer*)

   5. _____

6. A skillful poet considers the number of _____ in each word of a poem. *(syllabication)*

6. _____

7. In court the lawyer _____ a little-known decision. *(citation)*

7. _____

8. _____ through bookstores is one of Loretta's favorite activities. *(browse)*

8. _____

9. The experienced reader can often sound out unfamiliar words _____. *(phonetics)*

9. _____

10. It is helpful to have a _____ in the back of a textbook. *(glossary)*

10. _____

READING COMPREHENSION

Each numbered sentence in the following passage contains an italicized vocabulary word or related form. After you have read the passage, you will complete an exercise.

A SHORT HISTORY OF DICTIONARIES

(1) The dictionary, which is now a vast storehouse of definitions, *etymologies,* and other information about words, had a humble beginning about fourteen hundred years ago in Europe. At that time, monks studied books and documents that were written in Latin. (2) When some of the monks *browsed* through the materials, they could not understand difficult Latin words. To help them, monks who had mastered Latin wrote definitions of difficult words in the margins. (3) Later monks translated the definitions into English and collected them into *glosssaries.*

(4) Although later writers gathered words into *compendiums,* these books did not contain accurate definitions. (5) The first *lexicographer* to attempt to write an accurate dictionary of the English language was Samuel Johnson, an English writer who lived in the 1700s.

The first American dictionary appeared in 1806. Entitled *A Compendious Dictionary of the English Language,* it was the work of Noah Webster. Webster attempted to make the spellings of words more standard. (6) His first dictionary includes words that are spelled *phonetically,* such as *thum* instead of *thumb* and *hed* instead of *head.* Only a few of Webster's changes, such as ending *theater* with *-er* instead of *-re,* caught on.

Another famous dictionary is *The Oxford English Dictionary,* a series of thirteen volumes providing detailed definitions. (7) In compiling this dictionary, the editors received thousands of words and *citations* from volunteer readers. When the dictionary was completed in 1928, it contained more than 400,000 entries.

(8) Early dictionaries were difficult for children to use, and even *abridged* dictionaries included words that children were not likely to look up. To help students, Edward L. Thorndike compiled the *Thorndike-Century Junior Dictionary,* which was published in 1935. Since then, other dictionaries, including the *Houghton Mifflin Student Dictionary,* have proven popular among both students and teachers.

(9) Today, all dictionaries give information about pronunciation, meaning, *syllabication,* and parts of speech. (10) In addition, some include *gazetteers* and short biographies of famous people. With these additional features, dictionaries are better able to give us an accurate picture of our changing language.

Words About Dictionaries   **5**

Each of the following statements corresponds to a numbered sentence in the passage. Each statement contains a blank and is followed by four answer choices. Decide which choice fits best in the blank. The word or phrase that you choose must express roughly the same meaning as the italicized word in the passage. Write the letter of your choice on the answer line.

1. Present dictionaries contain much information about words, including
   _____ .
   a. definitions
   b. sentences
   c. pronunciation marks
   d. word histories

   1. _____

2. When monks _____, they sometimes did not understand difficult Latin words.
   a. went to church
   b. translated books
   c. looked casually through books
   d. read books closely

   2. _____

3. Later monks collected the definitions in the margins into _____ .
   a. encyclopedias
   b. lists of words and definitions
   c. pronunciations of names
   d. spelling rules

   3. _____

4. Early _____ did not contain accurate definitions.
   a. Latin documents
   b. collections of words
   c. encyclopedias
   d. indexes

   4. _____

5. Samuel Johnson was an early _____ .
   a. writer of essays   b. drama critic   c. dictionary writer   d. monk

   5. _____

6. Noah Webster tried to get people to spell _____ .
   a. by sound   b. by memory   c. correctly   d. in old-fashioned ways

   6. _____

7. For *The Oxford English Dictionary*, volunteer readers sent in words and _____ .
   a. histories   b. articles   c. symbols   d. quotations

   7. _____

8. Even _____ dictionaries had words that children were not likely to use.
   a. picture   b. computer   c. shortened   d. difficult

   8. _____

9. Modern dictionaries give information about parts of speech, pronunciation, meaning, and _____ .
   a. division of words into units of sound
   b. geographical locations
   c. histories of words
   d. famous people

   9. _____

10. _____ and short biographies may be found in some dictionaries.
    a. Lists of newspapers
    b. Famous quotations
    c. Lists of symbols
    d. Information about places

    10. _____

WRITING ASSIGNMENT

Select a topic in which you are especially interested, such as music, sports, computers, television, or photography. Acting as a lexicographer, create a dictionary of terms that are commonly used in that field. In your dictionary you should show each term, its syllabication, its part of speech, and its definition. Write the definitions of the terms in your own words, and include at least ten terms. Make sure that your definitions are clear to someone who has little knowledge about this field.

$\mathbf{A}$lthough most people associate teaching with school, teaching also occurs in many other places. You have probably had many teaching experiences already, such as telling a friend how to make a basketball shot or showing a child how to tie shoelaces. The words you will study in this lesson may help you to become a more effective teacher, for they will make you aware of different methods of explaining, instructing, and showing.

WORD LIST

academic
clarify
confide
disclose
enlighten
exhibit
expound
ingrained
sage
seminar

DEFINITIONS

After you have studied the definitions and example for each word, write the vocabulary word on the line to the right.

1. **academic** (ăk′ə-děm′ĭk) *adjective*   Scholarly; relating to general or liberal arts courses rather than to vocational education. (From the Greek word *Akadēmia,* the name of the school where the philosopher Plato taught)

   Related Words   **academically** *adverb;* **academy** *noun*
   Example   English, social studies, mathematics, science, and foreign languages are *academic* courses.

1. _____

2. **clarify** (klăr′ə-fī′) *verb*   To make clear or easy to understand. (From the Latin words *clarus,* meaning "clear," and *facere,* meaning "to make")

   Related Word   **clarification** *noun*
   Example   The article was difficult to understand because the writer had not *clarified* the directions for building a birdhouse.

2. _____

3. **confide** (kən-fīd′) *verb*   To share a secret (with) in private. (From the Latin *confidere,* meaning "to trust with confidence")

   Related Words   **confidence** *noun;* **confidential** *adjective*
   Example   Laurel wanted to know her roommate better before she *confided* in her.

3. _____
See *disclose.*

4. **disclose** (dĭ-sklōz′) *verb*   To uncover or bring into view; to reveal; to make known.

   Related Word   **disclosure** *noun*
   Example   Aunt Tillie will not read movie reviews because they *disclose* the endings.

4. _____
USAGE NOTE: *Disclose* means "to bring into the open." *Confide* implies secrecy.

5. **enlighten** (ĕn-līt′n) *verb* To furnish with information or knowledge; to inform; to give new insight.

   Related Word enlightenment *noun*
   Example The cooking instructor's helpful hints *enlightened* us about the best way to knead bread.

5. _____

6. **exhibit** (ĭg-zĭb′ĭt) *verb* To show or display; to present to public view. *noun* A display; something displayed. (From the Latin *ex-*, meaning "out," and *habere*, meaning "to hold")

   Related Word exhibition *noun*
   Example Marathon runners *exhibit* strength and courage.

6. _____
USAGE NOTE: Compare *exhibit* with *inhibit*, which means "to hold back"

7. **expound** (ĭk-spound′) *verb* To make a detailed statement on a topic. (From the Latin *ex-*, meaning "out," and *ponere*, meaning "to place")

   Example The director of the trailside museum will *expound* on the causes of the historic battle.

7. _____

8. **ingrained** (ĭn-grānd′) *adjective* Impressed firmly on the mind; established deeply.

   Example For Richard, reading the newspaper every morning was an *ingrained* habit.

8. _____
USAGE NOTE: *Ingrained* can also mean "worked deeply into the texture or fiber"—into the *grain*—a physical action.

9. **sage** (sāj) *noun* A person who is respected for experience, judgment, and wisdom. *adjective* Showing wisdom and good judgment. (From the Latin word *sapere*, meaning "to be wise")

   Related Words sagacity *noun;* sagely *adverb*
   Example Confucius was a beloved *sage* whose wise words are still respected by many.

9. _____

10. **seminar** (sĕm′ə-när′) *noun* A group discussion involving an exchange of ideas on a particular topic; a conference.

    Example Gina is attending a *seminar* on fourteenth-century painters.

10. _____

EXERCISE 1 WRITING CORRECT WORDS

On the answer line, write the word from the vocabulary list that fits
each definition.

1. To provide with new information

2. To make a detailed statement on a topic

3. A conference where a specific topic is discussed

4. To show, display, or present to the public

5. Relating to liberal arts rather than to vocational courses

6. To tell something in secret

7. A wise, respected person

8. To make clear or easy to understand

9. To uncover; to reveal; to make known

10. Impressed firmly on the mind

1. _____

2. _____

3. _____

4. _____

5. _____

6. _____

7. _____

8. _____

9. _____

10. _____

EXERCISE 2 USING WORDS CORRECTLY

Decide whether the italicized vocabulary word has been used correctly in the
sentence. On the answer line, write *Correct* for correct use and *Incorrect* for
incorrect use.

1. Joshua has been exposed to chicken pox, but he has not *exhibited* any
symptoms yet.

2. Kyla *clarified* the instructions for the experiment.

3. Peter's team placed first in the swimming *seminar* this afternoon.

4. A *sage* is a poor person to ask for advice.

5. Leaving a building at the sound of a fire alarm is an *ingrained* action for
most people.

6. Brianna was angry when she overheard two girls discussing the
information that she had *confided* to one of them.

7. It is important to *expound* the old paint before applying a fresh coat.

8. In some mystery novels, the detective gathers together all the suspects at
the end and *discloses* the name of the guilty person.

9. Shayna chose the most *academic* flowers she could find for the banquet.

10. Theo hoped that the fish would *enlighten* the bait.

1. _____

2. _____

3. _____

4. _____

5. _____

6. _____

7. _____

8. _____

9. _____

10. _____

EXERCISE 3 CHOOSING THE BEST DEFINITION

For each italicized word in the following sentences, write the letter of the best
definition on the answer line.

1. The science lesson *enlightened* the children about sharks.
   a. reached   **b.** informed   **c.** frightened   **d.** convinced

1. _____

2. Many companies hold *seminars* to train employees.
   a. conferences   **b.** equipment   **c.** visits   **d.** tryouts

2. _____

3. As Rex *expounded* the finer points of playing football, Tad had trouble staying awake.
   a. pleaded   **b.** produced   **c.** received   **d.** explained

3. _____

4. Because of their outstanding *academic* program, the students improved their study habits.
   a. primary   **b.** useful   **c.** tough   **d.** scholarly

4. _____

5. Even at a young age, Julian *exhibited* a talent for acting.
   a. lacked   **b.** forgot   **c.** showed   **d.** taught

5. _____

6. Melissa *confided* all her secrets to her cat.
   a. entrusted   **b.** recalled   **c.** traded   **d.** excused

6. _____

7. The professor asked one of the students to *clarify* the point of law that the class was discussing.
   a. repeat   **b.** measure   **c.** make clear   **d.** follow through

7. _____

8. Jodi's report *disclosed* some little-known historical facts.
   a. canceled   **b.** revealed   **c.** corrected   **d.** spoiled

8. _____

9. In ancient cultures the oldest member of the tribe was often looked upon as a *sage*.
   a. wise person   **b.** hunter   **c.** magician   **d.** doctor

9. _____

10. Rising early was an *ingrained* pattern of behavior at the camp.
    a. forgotten   **b.** criticized   **c.** established   **d.** unnecessary

10. _____

EXERCISE 4   USING DIFFERENT FORMS OF WORDS

Decide which form of the vocabulary word in parentheses best completes the sentence. The form given may be correct. Write your answer on the answer line.

1. The jury asked the judge for a _____ of the charges against the defendant. *(clarify)*

1. _____

2. The opportunity for taking her best friend into her _____ came and went. *(confide)*

2. _____

3. Federal law requires financial _____ by anyone running for a federal office. *(disclose)*

3. _____

4. A display at an art museum is referred to as an exhibit or as an _____. *(exhibit)*

4. _____

5. Uncle Jerome _____ imparted his advice to his nephews. *(sage)*

5. _____

6. Dr. Lima grabbed the opportunity to _____ on his research project. *(expound)*

6. _____

7. Kathleen's counselor advised her to choose an _____ challenging program. *(academic)*

7. _____

8. Please keep this message _____. *(confide)*

8. _____

9. _____ students is the goal of every teacher. *(enlighten)*

9. _____

10. Emil liked the _____ because it provided opportunity for discussion. *(seminar)*

10. _____

READING COMPREHENSION

Each numbered sentence in the following passage contains an italicized vocabulary word or related form. After you read the passage, you will complete an exercise.

HELEN KELLER: AN INSPIRING EXAMPLE

For years, Eileen had dreamed of being an actress. She had been in several plays in elementary school but had had a bad experience in a Thanksgiving production. (1) Dressed as a pumpkin and ready to *expound* on how good the harvest had been, she suddenly forgot her lines. (2) Her silence *disclosed* her stage fright. (3) The incident left her with an *ingrained* nervousness about acting for audiences.

Now, several years later, her class was planning a play. (4) Because Eileen wanted to try out for a part, she decided to *confide* her fears to the director. Ms. Estes was sympathetic and

comforting. (5) She gave Eileen a *sage* smile as she handed her a copy of the script. "This play will inspire you," Ms. Estes said.

When she began reading *The Miracle Worker*, Eileen saw immediately what Ms. Estes meant. The play was about Helen Keller whose sight and hearing had been destroyed by a serious illness when she was eighteen months old. (6) She was almost totally isolated from the people around her until Anne Sullivan came to *enlighten* her eager mind. From this patient and skilled woman, Helen learned the manual alphabet and the techniques of reading and writ-

ing Braille. By the age of sixteen, Helen had enrolled at Radcliffe College. (7) There Anne Sullivan helped Helen by *clarifying* class lectures and discussions. (8) Helen took the regular *academic* program.

Helen Keller devoted her life to helping others. (9) She went on many speaking tours, led *seminars* at special schools for the blind and deaf, and wrote newspaper articles and books.

Ms. Estes was right. (10) If Helen Keller was able to succeed in the face of almost impossible odds, then Eileen could certainly *exhibit* the courage to try out for the part of Helen in the play.

READING COMPREHENSION EXERCISE

Each of the following statements corresponds to a numbered sentence in the passage. Each statement contains a blank and is followed by four answer choices. Decide which choice fits best in the blank. The word or phrase that you choose must express roughly the same meaning as the italicized word in the passage. Write the letter of your choice on the answer line.

1. Eileen forgot her lines just as she was about to _____ the harvest.
   a. think about   **b.** identify   **c.** talk about   **d.** delay

   1. _____

2. Unfortunately, Eileen _____ her nervousness to the audience.
   a. revealed   **b.** proved   **c.** passed on   **d.** extended

   2. _____

3. After the incident Eileen's stage fright was _____.
   a. over   **b.** easily outgrown   **c.** rare   **d.** firmly established

   3. _____

4. Eileen _____ the director with an honest explanation of her fears.
   a. fooled   **b.** confronted   **c.** entrusted   **d.** amused

   4. _____

5. Ms. Estes gave Eileen a _____ smile because she understood how Eileen felt.
   a. silly   b. wise   c. mocking   d. brave

5. _____

6. Helen Keller could not communicate with other people until Anne Sullivan arrived to _____ her.
   a. provide knowledge for   c. influence
   b. take care of   d. study

6. _____

7. Helen needed Anne Sullivan's help to make information from class lectures and discussions _____ .
   a. faster to locate   c. easier to understand
   b. more traditional   d. more up-to-date

7. _____

8. In spite of her handicaps, Helen took _____ courses with the other students.
   a. science   b. liberal arts   c. language   d. history

8. _____

9. Helen Keller led _____ at special schools for the blind and deaf.
   a. marches   b. performances   c. conferences   d. awards

9. _____

10. *The Miracle Worker* inspired Eileen to _____ courage and overcome her stage fright.
    a. display   b. copy   c. believe in   d. borrow

10. _____

WRITING ASSIGNMENT

The principal of your school has just asked you to be the chairperson of this year's activity fair. Using five words from this lesson, write a short speech that explains the purpose of the fair and tells about some of the events in it. Underline the vocabulary words that you use. Teacher sponsors and members of school teams and clubs make up the audience whom you will address.

VOCABULARY ENRICHMENT

The word *academic*, which appears in this lesson, has an interesting history. The Greek philosopher Plato decided to set up a school to train citizens for political service. According to a legend, he located the school in a grove of trees that was once owned by a Greek hero named Academus. The school, built around 387 B.C., was therefore called the Academy.

Although Plato's aim was to train political leaders, his school soon became well known for its courses of study in astronomy, biology, natural science, political science, mathematics, and law. Students discussed and suggested solutions for challenging problems. Many historians consider the Academy to have been the first university. From Plato's Academy we have inherited the word *academic*, as well as the scholarly approach to learning that characterizes history, political science, biology, chemistry, and other fields.

Activity In a dictionary look up the following school-related words, and write their definitions and their Greek or Latin roots. Then explain in writing the connection between the root and the definition.

1. sophomore 2. junior 3. senior 4. student

LESSON 3 THE ROOTS *-GRAPH-* AND *-GRAM-*

3

The Greek root *-graph-* and its related form *-gram-* serve as the basis of many of our English words. In ancient Greek, the word *graphein* meant "to write." Therefore, words like *phonograph* and *photograph* can be translated as "writing in sound" and "writing in light." The Greek word *gramma*, which is related to *graphein*, means "letter" or "something written." Words like *diagram*, "sketch or drawing," and *grammar*, "the rules of language," are derived from the root *-gram-*. All the words in this lesson are from the roots *-graph-* and *-gram-*.

WORD LIST

calligraphy
cartography
epigram
graphic
holography
monogram
monograph
seismograph
stenography
typography

DEFINITIONS

After you have studied the definitions and example for each word, write the vocabulary word on the line to the right.

1. **calligraphy** (kə-lĭg′rə-fē) *noun*   The art of fine handwriting; elegant and ornamental penmanship. (From the Greek words *kallos*, meaning "beauty," and *graphein*, meaning "to write")

   Related Word   **calligrapher** *noun*
   Example   Sara purchased a set of special pens for her *calligraphy* course.

   1. _____

2. **cartography** (kär-tŏg′rə-fē) *noun*   The science or technique of making maps or charts. (From the French word *carte*, meaning "map," and the Greek word *graphein*)

   Related Word   **cartographer** *noun*
   Example   *Cartography* requires scientists to survey Earth's surface.

   2. _____

3. **epigram** (ĕp′ĭ-grăm′) *noun*   A short, clever saying or poem. (From the Greek *epi-*, meaning "on," and *gramma*, meaning "something written")

   Example   To emphasize the value of hard work, Benjamin Franklin created the *epigram* "Little strokes fell great oaks."

   3. _____

4. **graphic** (grăf′ĭk) *adjective*   **a.** Described in a clear, effective, and vivid manner.   **b.** Referring to ways of printing words and pictures. (From the Greek word *graphein*)

   Related Words   **graphically** *adverb*; **graphics** *noun*
   Example   A *graphic* description of Dallas's skyline would help a person to visualize the scene.

   4. _____

© Great Source DO NOT COPY

The Roots *-graph-* and *-gram-*   13

5. **holography** (hō-lŏg′rə-fē) *noun*   A method of photography in which an image is recorded on a photographic plate or film by means of laser light. When the pattern on the plate or film is exposed to visible light, a three-dimensional image of an object or scene is formed. (From the Greek words *holos*, meaning "whole," and *graphein*)

   Example   The *holography* exhibit at the Science Museum featured realistic photographs of the brain.

   5. _____

6. **monogram** (mŏn′ə-grăm′) *noun*   A design composed of one or more letters, usually the initials of a person's name. (From the Greek words *monos*, meaning "single," and *gramma*)

   Example   Kurt wore a shirt with his *monogram* on the pocket.

   6. _____

7. **monograph** (mŏn′ə-grăf′) *noun*   A scholarly report on a single specialized subject. (From the Greek words *monos*, meaning "single," and *graphein*)

   Example   Professor Ames wrote a *monograph* on the symbolism in William Faulkner's novels.

   7. _____

8. **seismograph** (sīz′mə-grăf′) *noun*   An instrument that measures and records the earth's vibrations. (From the Greek words *seismos*, meaning "earthquake," and *graphein*)

   Related Words **seismographic** *adjective;* **seismography** *noun*
   Example   *Seismographs* help to warn us of earthquakes.

   8. _____

9. **stenography** (stə-nŏg′rə-fē) *noun*   A method of rapid handwriting in which symbols represent letters, words, and phrases; shorthand. (From the Greek words *stenos*, meaning "narrow," and *graphein*)

   Related Words **stenographer** *noun;* **stenographic** *adjective*
   Example   Court reporters once used *stenography* to record every word spoken at a trial.

   9. _____

10. **typography** (tī-pŏg′rə-fē) *noun*   The appearance of printed material. Typography refers to the style, size, and spacing of letters set in type and to the arrangement of words on the printed page. (From the Greek words *typos*, meaning "impression," and *graphein*)

    Related Words **typographer** *noun;* **typographical** *adjective*
    Example   Styles of *typography* have changed greatly in the last hundred years.

    10. _____

EXERCISE 1 WRITING CORRECT WORDS

On the answer line, write the word from the vocabulary list that fits
each definition.

1. Fine handwriting; ornamental penmanship

2. Described in a vivid manner; referring to techniques used to reproduce
   words and pictures

3. A scholarly study on a specialized subject

4. An instrument for measuring earthquake vibrations

5. The appearance of a printed page

6. Mapmaking

7. Shorthand writing

8. A design composed of one or more initials

9. A short, clever saying or poem

10. A process in which a three-dimensional image is created by the
    intersecting beams of a laser

1. _____

2. _____

3. _____

4. _____

5. _____

6. _____

7. _____

8. _____

9. _____

10. _____

EXERCISE 2 USING WORDS CORRECTLY

Decide whether the italicized vocabulary word has been used correctly in the
sentence. On the answer line, write *Correct* for correct use and *Incorrect* for
incorrect use.

1. Some computer software can create charts, drawings, and other *graphic*
   displays.

2. Mr. Brady was very particular about the *typography* of the menu for his
   restaurant.

3. Eduardo had to take a course in *cartography* before he could teach English.

4. One of the tests a doctor uses to diagnose illness is an *epigram*.

5. Archie hoped that a *stenography* course would help him to take better
   class notes.

6. Sabrina used a *seismograph* to draw animals.

7. Betty addressed the wedding invitations in *calligraphy*.

8. Tyler received a ring with his *monogram* on it.

9. Winifred observed the stars through a large *monograph*.

10. The electrician repaired the wiring by using *holography*.

1. _____

2. _____

3. _____

4. _____

5. _____

6. _____

7. _____

8. _____

9. _____

10. _____

Decide which vocabulary word or related form best completes the sentence.
Write the letter of that word on the answer line.

1. The author used a(n) _____ to begin each chapter.
   a. epigram   b. cartography   c. seismograph   d. holography

1. _____

2. A bold _____ design makes a good trademark.
   a. epigram   b. stenographic   c. graphic   d. seismographic

2. _____

3. _____ is a type of photography.
   a. Typography   b. Stenography   c. Calligraphy   d. Holography

3. _____

4. The use of some symbols from _____ enabled Siobhan to take notes quickly in class.
   a. stenography   b. seismography   c. typography   d. cartography

4. _____

5. The _____ of a newspaper may be changed to give it a new look.
   a. calligraphy   b. cartography   c. seismography   d. typography

5. _____

6. Stores often include a free _____ on bath towels.
   a. epigram   b. monogram   c. monograph   d. seismograph

6. _____

7. New land-surveying techniques have improved _____.
   a. stenography   b. cartography   c. calligraphy   d. seismography

7. _____

8. The readings on the _____ indicated that a major volcanic eruption was likely to occur.
   a. seismograph   b. monogram   c. monograph   d. epigram

8. _____

9. The art teacher wrote each student's name in _____ on the certificates.
   a. typography   b. stenography   c. calligraphy   d. cartography

9. _____

10. The professor's _____ on solar energy was published recently.
   a. monogram   b. hologram   c. seismograph   d. monograph

10. _____

Decide which form of the vocabulary word in parentheses best completes the
sentence. The form given may be correct. Write your answer on the answer line.

1. One should always proofread for _____ errors. (*typography*)

1. _____

2. Early _____ had to draw maps by hand. (*cartography*)

2. _____

3. The _____ readings indicated that the earthquake's aftershocks continued for two days. (*seismograph*)

3. _____

4. The judge asked the court _____ to read the witness's answer. (*stenography*)

4. _____

5. It takes much practice to become a good _____. (*calligraphy*)

5. _____

6. Cynthia designs computer _____. (*graphic*)

6. _____

7. The small publishing company printed only _____. (*monograph*)

7. _____

8. She needs a secretary with excellent _____ skills. (*stenography*)

8. _____

9. The nature exhibit _____ displayed the splendor of the wildlife areas. (*graphic*)

9. _____

10. Laser _____ has recently become common in industry. (*holography*)

10. _____

READING COMPREHENSION

Each numbered sentence in the following passage contains an italicized vocabulary word. After you read the passage, you will complete an exercise.

CHARTING THE WORLD

(1) Early European explorers had few accurate maps to guide them, for *cartography* was largely based on guesswork. In 1492, for example, Christopher Columbus thought that he had reached India when he had actually reached America. His map showed the earth to be smaller than it really is, and India lay far beyond where he thought it should be.

Although early maps may not have been accurate, they were beautiful. (2) Using the delicate brush strokes of *calligraphy*, mapmakers wrote the names of the four winds. (3) In addition to drawing land masses and bodies of water, they included *graphic* representations of the plants and animals that they believed to inhabit different lands. (4) If they lacked knowledge about the geography of a particular area, they sometimes included an appropriate *epigram* or quotation. (5) Cartographers nearly always signed their maps with decorative *monograms.*

During the late fifteenth century, scholars rediscovered and translated the writings of Ptolemy, a famous Greek mathematician and cartographer who had lived during the second century A.D. (6) Ptolemy's *monographs* on mapmaking became very helpful to mapmakers centuries later.

The invention of printing in the fifteenth century also revolutionized cartography in several ways. The printing press made more maps available to mapmakers, who then could compare their maps and learn from one another. (7) Printing also standardized the *typography* of maps.

Today, mapmaking is a highly specialized science. Modern instruments make observation and measurement precise. (8) A complex system of symbols, such as those used in *stenography*, allows the mapmaker to include large amounts of information in small spaces. Computers have streamlined many mapping operations, and some maps are being produced solely by machines. (9) *Holography* soon may be used to produce realistic, three-dimensional maps.

All of these modern methods have led to the development of many different types of maps. (10) Information collected from *seismographs* even allows mapmakers to chart places where earthquakes could occur. Unlike the maps of yesterday, maps today are highly technical and exact representations of the world around us.

Each of the following statements corresponds to a numbered sentence in the passage. Each statement contains a blank and is followed by four answer choices. Decide which choice best fits in the blank. The word or phrase that you choose must express roughly the same meaning as the italicized word in the passage. Write the letter of your choice on the answer line.

1. Early explorers could not rely on the inexact results of early _____.
   a. decorative writing
   b. technical instruments
   c. printing
   d. mapmaking

   1. _____

2. Early cartographers used _____ to write the names of the four winds.
   a. elegant handwriting
   b. printing presses
   c. watercolors
   d. ancient symbols

   2. _____

3. Many mapmakers included _____ plants and animals on their maps.
   a. witty poems about
   b. quotations about
   c. vivid pictures of
   d. histories of

   3. _____

4. A mapmaker might include a _____ if geographical information were not available.
   a. short, clever saying
   b. long explanation
   c. design
   d. diagram

   4. _____

5. Mapmakers signed their maps with _____.
   a. symbols
   b. designs using their initials
   c. their names
   d. self-portraits

   5. _____

6. Ptolemy, a Greek mapmaker, wrote _____ about map-making.
   a. long poems
   b. scholarly reports
   c. short summaries
   d. outlines

   6. _____

7. Printing made the _____ of maps more standard than it had been.
   a. size   b. color   c. boundary   d. appearance

   7. _____

8. Mapmakers can fit large amounts of information into small spaces by using symbols like those used in _____.
   a. photography   b. poetry   c. shorthand writing   d. medicine

   8. _____

9. _____ may make future maps more realistic.
   a. Laser-image photography
   b. New measuring instruments
   c. Space capsules
   d. Better colors

   9. _____

10. Information from _____ allows mapmakers to chart the location of earthquakes.
    a. machines that measure vibrations
    b. special studies
    c. a collection of symbols
    d. ancient documents that explain natural occurrences

   10. _____

WRITING ASSIGNMENT

From this lesson, choose one vocabulary word that refers to a topic that interests you, and do some library research about that subject. For example, you might read about the history of calligraphy in an encyclopedia or about specific lettering techniques in an art book. Assume that your classmates know nothing about your topic. Write a summary of the information to share what you learn.

DICTIONARY SKILLS
FINDING THE APPROPRIATE DEFINITION

Many words in a dictionary have more than one definition. When you look up a word, you must decide which definition fits the meaning of the sentence in which the word is being used.

PROCEDURE

1. *Read all of the definitions in an entry.* Suppose that you do not know the meaning of *migrated* in the following sentence. You look it up in the dictionary and read both definitions.

   During the 1849 Gold Rush, many people migrated *to California.*

   > **mi•grate** (mī′grāt′) *v.* **mi•grat•ed, mi•grat•ing.**
   > **1.** To move from one country or region and settle in another. **2.** To move regularly to a different region, especially at a particular time of the year: *Many birds migrate to southern regions in the fall.*

2. *If there is more than one entry of a word, read each entry completely.* Some words are homographs—they are spelled the same way but are completely different in meaning, origin, and sometimes pronunciation. Homographs have separate dictionary entries, each printed with a raised number. Suppose that you do not know what *refuse* means in the following sentence. When you look up *refuse* in the dictionary, you find that it is a homograph.

   We took the refuse *to the town dump.*

   > **re•fuse¹** (rĭ•fyōōz′) *v.* **re•fused, re•fus•ing.**
   > **1.** To decline to do (something). **2.** To decline to accept; turn down: *refuse an offer.* **3.** To decline to give: *refused permission.*
   > **ref•use²** (rĕf′yōōs) *n.* Worthless matter; waste.

3. *Read the sentence in which you found the word, substituting each definition for the word.* The one that makes the most sense is the correct definition.

   During the 1849 Gold Rush, many people moved from other regions of the country and settled *in California.*

   We took the worthless matter *to the town dump.*

   For *migrated* the first definition in the entry is the correct one.
   For *refuse* the second entry gives the right definition.

Using the dictionary entries provided, find the appropriate definition of the italicized word in each of the following sentences. *Step 1:* Write the appropriate definition. *Step 2:* Write a sentence of your own in which you use the word according to the same definition.

1. The jet *soared* over our heads and away from the airport.

   Definition _____

   Sentence _____

2. In the movie, Count Dracula wore a dark *cape.*

   Definition _____

   Sentence _____

3. The *cape* has beautiful beaches.

   Definition _____

   Sentence _____

4. The dairy cows were *grazing* in the meadow.

   Definition _____

   Sentence _____

5. The prices of concert tickets have *soared* lately.

   Definition _____

   Sentence _____

6. The runner *grazed* the wall as she entered the stadium.

   Definition _____

   Sentence _____

cape[1] (kāp) *n.* A sleeveless outer garment fastened at the throat and worn hanging loose over the shoulders.

cape[2] (kāp) *n.* A point of land projecting into a sea or other body of water.

graze[1] (grāz) *v.* **grazed, graz•ing.** **1.** To feed on growing grasses and herbage: *Cattle graze on the grass.* **2.** To put (livestock) out to feed: *They graze cattle and sheep on the plains.*

graze[2] (grāz) *v.* **grazed, graz•ing.** To touch or scrape lightly in passing: *The suitcase grazed her leg and tore her stocking.* —*n.* A light touch or scrape in passing.

soar (sôr) or (sōr) *v.* **1.** To rise, fly, or glide high, especially by using rising air currents and moving with little apparent effort, as eagles and hawks do. **2.** To rise suddenly and rapidly, especially above what is normal: *The cost of living soared.*

Enthusiasm, an intense feeling for or interest in something, is an important factor in success. An enthusiasm for playing the violin or guitar inspires musicians to put in the long hours of practice to master it. An enthusiasm for helping others motivates people to serve in the Peace Corps or in other volunteer organizations. Enthusiasm for curing disease will often lead to the years of research to develop new medicines that enable all of us to lead healthier lives. As the famous American author Ralph Waldo Emerson once wrote, "Nothing great was ever achieved without enthusiasm." This lesson contains words that will help you to express your own enthusiasm about activities that you enjoy.

WORD LIST

allure
avid
exhilarate
exult
fanatic
fervor
jubilant
motivate
zealous
zest

DEFINITIONS

After you have studied the definitions and example for each word, write the vocabulary word on the line to the right.

1. **allure** (ə-lŏor′) *noun*   A strong attraction or fascination.   *verb*   To attract or tempt.

   Example   Ron could not resist the *allure* of the sea and joined the navy.

1. _____

   MEMORY CUE: The word *allure* has *lure* in it.

2. **avid** (ăv′ĭd) *adjective*   Eager; very enthusiastic. (From the Latin word *avere*, meaning "to desire")

   Related Words   **avidity** *noun*; **avidly** *adverb*
   Example   An *avid* reader may finish two books a week.

2. _____

3. **exhilarate** (ĭg-zĭl′ə-rāt′) *verb*   **a.** To make extremely happy; to inspire. **b.** To refresh or invigorate. (From the Greek word *hilaros*, meaning "cheerful")

   Related Word   **exhilaration** *noun*
   Example   *Exhilarated* by their first prize in the debate contest, the students ran off the bus shouting, "We won!"

3. _____

4. **exult** (ĭg-zŭlt′) *verb*   To rejoice greatly. (From the Latin *ex-*, meaning "out," and *salire*, meaning "to leap")

   Related Words   **exultant** *adjective*; **exultation** *noun*
   Example   The students *exulted* after their team won the state championship.

4. _____

   USAGE NOTE: *Exult* means "to express joy." *Exalt* means "to raise in positions or status."

5. **fanatic** (fə-nătʹĭk) *noun*   A person who believes in a cause or an idea to an extent that is unreasonable or abnormal. (From the Latin word *fanaticus*, meaning "inspired by a god")

   Related Words   **fanatical** *adjective;* **fanatically** *adverb;* **fanaticism** *noun*
   Example   *Fanatics* often do not listen to those who have opposing viewpoints.

5. _____
MEMORY CUE: The word *fan* comes from *fanatic.*

6. **fervor** (fûrʹvər) *noun*   A state of great or intense emotion. (From the Latin word *fervere*, meaning "to boil")

   Related Word   **fervent** *adjective*
   Example   With great *fervor*, the scientist told the group about her theory.

6. _____

7. **jubilant** (jo͞oʹbə-lənt) *adjective*   Full of joy; in a rejoicing mood. (From the Latin word *jubilare*, meaning "to raise a shout of joy")

   Related Word   **jubilation** *noun*
   Example   Mary was *jubilant* when she was selected for the varsity squad.

7. _____

8. **motivate** (mōʹtə-vātʹ) *verb*   To provide with an incentive or a reason to act in a certain way. (From the Latin word *movere*, meaning "to move")

   Related Words   **motivation** *noun;* **motive** *noun*
   Example   His intense desire to win *motivated* Brad to shoot baskets for hours.

8. _____

9. **zealous** (zĕlʹəs) *adjective*   Fiercely dedicated, especially in pursuing a cause, an ideal, or a goal.

   Related Words   **zeal** *noun;* **zealot** *noun;* **zealously** *adverb*
   Example   Betsy was *zealous* in her campaign for class president.

9. _____

10. **zest** (zĕst) *noun*   Spirited enjoyment; eagerness.

    Related Words   **zestful** *adjective;* **zestfully** *adverb*
    Example   With great *zest* Isabel planned the birthday party for her father.

10. _____

EXERCISE 1 WRITING CORRECT WORDS

On the answer line, write the word from the vocabulary list that best fits each definition.

1. To make very happy; invigorate

2. A person who has an extreme belief in a cause

3. A strong attraction

4. Fiercely dedicated to a cause or a goal

5. Full of joy

6. To provide with a reason to do something

7. Spirited enjoyment; gusto

8. Eager or enthusiastic

9. A state of intense emotion

10. To rejoice greatly

1. _____

2. _____

3. _____

4. _____

5. _____

6. _____

7. _____

8. _____

9. _____

10. _____

EXERCISE 2 USING WORDS CORRECTLY

Each of the following questions contains an italicized vocabulary word. Decide the answer to the question, and write *Yes* or *No* on the answer line.

1. Might a citizen who is *zealous* about safety argue in favor of installing a traffic light at a dangerous intersection?

2. Would a person who is *avid* about golf try to avoid playing it?

3. Is a *fanatic* likely to be influenced by someone with a different opinion?

4. Is a swim in a cool pond likely to be *exhilarating*?

5. Would a *jubilant* person burst into tears of sadness?

6. Would living in Florida have great *allure* for someone who prefers cold weather?

7. Would the supporters of a candidate *exult* if that person lost an election?

8. Might a speaker show *fervor* by raising her voice and gesturing enthusiastically with her hands?

9. Would a person who is full of *zest* seem bored by most activities?

10. Would a *motivated* coin collector be alert for opportunities to obtain more coins?

1. _____

2. _____

3. _____

4. _____

5. _____

6. _____

7. _____

8. _____

9. _____

10. _____

EXERCISE 3 CHOOSING THE BEST DEFINITION

For each italicized vocabulary word or related form in the following
sentences, write the letter of the best definition on the answer line.

1. Jody was a Red Sox *fanatic*.
   a. strong believer **b.** occasional fan **c.** dreamer   **d.** authority

   1. _____

2. Leroy read the speech from *Hamlet* with such *fervor* that his voice
   trembled.
   a. happiness   **b.** intensity   **c.** lack of interest **d.** fear

   2. _____

3. When our soccer team won the finals, the whole school *exulted* in the
   victory.
   a. shared   **b.** rejoiced   **c.** mourned   **d.** ignored

   3. _____

4. Carl is so *zealous* about the need for peace that he has written a book on
   the subject.
   a. apathetic   **b.** knowledgeable **c.** dedicated   **d.** brave

   4. _____

5. My grandmother, who is sixty, still plays tennis with energy and *zest*.
   a. enthusiasm   **b.** suffering   **c.** strength   **d.** weakness

   5. _____

6. Ruth found the prospect of riding a raft down the Snake River *alluring*.
   a. frightening   **b.** boring   **c.** peculiar   **d.** attractive

   6. _____

7. Despite the danger, the hikers were *exhilarated* by their climb up steep,
   narrow trails.
   a. worried   **b.** worn out   **c.** invigorated   **d.** scared

   7. _____

8. Julio has an *avid* interest in archaeology.
   a. mysterious   **b.** enthusiastic   **c.** mild   **d.** humorous

   8. _____

9. Even before time ran out, *jubilant* fans stood at the sidelines of the football
   field.
   a. gloomy   **b.** overjoyed   **c.** critical   **d.** dangerous

   9. _____

10. Jason uses a carrot to *motivate* his mule to pull the wagon.
    a. persuade   **b.** punish   **c.** discourage   **d.** ask

    10. _____

EXERCISE 4 USING DIFFERENT FORMS OF WORDS

Decide which form of the word in parentheses best completes the sentence.
The form given may be correct. Write your answer on the answer line.

1. Lisa certainly plays tennis _____! *(zest)*

   1. _____

2. We took an _____ swim in a spring-fed lake. *(exhilarate)*

   2. _____

3. Our math teacher _____ reads software magazines. *(avid)*

   3. _____

4. Pat is _____ about the need to preserve the environment. *(zealous)*

   4. _____

5. The _____ graduates cheered at the end of the ceremony. *(exult)*

   5. _____

6. The prosecutor will prove that the defendant had both a _____ and an
   opportunity to commit the crime. *(motivate)*

   6. _____

7. The family reunion last summer was a time of _____ for all of us. *(jubilant)*

   7. _____

8. Julie's most ____ wish is to get a job as a lifeguard. *(fervor)*

    8. _____

9. Part of the ____ of the restaurant is its elegant appearance. *(allure)*

    9. _____

10. In the novel *Moby Dick*, Captain Ahab pursues the white whale with single-minded ____. *(fanatic)*

    10. _____

READING COMPREHENSION

Each numbered sentence in the following passage contains an italicized vocabulary word or related form. After you read the passage, you will complete an exercise.

SPARTACUS: REBEL AGAINST ROME

Spartacus was a Roman slave who led a revolt against the Roman Empire in the years from 73 B.C. to 71 B.C. **(1)** Because of his *zealous* struggle against his Roman captors, he became a symbol of the struggle for freedom.

Originally a member of a group of nomadic herders from near Greece, Spartacus later served in the Roman army. After deserting the army, he was captured and enslaved by the Romans. **(2)** Because Spartacus fought with great *fervor,* the Romans made him a gladiator, a man or woman who fought other warriors or wild beasts. **(3)** Roman citizens were *avid* followers of the gladiator contests, in which men and women displayed their fighting abilities.

(4) Driven by the *allure* of freedom, Spartacus escaped and hid on Vesuvius, a volcano south of Rome. **(5)** There he attracted an army of seventy thousand rebel slaves, who *exulted* in their newfound freedom. **(6)** The army, which supported Spartacus *fanatically,* succeeded in defeating the Roman army. **(7)** The former slaves were *jubilant* over their success.

By 71 B.C., Spartacus grew weary of fighting and decided to lead the slave army out of Italy. **(8)** His followers, however, who were still *exhilarated* by their success, planned an attack on Rome. **(9)** In the following battle, the slaves did not fight with the *zest* they had shown earlier, and the fresh Roman army defeated them. Spartacus died on the battlefield, and the Romans condemned his followers to death. **(10)** In spite of his defeat, Spartacus set an example that has *motivated* many others to fight for their freedom.

READING COMPREHENSION EXERCISE

Each of the following statements corresponds to a numbered sentence in the passage. Each sentence contains a blank and is followed by four answer choices. Decide which choice fits best in the blank. The word or phrase that you choose must express roughly the same meaning as the italicized word in the passage. Write the letter of your choice on the answer line.

1. Spartacus carried on a _____ fight for freedom.
   a. jealous　　b. foolish　　c. dedicated　　d. successful

2. He was made a gladiator because he fought with _____.
   a. intelligence　　b. care　　c. tricks　　d. intensity

3. The Romans followed the gladiator contests _____.
   a. eagerly
   b. with mild interest
   c. only now and then
   d. in a polite way

4. The _____ of freedom led Spartacus to escape.
   a. attraction　　b. question　　c. fear　　d. impossibility

5. Spartacus's army _____ their freedom.
   a. wasted　　b. rejoiced in　　c. rejected　　d. politely asked for

6. The army supported Spartacus _____.
   a. unwillingly
   b. occasionally
   c. with unusual enthusiasm
   d. obediently

7. The slaves were _____ about their success.
   a. overjoyed　　b. thoughtful　　c. worried　　d. foolish

8. Spartacus's followers, who were still _____, planned to attack Rome.
   a. exhausted　　b. well rested　　c. well trained　　d. inspired

9. In the final battle, the slaves fought with less _____.
   a. skill　　b. fear　　c. knowledge　　d. spirit

10. The example of Spartacus has _____ others.
    a. disgusted　　b. influenced　　c. fooled　　d. discouraged

1. _____
2. _____
3. _____
4. _____
5. _____
6. _____
7. _____
8. _____
9. _____
10. _____

PRACTICE WITH ANALOGIES

See pages 52, 78, and 98 for some other strategies to use with analogies.

An analogy compares word pairs that are related in some way. An analogy can be expressed in a sentence or with colons.

Oxygen is to gas as ivy is to vine.
OXYGEN : GAS :: ivy : vine

Strategy To complete an analogy, find the relationship between the words in the first pair. The second pair must have the same relationship. *Oxygen* is a type of gas as *ivy* is a type of vine. The relationship is "type of."

Directions Write a vocabulary word or a form of it to complete each analogy.

1. Terms is to glossary as places is to _____. (*Lesson 1*)

2. Elusive is to catch as _____ is to resist. (*Lesson 4*)

3. Chat is to converse as _____ is to read. (*Lesson 1*)

4. Abbreviate is to word as _____ is to book. (*Lesson 1*)

1. _____
2. _____
3. _____
4. _____

Each of the arts has its special vocabulary. In the performing arts, such as drama, opera, the dance, and concert music, performers must understand the particular language used in their profession. The visual arts, such as painting, sculpture, and architecture, also have special vocabularies. Many people find it useful to gain some knowledge of these vocabularies in order to discuss the arts and gain greater appreciation of them. In this lesson you will learn words referring to the arts.

DEFINITIONS

After you have studied the definitions and example for each word, write the vocabulary word on the line to the right.

1. **audition** (ô-dĭsh'ən) *noun* A performance to demonstrate ability or skill; a tryout. *verb* To perform to demonstrate one's skill. (From the Latin word *audire*, meaning "to hear")

    Example Each dancer had an *audition* before being offered a job with the troupe.

    1. _____

2. **ceramics** (sə-răm'ĭks) *noun* **a.** Objects made from clay and hardened by intense heat. **b.** The art or technique of making such objects. (From the Greek word *keramos*, meaning "potter's clay")

    Related Words **ceramic** *noun;* **ceramic** *adjective*
    Example Daria made beautiful *ceramics* in her art class.

    2. _____

3. **classical** (klăs'ĭ-kəl) *adjective* **a.** Pertaining to Western European arts of the seventeenth and eighteenth centuries, particularly drama, music, ballet, and architecture. **b.** Pertaining to the culture of ancient Greece or Rome.

    Related Words **classic** *adjective;* **classic** *noun;* **classics** *noun*
    Example Beethoven is considered by many to be the greatest *classical* composer.

    3. _____

4. **daub** (dôb) *verb* To apply paint or color with crude strokes. (From the Latin word *dealbare*, meaning "to whitewash")

    Example Painters who *daub* at the canvas are usually lacking in skill.

    4. _____

5. **medley** (mĕd′lē) *noun*   **a.** A musical arrangement made from a series of melodies from various sources.   **b.** A mixture, a hodgepodge.

   Example   We sang a *medley* of old songs at camp.

6. **melodious** (mə-lō′dē-əs) *adjective*   Having a pleasing succession of sounds; pleasant to hear.

   Related Word   **melody** *noun*
   Example   The bird's song was clear and *melodious.*

7. **orchestrate** (ôr′kĭ-strāt′) *verb*   To arrange music for performance by various instruments in a musical ensemble such as an orchestra. (From the Greek word *orkheisthai,* meaning "to dance")

   Related Words   **orchestra** *noun;* **orchestral** *adjective;* **orchestration** *noun*
   Example   Although Modest Mussorgsky composed *Pictures at an Exhibition* for solo piano, Maurice Ravel *orchestrated* it.

8. **palette** (păl′ĭt) *noun*   **a.** A thin board on which an artist mixes different paints.   **b.** A painter's range of colors.

   Example   When Johanna dropped her *palette,* all the colors ran together.

   USAGE NOTE: Do not confuse *palette* with *palate* ("the roof of the mouth") or *pallet* ("small bed").

9. **pantomime** (păn′tə-mīm′) *noun*   Acting that consists mostly of gesture and is performed without speech.   *verb*   To perform using pantomime.

   Example   To show fear in *pantomime,* you might hold your hands up, open your eyes and mouth wide, and look scared.

   USAGE NOTE: One who performs pantomime is called a *mime.*

10. **texture** (tĕks′chər) *noun*   The feel of the surface of an object. (From the Latin word *textum,* meaning "woven")

    Example   A picture with thick layers of paint, called *impasto,* has a rough *texture.*

5. _____

6. _____

7. _____

8. _____

9. _____

10. _____

Word History: palette

Latin: pala=shovel

   Artists often use a *palette,* a thin board with a hole for the thumb, on which to mix their paints before they apply them to the canvas. The word *palette,* meaning "little shovel," comes from the Latin word *pala,* meaning "shovel." The thin, flat head of a *pala,* or "shovel," became the artist's *palette* because of the useful shape on which paints could be spread and blended easily.

EXERCISE 1 WRITING CORRECT WORDS

On the answer line, write the word from the vocabulary list that fits each definition.

1. To apply color crudely

2. Containing a pleasant combination of sounds

3. A board on which to mix paints

4. Objects made from clay and hardened by heat

5. A performance by an actor or a musician to demonstrate ability

6. A form of drama in which actors use gestures and no words

7. A musical arrangement made from a number of different songs

8. Referring to the culture of eighteenth-century Western Europe

9. To arrange music for performance by an ensemble

10. The feel of a surface

1. _____

2. _____

3. _____

4. _____

5. _____

6. _____

7. _____

8. _____

9. _____

10. _____

EXERCISE 2 USING WORDS CORRECTLY

Each of the following questions contains an italicized vocabulary word. Decide the answer to the question, and write *Yes* or *No* on the answer line.

1. Does the *texture* of clay change when the clay is heated?

2. Would someone enjoy listening to a *melodious* song?

3. Must one *orchestrate* music to be played on a single violin?

4. Is *classical* ballet the same as modern dance?

5. Might a painter mix colors on a *palette* before applying the paint to canvas?

6. Is a *medley* a song that repeats the same tune over and over?

7. Are young children likely to *daub* on a canvas?

8. Is the main purpose of an *audition* to entertain a paying audience?

9. Does *pantomime* involve memorizing long speeches?

10. Is a person who makes beautiful clay bowls skillful at *ceramics?*

1. _____

2. _____

3. _____

4. _____

5. _____

6. _____

7. _____

8. _____

9. _____

10. _____

Decide which vocabulary word or related form best completes the sentence, and write the letter of your choice on the answer line.

1. The sculpture had a very bumpy _____.
   a. medley   **b.** texture   **c.** ceramics   **d.** palette

   1. _____

2. We listened to a long and varied _____ on the radio.
   a. palette   **b.** pantomime   **c.** medley   **d.** texture

   2. _____

3. The children admired the _____ in the pottery shop.
   a. ceramics   **b.** pantomime   **c.** audition   **d.** medley

   3. _____

4. Music students may learn to _____ a piece for a string quartet.
   a. orchestrate   **b.** daub   **c.** pantomime   **d.** audition

   4. _____

5. Did William's _____ please the orchestra conductor?
   a. palette   **b.** ceramics   **c.** pantomime   **d.** audition

   5. _____

6. Paula mixed colors haphazardly on her _____.
   a. medley   **b.** palette   **c.** ceramics   **d.** pantomime

   6. _____

7. My father prefers _____ music to popular music.
   a. classical   **b.** textured   **c.** pantomime   **d.** medley

   7. _____

8. _____ warbling filled the air outside my window.
   a. Orchestrated   **b.** Classical   **c.** Melodious   **d.** Textural

   8. _____

9. Eugenia carelessly _____ at the canvas with her paintbrush.
   a. orchestrated   **b.** daubed   **c.** pantomimed   **d.** auditioned

   9. _____

10. He loved to watch _____ and guess what the actors were doing.
    a. ceramics   **b.** orchestration   **c.** medley   **d.** pantomime

    10. _____

For each italicized vocabulary word in the following sentences, write the letter of the best definition on the answer line.

1. In *ceramics*, an artist works with _____.
   a. a material such as clay   **c.** household items
   b. paints and a canvas   **d.** steel or other metals

   1. _____

2. An artist uses a *palette* as a _____.
   a. tool with which to apply paint to a canvas
   b. knife to remove splattered paint
   c. surface on which to mix colors
   d. container for paints

   2. _____

3. *Melodious* sounds are _____.
   a. lively   **b.** frightening   **c.** abrupt   **d.** pleasing

   3. _____

4. In *pantomime*, the performers _____.
   a. use gestures   **b.** are not seen   **c.** speak loudly   **d.** are seated

   4. _____

5. An *audition* may require _____.
   a. construction work   **c.** writing and spelling
   b. acting or singing   **d.** sleeping

   5. _____

6. An artist who *daubs* at a canvas _____.
   a. paints in detail
   b. paints skillfully
   c. uses two colors
   d. applies crude strokes

6. _____

7. *Texture* refers to _____.
   a. smell   b. color   c. surface   d. drama

7. _____

8. A *medley* is a musical arrangement _____.
   a. using tunes from various sources
   b. that lasts under two minutes
   c. composed solely for orchestra
   d. played only in churches

8. _____

9. *Classical* music goes back to seventeenth-century _____.
   a. Europe   b. America   c. Asia   d. guitars

9. _____

10. To *orchestrate* is to _____.
    a. sing   b. conduct orchestras   c. arrange music   d. design instruments

10. _____

READING COMPREHENSION

Each numbered sentence in the following passage contains an italicized vocabulary word. After you read the passage, you will complete an exercise.

SCHOOLS FOR THE TALENTED

In some large cities in the United States, school systems have established special schools for intensive study in a specific area, such as the performing arts or the visual arts. (1) Students generally must pass an examination or an *audition* and must display exceptional talent in order to be admitted.

The courses offered in a school for performing arts are varied. (2) In a school specializing in music, for example, the students might study *classical* music. (3) Many of them will learn to compose and *orchestrate* musical pieces such as concertos. Some will study singing and others will study various instruments. Drama is also a popular field of study. (4) Students study acting, *pantomime,* movement, lighting, and set design.

At the close of the school year, the music students and the

drama students typically team up and put on a large-scale musical production. (5) In such a production, one might hear the drama students performing the *melodious* compositions of the music students. (6) A *medley* of songs might be sung to keep the evening interesting.

Other schools concentrate on visual arts rather than performing arts. (7) Students in these schools do not just play with clay or *daub* paint on canvas. (8) Those making *ceramics* learn to use kilns, the special ovens for baking clay. (9) The painter learns to blend subtle colors on a *palette.* (10) The sculptor learns how to apply *textures* to different materials such as clay and marble.

Each of the following statements corresponds to a numbered sentence in the passage. Each statement contains a blank and is followed by four answer choices. Decide which choice fits best in the blank. The word or phrase that you choose must express roughly the same meaning as the italicized word in the passage. Write the letter of your choice on the answer line.

1. In order to be admitted to special schools for the arts, a student must _____.
   a. fill out an application
   b. live in the area
   c. be recommended
   d. have a tryout

   1. _____

2. The music student might study _____ music.
   a. eighteenth-century European
   b. ancient Hebrew
   c. folk
   d. African

   2. _____

3. Although music students learn to play music, they may also learn to _____.
   a. play instruments
   b. conduct music
   c. arrange music
   d. write music reviews

   3. _____

4. In addition to reading plays aloud, students of drama learn to _____.
   a. apply make-up
   b. make costumes
   c. direct
   d. act using gestures alone

   4. _____

5. Sometimes drama students perform the _____ creations of the music department.
   a. original
   b. artistic
   c. pleasant-sounding
   d. modern-sounding

   5. _____

6. The evening might include a(n) _____ of songs.
   a. abundance   b. series   c. majority   d. pantomime

   6. _____

7. Art students do not merely _____.
   a. paint crudely
   b. make mistakes
   c. sketch
   d. learn perspective

   7. _____

8. The student _____ will learn about kilns.
   a. making sketches
   b. taking photographs
   c. working with clay
   d. learning sculpting

   8. _____

9. The artist will mix color on a(n) _____.
   a. brush   b. board   c. easel   d. canvas

   9. _____

10. Materials that can be sculpted have various _____.
    a. weights   b. surfaces   c. colors   d. shapes

    10. _____

WRITING ASSIGNMENT

Imagine that you are writing a brochure for new students at your school. Describe for them the opportunities for creative expression at the school. Use five of the words from this lesson, and make your composition two or three paragraphs long.

LESSON 6 LITERATURE

Literature is writing done in a particularly creative or artistic way. For thousands of years, literature has entertained, informed, and inspired people. The earliest type known to us describes battles of legendary heroes such as Achilles and Odysseus. This early literature probably developed from storytelling.

Contemporary literature is more varied. Today's reader can choose poetry, drama, novels, biographies, or any of a number of other kinds of writing. The following words relate to literature.

WORD LIST

allusion
anthology
dialogue
episode
foreshadow
image
literary
pseudonym
serialize
volume

DEFINITIONS

After you have studied the definitions and example for each word, write the vocabulary word on the line to the right.

1. **allusion** (ə-lōō′zhən) *noun*   An indirect reference to or mention of something.

    Related Word   **allude** *verb*
    Example   The author made several *allusions* to Greek and Roman myths.

    1. _____
    USAGE NOTE: Do not confuse *allusion* and *illusion*. An illusion is a false impression.

2. **anthology** (ăn-thŏl′ə-jē) *noun*   A collection of writings by various authors. (From the Greek words *anthos*, meaning "flower," and *logia*, meaning "collection")

    Related Word   **anthologize** *verb*
    Example   An *anthology* of great American literature might include selections from such authors as Ernest Hemingway, John Steinbeck, and F. Scott Fitzgerald.

    2. _____

3. **dialogue** (dī′ə-lôg′) *noun*   Conversation, especially in a book, play, film, or television presentation. (From the Greek word *dialogos*, meaning "conversation")

    Example   Sir Arthur Conan Doyle captured English characteristics perfectly in the *dialogue* he wrote for Sherlock Holmes and Dr. Watson.

    3. _____

4. **episode** (ĕp′ĭ-sōd′) *noun*   One part or one event in a series. (From the Greek word *epeisodion*, meaning "additional story")

    Related Word   **episodic** *adjective*
    Example   The most famous *episode* in *Gone with the Wind* is probably the burning of Atlanta.

    4. _____

5. **foreshadow** (fôr-shǎd′ō) *verb*   To give a hint of something that will happen later.

   Example   In a movie the view of a figure lurking in a dark alley might *foreshadow* a crime.

   5. _____

6. **image** (ĭm′ĭj) *noun*   **a.** A vivid word picture or description of something. **b.** A mental picture, impression, or idea.

   Related Words   **imagery** *noun;* **imagine** *verb*
   Example   A poem by Robert Francis presents the *image* of a ballplayer stealing a base.

   6. _____

7. **literary** (lĭt′ə-rĕr′ē) *adjective*   Having to do with literature, books, or writing. (From the Latin noun *littera,* meaning "letter")

   Example   Many famous *literary* works have been adapted for the theater, movies, and television.

   7. _____

8. **pseudonym** (sōōd′n-ĭm′) *noun*   A fictional name used by an author; a pen name. (From the Greek *pseudēs,* meaning "false," and *onoma,* meaning "name")

   Example   The author Samuel Langhorne Clemens used the *psuedonym* "Mark Twain," a Mississippi riverboat term.

   8. _____

9. **serialize** (sîr′ē-ə-līz′) *verb*   To present in a number of parts, one after the other. (From the Latin word *serere,* meaning "to join")

   Related Words   **serial** *noun;* **serial** *adjective;* **serialization** *noun;* **serially** *adverb*
   Example   The novel was *serialized* for television.

   9. _____

10. **volume** (vŏl′yōōm) *noun*   **a.** A book.   **b.** One book of a set. (From the Latin word *volumen,* meaning "a roll of writing")

    Example   A publisher might use two or three *volumes* for an edition of Shakespeare's works.

    10. _____

EXERCISE 1 WRITING CORRECT WORDS

On the answer line, write the word from the vocabulary list that best fits each definition.

1. Indirect reference or mention of something

2. Conversation

3. To hint or suggest before something happens

4. Collection of writings by various authors

5. To present one part at a time

6. One book in a set

7. One part in a series

8. A vivid description

9. A pen name

10. Referring to books and writing

1. _____

2. _____

3. _____

4. _____

5. _____

6. _____

7. _____

8. _____

9. _____

10. _____

EXERCISE 2 USING WORDS CORRECTLY

Each of the following statements contains an italicized vocabulary word. Decide whether the sentence is true or false, and write *True* or *False* on the answer line.

1. Situation comedies on television are usually shown one *episode* per week.

2. When authors write realistic *dialogue*, their characters seem believable.

3. "Herculean strength" is an *allusion* to Hercules, the mythical Greek hero of enormous strength.

4. Newspapers are likely to *serialize* a short article.

5. When you apply for a driver's license, you must give your correct *pseudonym* and address.

6. Cloudy skies often *foreshadow* rain.

7. *Anthology* is one of the physical sciences.

8. Paintings are not considered *literary* works.

9. A story about two people swimming would probably contain an *image* of water.

10. An encyclopedia usually has many *volumes*.

1. _____

2. _____

3. _____

4. _____

5. _____

6. _____

7. _____

8. _____

9. _____

10. _____

EXERCISE 3 CHOOSING THE BEST WORD

Decide which vocabulary word or related form best completes the sentence, and write the letter of your choice on the answer line.

1. His name, Thomas Jefferson Coolidge, makes a(n) _____ to his famous ancestor, the third president of the United States.
   a. anthology   **b.** dialogue   **c.** image   **d.** allusion

   1. _____

2. George Eliot was the _____ of the English novelist whose real name was Mary Ann Evans.
   a. pseudonym   **b.** image   **c.** allusion   **d.** serial

   2. _____

3. In English classes one often studies such _____ forms as poetry, drama, and short stories.
   a. serialized   **b.** episodic   **c.** literary   **d.** foreshadowed

   3. _____

4. Some of Charles Dickens's books were originally _____ in weekly or monthly publications.
   a. foreshadowed   **b.** serialized   **c.** alluded to   **d.** anthologized

   4. _____

5. My sister does her homework early on Mondays so that she won't miss a single _____ of her favorite comedy on television.
   a. episode   **b.** volume   **c.** image   **d.** dialogue

   5. _____

6. Some of Shakespeare's _____ between Romeo and Juliet is very witty.
   a. anthologies   **b.** foreshadowing   **c.** dialogue   **d.** allusion

   6. _____

7. Stories by Gogol might be included in a(n) _____ of humorous writings.
   a. allusion   **b.** foreshadowing   **c.** image   **d.** anthology

   7. _____

8. "With drums and guns, and guns and drums," a line in an Irish ballad, contains military _____.
   a. images   **b.** pseudonyms   **c.** volumes   **d.** dialogues

   8. _____

9. A composer might use a storm in an opera to _____ a coming disaster.
   a. serialize   **b.** foreshadow   **c.** anthologize   **d.** imagine

   9. _____

10. Tom keeps a(n) _____ of short stories by his bed so that he can read before going to sleep.
    a. volume   **b.** episode   **c.** dialogue   **d.** allusion

    10. _____

EXERCISE 4 CHOOSING THE BEST DEFINITION

For each italicized vocabulary word or related form in the following sentences, write the letter of the best definition on the answer line.

1. Poems by Robert Frost have been *anthologized* numerous times.
   a. included in collections of writings   **c.** collected in libraries
   b. illustrated   **d.** taught in schools

   1. _____

2. Leopold Senghor is an important political and *literary* figure in Africa.
   a. involved with the theater   **c.** involved with the government
   b. involved with writing   **d.** involved with sports

   2. _____

3. Maria's new *volume* on World War II was reviewed in the *Los Angeles Times*.
   a. large amount   **c.** essay
   b. book   **d.** part of a television show

   3. _____

4. Bill's half of the *dialogue* on the phone was "Yes," "No," "Yes, all right," and "Good-by."
   a. argument   **b.** lecture   **c.** conversation   **d.** interview

4. _____

5. A skillful writer can weave a series of *episodes* into a play or novel.
   a. references   **b.** conversations   **c.** pictures   **d.** events

5. _____

6. A candidate for political office works hard to create a favorable public *image.*
   a. impression   **b.** vote   **c.** policy   **d.** speech

6. _____

7. The suspect said he was using a *pseudonym,* but the police said it was an alias.
   a. pen name   **b.** false name   **c.** new name   **d.** surname

7. _____

8. At the party Joan *alluded* to her accomplishments as a cowhand.
   a. discussed   **b.** referred   **c.** exaggerated   **d.** forgot

8. _____

9. When people talk about daytime television *serials,* they usually mean soap operas.
   a. news programs   **c.** romantic programs
   b. programs shown in parts   **d.** adventure programs

9. _____

10. The candidate's decision to run for office was *foreshadowed* by her many public appearances.
    a. changed   **b.** announced   **c.** undermined   **d.** hinted at

10. _____

READING COMPREHENSION

Each numbered sentence in the following passage contains an italicized vocabulary word or related form. After you read the passage, you will complete an exercise.

CHARLES DICKENS: AUTHOR AND REFORMER

The great English author Charles Dickens was a life-long champion of social justice. (1) In fact, his own childhood *foreshadowed* the lives of the characters in his novels. Poverty forced Dickens at the age of twelve to quit school and work in a shoe polish factory. He never forgot that experience. (2) *Images* of poverty appear in many of his novels.

(3) Dickens began his *literary* career by writing articles for newspapers. (4) He often used the *pseudonym* "Boz." (5) When he was twenty-four years old, several of these articles were published in one *volume* called *Sketches by Boz.*

Dickens's first publications were humorous. However, as his fame grew, he began to write more about social problems. Dickens's novel *Oliver Twist* dealt with cruelty toward orphaned children. (6) Dickens used Oliver's story to *allude* to the social system in England. (7) He used the slang of poor people and even criminals in some of

the *dialogue* he wrote.

(8) A London newspaper first published *Oliver Twist* in *serialized* form. (9) People waited eagerly for each *episode* to appear. In addition to entertaining readers, however, Oliver's story made the public aware of the need to protect orphaned children.

(10) Dickens's work often appears in *anthologies* of great literature. His compassion for poor people inspired many of the English to work for improvements in the quality of life of the poor.

Each of the following statements corresponds to a numbered sentence in the passage. Each statement contains a blank and is followed by four answer choices. Decide which choice fits best in the blank. The word or phrase that you choose must express roughly the same meaning as the italicized word in the passage. Write the letter of your choice on the answer line.

1. Dickens's childhood _____ the lives of some of his characters.
   a. created again
   b. suggested beforehand
   c. darkened
   d. produced

   1. _____

2. _____ of poverty appear in his novels.
   a. Stories   b. Pieces   c. Books   d. Pictures

   2. _____

3. Dickens began his _____ career by writing articles for newspapers.
   a. speaking   b. traveling   c. writing   d. acting

   3. _____

4. He used the _____ "Boz."
   a. title   b. pen name   c. character   d. book

   4. _____

5. Articles were published in one _____ called *Sketches by Boz*.
   a. week   b. newspaper   c. year   d. book

   5. _____

6. Oliver Twist's story _____ the social system.
   a. refers to   b. never mentions   c. changes   d. destroys

   6. _____

7. Dickens used the slang of poor people and criminals in some of the _____ he wrote.
   a. conversations   b. words   c. descriptions   d. novels

   7. _____

8. *Oliver Twist* was first published _____.
   a. weekly
   b. in its entirety
   c. in parts
   d. with illustrations

   8. _____

9. People waited eagerly for each _____ to appear.
   a. novel   b. book   c. volume   d. part

   9. _____

10. Dickens's work appears in _____ of great literature.
    a. summaries   b. collections   c. libraries   d. bookstores

    10. _____

Directions   On the answer line, write the vocabulary word or a form of it that completes each analogy.

See pages 26, 52, 78, and 98 for some strategies to use with analogies.

1. Collage is to images as _____ is to songs. *(Lesson 5)*

   1. _____

2. Volume is to set as _____ is to series. *(Lesson 6)*

   2. _____

3. Alias is to criminal as _____ is to author. *(Lesson 6)*

   3. _____

4. Fragrant is to smell as _____ is to sound. *(Lesson 5)*

   4. _____

5. Tryout is to team as _____ is to play. *(Lesson 5)*

   5. _____

6. Solo is to duet as monologue is to _____. *(Lesson 6)*

   6. _____

DICTIONARY SKILLS

PART-OF-SPEECH LABELS

Many words function as more than one part of speech. To find the correct dictionary definition of such a word, you need to know how to read part-of-speech labels in the entries. These labels are usually abbreviations. For example, *v.* means "verb" and *n.* means "noun." A key to the abbreviations is given in the front of most dictionaries.

To find the appropriate definition for a word that functions as more than one part of speech, use the following strategies.

PROCEDURE

1. *Determine the part of speech of the word in the sentence.* In the following sentence, *delegated* is used as a verb.

   We *delegated* the job to Betty.

2. *Read all of the dictionary definitions for the word used as that part of speech.* In a dictionary entry, the part-of-speech label is italicized and comes before the definition. Here is the entry for *delegate.*

   > **del•e•gate** (dĕl′ĭ-gāt′) *or* (-gĭt) *n.* **1.** A person chosen to speak and act for another person or for a group to which he belongs; a representative; agent. **2.** A person who represents a Territory of the United States in the House of Representatives. **3.** A member of the lower house of the legislature of Maryland, Virginia, or West Virginia. —*v.* (dĕl′ĭ-gāt′) **del•e•gat•ed, del•e•gat•ing 1.** To select (a person) as a representative. **2.** To appoint (a person) as agent: *delegated him to study the problem.* **3.** To give or entrust to an agent or representative: *delegate power.*

   The entry shows that *delegate* may be a noun or a verb. You should read the verb definitions.

3. *Decide which definition best fits the meaning of the sentence.* For *delegate* as it is used in the sentence above, the third verb definition is correct: "To give or entrust to an agent or representative." A clue in deciding on this definition is the entry's example, *"delegate power."* In this example the word is used in the same way that it is in the sentence "We *delegated* the job to Betty."

Using the dictionary entries at the end of this exercise, write the part of speech and the correct definition of the italicized word in each of the following sentences.

1. The *bait* had fallen off the fishhook.

   Part of Speech _____

   Definition _____

2. Julie invested her *capital* in stocks and bonds.

   Part of Speech _____

   Definition _____

3. As a boy, Ben used to *bait* his younger brother.

   Part of Speech _____

   Definition _____

4. Parker could not *fathom* the meaning of the poem.

   Part of Speech _____

   Definition _____

5. That word begins with a *capital*.

   Part of Speech _____

   Definition _____

6. The water was twelve *fathoms* deep.

   Part of Speech _____

   Definition _____

7. Ottawa is the *capital* of Canada.

   Part of Speech _____

   Definition _____

bait (bāt) *n.* **1.** Food placed on a hook or in a trap to lure fish, birds, or other animals. **2.** Anything used to lure or entice. —*v.* **1.** To put bait on: *bait a fishhook.* **2.** To set dogs upon (a chained animal) for sport. **3.** To torment with repeated verbal attacks, insults, or ridicule.

cap•i•tal (kăp'ĭ-tl) *n.* **1.** A city that is the seat of a state or national government. **2.** Wealth or property that is invested to produce more wealth. **3.** A *capital letter.* **4.** The top part, or head, of a pillar or column. —**modifier:** *capital investments; capital gains.* —*adj.* **1.** First and foremost; principal. **2.** Excellent: *a capital fellow.* **3.** Punishable by or involving death: *a capital offense; capital punishment.*

fath•om (făth'əm) *n., pl.* **fath•oms** or **fath•om.** A unit of length equal to six feet, used mainly in measuring and expressing depths in the ocean. —*v.* **1.** To measure the depth of; sound. **2.** To get to the bottom of; comprehend: *His motives are very difficult to fathom.* —**fath'om•a•ble** *adj.*

For thousands of years, people have studied plants and animals. Early Egyptians wrote descriptions of plants. Greek and Roman doctors grew plants and used them to cure diseases. So far as we know, the philosopher Aristotle made the first scientific observations of animals. Today, scientists continue to study plants and animals, both in the wild and in controlled environments. In this lesson you will learn words that they use to discuss plants and animals.

WORD LIST

arboretum
aviary
botany
chameleon
cultivate
habitat
nurture
talon
terrarium
zoology

DEFINITIONS

After you have studied the definitions and example for each word, write the vocabulary word on the line to the right.

1. **arboretum** (är′bə-rē′təm) *noun*   A park where trees and shrubs are displayed and studied. (From the Latin word *arbor*, meaning "tree")

   1. _____

   Example   An *arboretum* often contains a section for rare plants.

2. **aviary** (ā′vē-ĕr′ē) *noun*   A structure for keeping birds in captivity, usually in a zoo or a wildlife park. (From the Latin word *avis*, meaning "bird")

   2. _____

   Example   We walked through the *aviary* that had the mynas and parrots.

3. **botany** (bŏt′n-ē) *noun*   The scientific study of plants. (From the Greek word *botanē*, meaning "plant")

   3. _____

   Related Words **botanical** *adjective;* **botanist** *noun*
   Example   By studying *botany*, one can learn more about the sources of many foods.

4. **chameleon** (kə-mēl′yən) *noun*   A small lizard that changes the color of its skin. (From the Greek words *khamai*, meaning "on the ground," and *leōn*, meaning "lion"

   4. _____

   Example   Usually the *chameleon* changes color to blend in with its surroundings.

5. **cultivate** (kŭl′tə-vāt′) *verb*   **a.** To prepare land for growing crops; to raise or tend plants or crops.   **b.** To promote the growth of friendships or interests. (From the Latin word *cultus*, meaning "having been tilled")

   Related Word   cultivation *noun*
   Example   You *cultivate* land by plowing and fertilizing it.

5. _____

6. **habitat** (hăb′ĭ-tăt′) *noun*   The environment in which a plant or animal normally lives. (From the Latin word *habitare*, meaning "to dwell")

   Related Word   habitation *noun*
   Example   The *habitat* of a gorilla is forested land in Africa.

6. _____

7. **nurture** (nûr′chər) *verb*   To nourish or feed; to help to grow or develop. (From the Latin word *nutrire*, meaning "to feed")

   Example   The kangaroo *nurtures* her young while carrying them about in her pouch.

7. _____

8. **talon** (tăl′ən) *noun*   The claw of a hawk, falcon, eagle, or other bird of prey. (From the Latin word *talus*, meaning "ankle")

   Example   Trainers of falcons must protect their arms from the birds' *talons* by wearing heavy leather gloves.

8. _____

9. **terrarium** (tə-râr′ē-əm) *noun*   A transparent container in which small plants or animals are kept. (From the Latin word *terra*, meaning "earth")

   Example   The bottom of a *terrarium* is usually covered with soil, stones, twigs, and leaves.

9. _____

10. **zoology** (zō-ŏl′ə-jē) *noun*   The scientific study of animals. (From the Greek word *zōion*, meaning "living being")

    Related Words   zoological *adjective*; zoologist *noun*
    Example   If you study *zoology*, you might learn about the many ways animals survive in winter.

10. _____
MEMORY CUE: A *zoo* has animals in it, and *zoology* is the study of animals.

Word History: aviary

Latin: avis=bird

If you go to the *aviary* at the zoo, you will no doubt see birds flying around in a huge structure that resembles a giant cage. The word *aviary* comes from the Latin root *avis*, meaning "bird," which becomes *avia-* when it occurs in other words dealing with birds and flight. Consider *aviator*, "a man who flies a plane," *aviatrix*, "a woman who flies a plane," and *aviation*, "the operation of aircraft." In ancient Roman times, special fortune tellers used to observe the flight and feeding patterns of *aves* or "birds" in order to predict the future. Based on this superstitious custom, the old Roman expression, "to have good bird," meant that these *avian* creatures blessed you with luck.

EXERCISE I WRITING CORRECT WORDS

On the answer line, write the word from the vocabulary list that fits each definition.

1. To prepare land for growing crops by plowing and fertilizing
2. A large enclosure for holding birds in captivity
3. To feed or to help animals to grow
4. A container in which small plants or animals are kept
5. A lizard that changes the color of its skin
6. A park for growing and exhibiting trees and shrubs
7. The scientific study of plants
8. The claw of a hunting bird
9. The environment in which a plant or animal usually lives
10. The scientific study of animals

1. _____
2. _____
3. _____
4. _____
5. _____
6. _____
7. _____
8. _____
9. _____
10. _____

EXERCISE 2 USING WORDS CORRECTLY

Each of the following questions contains an italicized vocabulary word. Decide the answer to the question, and write *Yes* or *No* on the answer line.

1. Would you expect to see many tall buildings in an *arboretum*?
2. Would you keep goldfish in your *terrarium*?
3. Could an eagle use its *talons* to catch mice?
4. Does a *habitat* describe how wolves howl?
5. Does *botany* include the study of mammals?
6. At the zoo could parrots live in the *aviary*?
7. Do farmers usually *cultivate* their land?
8. Is it important for adult animals to *nurture* their young?
9. Can you include the *chameleon* in a list of animals that disguise themselves?
10. Would someone study rare species of orchids in a *zoology* class?

1. _____
2. _____
3. _____
4. _____
5. _____
6. _____
7. _____
8. _____
9. _____
10. _____

EXERCISE 3 CHOOSING THE BEST WORD

Decide which vocabulary word best completes the sentence, and write the letter of your choice on the answer line.

1. A hawk can still hunt well even if it loses one _____.
   a. aviary   **b.** habitat   **c.** terrarium   **d.** talon

   1. _____

2. Through recent studies, scientists have learned that wolves help to _____ pups from other wolves' litters.
   a. nurture   **b.** talon   **c.** cultivate   **d.** habitat

   2. _____

3. In order to grow crops, the pioneers had to _____ the land.
   a. talon   **b.** habitat   **c.** cultivate   **d.** nurture

   3. _____

4. The songs of many birds make the _____ one of the noisiest places in the zoo.
   a. aviary   **b.** terrarium   **c.** arboretum   **d.** habitat

   4. _____

5. Some people who study _____ worry about the effects of pesticides on wild animals.
   a. terrariums   **b.** arboretums   **c.** zoology   **d.** talons

   5. _____

6. If you put toads and turtles in your _____, you must remember to feed them.
   a. aviary   **b.** terrarium   **c.** botany   **d.** arboretum

   6. _____

7. The elephant's natural _____ in Africa has been shrinking because people have been cultivating more of the land.
   a. terrarium   **b.** aviary   **c.** botany   **d.** habitat

   7. _____

8. One requirement for the course in _____ is to make a collection of wild flowers.
   a. aviary   **b.** habitat   **c.** botany   **d.** zoology

   8. _____

9. On hot summer days, the shady _____ is one of the coolest places in the city.
   a. zoology   **b.** botany   **c.** terrarium   **d.** arboretum

   9. _____

10. _____ are difficult to observe in the wild because they often change color to match their surroundings.
    a. Talons   **b.** Chameleons   **c.** Terrariums   **d.** Aviaries

    10. _____

EXERCISE 4 USING DIFFERENT FORMS OF WORDS

Decide which form of the vocabulary word in parentheses best completes the sentence. The form given may be correct. Write your answer on the answer line.

1. Large commercial farms have thousands of acres under _____. *(cultivate)*

   1. _____

2. The largest birds at the zoo were kept in the _____. *(aviary)*

   2. _____

3. Sometimes a zoo is called a _____ garden. *(zoology)*

   3. _____

4. Hawks, eagles, and falcons all have _____. *(talon)*

   4. _____

5. If you want to have this rare plant identified, show it to a _____. *(botany)*

   5. _____

6. Certain tropical fish cannot survive outside their natural _____. *(habitat)*

   6. _____

44   Plants and Animals

7. _____ often give names to the whales they study for many years. *(zoology)*   7. _____

8. The _____ garden contained more than eighty-five varieties of plants. *(botany)*   8. _____

9. In some species of animals, both parents _____ the young. *(nurture)*   9. _____

10. Before planning our city's new park, the designers will visit _____ in several other cities. *(arboretum)*   10. _____

READING COMPREHENSION

Each numbered sentence in the following passage contains an italicized vocabulary word or related form. At the end of the passage, you will complete an exercise.

A TOUR OF THE SAN DIEGO ZOO

During my vacation last year, I enjoyed a fascinating trip to the San Diego Zoo. **(1)** Beneath brilliant California skies, the lush greenery reminded me of pictures in my *botany* book. **(2)** Flamingos with bright pink bodies wandered through the grounds, which are *cultivated* by teams of gardeners.

(3) As I took the zoo train around the eighteen-hundred-acre wildlife park, I heard chirps and twitters coming from the large outdoor *aviary.* **(4)** In this *habitat* rare tropical birds make their home. I first stopped to see the hawks and falcons, which live in a special area of the park for birds that hunt. **(5)** Having observed their sharp *talons*, I now understand why they are such successful hunters.

Next, I traveled to the reptile exhibits. **(6)** Looking into one *terrarium*, I glimpsed a small, poisonous coral snake curled under a rock. **(7)** In another, a little *chameleon*, nervously clinging to a branch, changed color as I watched.

I enjoyed seeing the many varieties of mammals in the zoo, especially the cuddly Australian koala bears and the lazy three-toed sloths. **(8)** I observed that the mothers of all these mammals, from monkeys to lions, *nurture* their young with great care.

(9) Before I left the zoo, I strolled through the Japanese garden, which is really a small *arboretum.* While I cooled off in the shade there, a peacock spread its flashy tail feathers and strutted across my path.

A one-day visit to the San Diego Zoo is not long enough to see everything. **(10)** I want to return again to view the fascinating examples of *zoological* life from around the world.

Each of the following statements corresponds to a numbered sentence in the passage. Each statement contains a blank and is followed by four answer choices. Decide which choice fits best in the blank. The word or phrase that you choose must express roughly the same meaning as the italicized word in the passage. Write the letter of your choice on the answer line.

1. The visitor to the zoo had seen similar greenery in a book about _____.
   a. animals   **b.** California   **c.** zoos   **d.** plants

   1. _____

2. The grounds in the zoo are _____ by many gardeners.
   a. watched   **b.** envied   **c.** cared for   **d.** enjoyed

   2. _____

3. Bird noises came from _____.
   a. the special enclosure for birds   **c.** a record
   b. people practicing bird calls   **d.** trees throughout the park

   3. _____

4. Many tropical birds live in this _____.
   a. playground   **c.** environment
   b. experimental building   **d.** laboratory

   4. _____

5. Birds of prey use their _____ to grab their victims.
   a. intelligence   **b.** good eyesight   **c.** speed   **d.** claws

   5. _____

6. The narrator saw a snake in _____.
   a. tall grass   **c.** an underground cave
   b. a transparent container   **d.** a cool building

   6. _____

7. When nervous, this _____ changes the color of its skin.
   a. butterfly   **b.** lizard   **c.** bear   **d.** bird

   7. _____

8. Mothers of all mammals _____ their young.
   a. care for   **b.** abandon   **c.** scold   **d.** play with

   8. _____

9. Before leaving the zoo, the visitor walked through _____.
   a. a transparent container   **c.** a park with special trees
   b. a park for birds   **d.** the reptile exhibit

   9. _____

10. The San Diego Zoo contains interesting _____ from all over the world.
    a. exhibits   **b.** visitors   **c.** plant life   **d.** animal life

    10. _____

Write a letter to someone who likes to observe plants and animals. Explain where in your community that person could go to see plants and animals. Describe what he or she would see. In your letter, use at least five words from this lesson, and underline them.

The English language is filled with words that have something to do with life. The roots -*bio*- and -*vit*- both come from words meaning "life." The root -*bio*- comes from the Greek word *bios*, and the root -*vit*- comes from the Latin word *vita*. The words *biology* and *vitamin* are derived from these roots. *Biology* is the study of living things, and *vitamins* are organic compounds necessary for maintaining normal life functions. In this lesson, you will learn other words that are related to life.

DEFINITIONS

After you have studied the definitions and example for each word, write the vocabulary word in the blank to the right.

1. **antibiotic** (ăn´tĭ-bī-ŏt´ĭk) *noun* A substance produced by certain fungi, bacteria, or other organisms. This substance stops the growth of harmful bacteria that can cause illness. *adjective* Of, using, or acting as an antibiotic. (From the Greek *anti-*, meaning "against," and *bios*, meaning "life")

   1. _____

   Example Penicillin is an effective *antibiotic* that is used against such infections as pneumonia.

2. **biopsy** (bī´ŏp´sē) *noun* **a.** The removal of tissue from a living person for examination or study. **b.** The study of such tissue. (From the Greek words *bios* and *opsis*, meaning "a sight")

   2. _____

   Example Hoping to identify the patient's disease, the doctor performed a *biopsy*.

3. **biosphere** (bī´ə-sfîr´) *noun* The part of Earth and its atmosphere in which living things exist. (From the Greek words *bios* and *sphaira*, meaning "sphere")

   3. _____

   Example Plants, animals, and human beings inhabit the *biosphere*.

4. **devitalize** (dē-vīt´l-īz´) *verb* To lower or destroy the physical energy or vigor of someone or something. (From the Latin *de-*, meaning "from," and *vita*, meaning "life")

   4. _____
   MEMORY CUE: Someone who is *devitalized* is lacking *vitality* or energy.

   Example A bad case of the flu *devitalized* Betsy for two weeks.

5. **microbe** (mī′krōb′) *noun*   A tiny life form that can be seen only through a microscope; a germ. (From the Greek words *mikros*, meaning "small," and *bios*)

   Example   Through years of study, scientists have discovered that *microbes* cause many diseases.

5. _____

6. **symbiosis** (sĭm′bē-ō′sĭs) *noun*   A close, beneficial relationship between two or more organisms. These organisms often, but not always, benefit each other. (From the Greek *syn-*, meaning "together," and *bios*)

   Related Word   **symbiotic** *adjective*
   Example   An alga and a fungus live together in beneficial *symbiosis* to create a plant called lichen.

6. _____

7. **viable** (vī′ə-bəl) *adjective*   **a.** Capable of continuing to live, grow, or develop under favorable conditions.   **b.** Capable of working successfully or effectively: *a viable plan*. (From the Latin word *vita*, meaning "life")

   Related Words   **viability** *noun;* **viably** *adverb*
   Example   When seeds from an ancient tomb were planted, they were found to be *viable*.

7. _____

8. **vitality** (vī-tăl′ĭ-tē) *noun*   **a.** Physical or mental energy; vigor.   **b.** The quality that distinguishes the living from the nonliving. (From the Latin word *vitalis*, meaning "alive")

   Related Word   **vital** *adjective*
   Example   Uncle Bob, who exercises two hours a day, is bursting with *vitality*.

8. _____

9. **vivacious** (vĭ-vā′shəs) *adjective*   Full of spirit; lively. (From the Latin word *vivere*, meaning "to live")

   Related Words   **vivaciously** *adverb;* **vivacity** *noun*
   Example   For Melanie and her *vivacious* party guests, there was always something to celebrate.

9. _____

10. **vivid** (vĭv′ĭd) *adjective*   **a.** Bright, distinct, and intense.   **b.** Creating lifelike images within the mind. (From the Latin word *vivere*, meaning "to live")

   Related Words   **vividly** *adverb;* **vividness** *noun*
   Example   Stan marveled at the *vivid* colors of the parrots in the zoo.

10. _____

EXERCISE I MATCHING WORDS AND DEFINITIONS

Match the definition in Column B with the word in Column A. Write the
letter of the correct definition on the answer line.

Column A

1. symbiosis
2. vivid
3. devitalize
4. biopsy
5. vivacious
6. microbe
7. antibiotic
8. viable
9. biosphere
10. vitality

Column B

a. lively and spirited
b. to lower the physical energy of
c. the removal of living tissue for study
d. bright and intense
e. tiny life form
f. physical or mental energy
g. the part of Earth and the atmosphere in which
living things exist
h. substance used to destroy or stop growth of
microorganisms
i. able to live or develop under favorable
conditions
j. the relationship of organisms living closely
together

1. _____
2. _____
3. _____
4. _____
5. _____
6. _____
7. _____
8. _____
9. _____
10. _____

EXERCISE 2 USING WORDS CORRECTLY

Each of the following questions contains an italicized vocabulary word.
Decide the answer to the question, and write *Yes* or *No* on the answer line.

1. Does an *antibiotic* promote the growth of bacteria?

2. Could a *biopsy* aid a doctor in the diagnosis of disease?

3. Does the sun form part of the *biosphere?*

4. Would a runner be *devitalized* after a twenty-six mile run?

5. Is a *microbe* a large organism that destroys bacteria?

6. Is there more than one organism involved in *symbiosis?*

7. Can a plan that will not work be described as *viable?*

8. Does two hours of aerobic exercise require great *vitality?*

9. Would a *vivacious* spectator sit quietly in the stands during an exciting
baseball game?

10. Is gray considered a *vivid* color?

1. _____
2. _____
3. _____
4. _____
5. _____
6. _____
7. _____
8. _____
9. _____
10. _____

EXERCISE 3 CHOOSING THE BEST WORD

Decide which vocabulary word or related form best completes the sentence,
and write the letter of your choice on the answer line.

1. When Harold was very ill, the doctor gave him a(n) _____ to fight the
infection.
   a. antibiotic   **b.** symbiosis   **c.** microbe   **d.** biopsy

1. _____

2. Janet's energetic lifestyle reflected her great _____.
   a. biosphere   **b.** vividness   **c.** symbiosis   **d.** vitality

   2. _____

3. The area of Earth called the _____ allows the growth of living things.
   a. symbiosis   **b.** biosphere   **c.** antibiotic   **d.** microbe

   3. _____

4. The runner was _____ by thirst during the last mile of the race.
   a. made viable   **b.** made vivid   **c.** made vivacious   **d.** devitalized

   4. _____

5. The scientists discovered a harmful _____.
   a. antibiotic   **b.** symbiosis   **c.** microbe   **d.** biosphere

   5. _____

6. The term _____ can be used to describe a close, beneficial relationship between two or more organisms.
   a. biopsy   **b.** symbiosis   **c.** biosphere   **d.** microbe

   6. _____

7. Doctors said that the patient's skin graft was _____.
   a. vivacious   **b.** vivid   **c.** symbiotic   **d.** viable

   7. _____

8. The doctor ordered a(n) _____ to help her in diagnosing the illness.
   a. biopsy   **b.** microbe   **c.** symbiotic   **d.** viable

   8. _____

9. The _____ young artist talked animatedly with every gallery owner at the party.
   a. viable   **b.** devitalized   **c.** vivacious   **d.** antibiotic

   9. _____

10. The novelist presented a(n) _____ picture of life in a frontier society.
    a. viable   **b.** antibiotic   **c.** symbiotic   **d.** vivid

    10. _____

EXERCISE 4 USING DIFFERENT FORMS OF WORDS

Decide which form of the italicized vocabulary word best completes the sentence. The form given may be correct. Write your answer on the answer line.

1. The physician studied a report on the patient's _____. *(biopsy)*

   1. _____

2. The tour guide waved _____ from the front seat of the bus. *(vivacious)*

   2. _____

3. Reaching the top of the mountain, the _____ group gave a weak cheer. *(devitalize)*

   3. _____

4. The Olympic champion _____ described the moment when she won a gold medal. *(vivid)*

   4. _____

5. The doctor decided to treat Ann's strep throat with an _____. *(antibiotic)*

   5. _____

6. The Portuguese man-of-war has a _____ relationship with small fish that live among its tentacles. *(symbiosis)*

   6. _____

7. Looking through the microscope, the scientist inspected the many _____. *(microbe)*

   7. _____

8. The use of pesticides resulted in a decrease in the _____ of the eagles' eggs. *(viable)*

   8. _____

9. Most viewers are awed by the _____ of Vincent Van Gogh's paintings. *(vivid)*

   9. _____

10. "All of the patient's _____ signs are good," the nurse told Dr. Freedman. *(vitality)*

    10. _____

50   The Roots -*bio*- and -*vit*-

READING COMPREHENSION

Each numbered sentence in the following passage contains an italicized vocabulary word or related form. At the end of the passage, you will complete an exercise.

IN QUEST OF GOOD BACTERIA: A TELEVISION INTERVIEW

ANNOUNCER: Tonight's interview will be conducted by our roving reporter, Jerry McDonald. (1) Regular Channel 95 viewers will remember Jerry for his *vivid* feature story about the changing seasons in our public parks. Tonight Jerry McDonald's probing interview takes him In Quest of—Good Bacteria.

JERRY: Thank you, John. *(pause)* To most of us, the word *bacteria* suggests the image of a dedicated scientist peering into a microscope in search of deadly germs. We are fortunate to have such a scientist with us this evening. Dr. June Miller, what are bacteria?

DR. MILLER: (2) First of all, Jerry, you should understand that bacteria are *microbes* and therefore cannot be seen with the naked eye.

JERRY: How can something so hard to see be so dangerous?

DR. MILLER: (3) By releasing poisonous substances into the bloodstream, harmful bacteria can quickly destroy healthy people's *vitality,* leaving them in a weakened condition.

JERRY: That's frightening! Where are these monsters lurking?

DR. MILLER: (4) Bacteria live in the bodies of organisms throughout the earth's *biosphere.* Plants, animals, and fish all can have bacteria. (5) All these germs need are the right living conditions in which to be *viable.*

JERRY: What types of diseases do bacteria cause?

DR. MILLER: One well-known type of bacteria is streptococcus. (6) Streptococcus is the cause of the *devitalizing* disease known as strep throat.

JERRY: (7) How can our viewers tell the difference between a strep throat and a routine sore throat? Would a doctor need to perform a *biopsy* on the infected throat?

DR. MILLER: That's not necessary, Jerry. A doctor merely needs to take a throat culture. The doctor swabs the infected throat area and then sends the culture to the laboratory for testing. (8) If the culture is positive, strep throat is then easily treated with an *antibiotic.*

JERRY: Are all bacteria harmful?

DR. MILLER: No, indeed. Surprisingly enough, Jerry, the beneficial bacteria far outnumber the harmful varieties. (9) For example, bacteria that live in *symbiotic* relationships with clover or bean crops enrich the soil by producing nitrogen.

ANNOUNCER: Thank you, Dr. Miller, and thank you, Jerry.

DR. MILLER: But there's so much more to say about good bacteria!

ANNOUNCER: And we say goodnight until next week when Jerry takes you In Quest of—

JERRY: (10) Calico Cats—Storybook Creatures or *Vivacious* House Pets?

READING COMPREHENSION EXERCISE

Each of the following statements corresponds to a numbered sentence in the passage. Each statement contains a blank and is followed by four answer choices. Decide which choice fits best in the blank. The word or phrase that you choose must express roughly the same meaning as the italicized word in the passage. Write the letter of your choice on the answer line.

1. Mr. McDonald's feature story on the changing seasons is described as _____.
   a. bright and clear   **c.** short and sweet
   b. long and tedious   **d.** loud and wild

   1. _____

2. Bacteria are _____.
   a. tiny life forms   **b.** blood cells   **c.** muscles   **d.** tissues

   2. _____

3. Harmful bacteria can quickly drain someone's _____.
   a. personality   **b.** aptitude   **c.** energy   **d.** savings

   3. _____

4. Bacteria can be found throughout that part of Earth where _____ exist.
   a. only desert animals   **c.** living organisms
   b. only sea creatures   **d.** only mammals

   4. _____

5. In favorable conditions, bacteria are _____.
   a. radioactive   **c.** likely to die
   b. capable of living   **d.** likely to become extinct

   5. _____

6. Streptococcus bacteria cause the _____ illness called strep throat.
   a. annoying   **b.** physically draining   **c.** life-enriching   **d.** deadly

   6. _____

7. Jerry wonders whether a(n) _____ is needed for strep throat diagnosis.
   a. x-ray   **c.** study of living tissue
   b. blood test   **d.** physical examination

   7. _____

8. Strep throat can be treated with _____.
   a. substances that attack microorganisms   **c.** vitamins
   b. ointments   **d.** cough medicines

   8. _____

9. Bacteria sometimes live in _____ relationships with certain crops.
   a. unusual   **b.** independent   **c.** unnecessary   **d.** mutually beneficial

   9. _____

10. Jerry's next "Quest" will deal with _____ calico cats.
    a. quiet   **b.** small-sized   **c.** high-spirited   **d.** very rare

    10. _____

PRACTICE WITH ANALOGIES

Strategy   Watch out for reversed elements in analogies.

   Incorrect   Actor is to cast as orchestra is to musician.
   Correct   Actor is to cast as musician is to orchestra.

Directions   On the answer line, write the letter of the phrase that best completes the analogy.

See pages 26, 78, and 98 for some other strategies to use with analogies.

1. Episode is to series as
   (A) tournament is to game   (B) game is to tournament

   1. _____

2. Song is to medley as
   (A) image is to collage   (B) collage is to image

   2. _____

3. Tree is to grove as
   (A) shrub is to thicket   (B) thicket is to shrub

   3. _____

4. Chapter is to book as
   (A) play is to act   (B) act is to play

   4. _____

5. Color is to spectrum as
   (A) letter is to alphabet   (B) alphabet is to letter

   5. _____

LESSON 9 COMMUNICATION

A familiar story concerns the shepherd who cries "Wolf!" in order to get his fellow villagers to pay him a visit on a lonely hillside. After he has played this trick two or three times, though, the townspeople ignore his cries when a wolf really does appear.

One important lesson of this fable involves communication. By using the word *wolf* to trick the villagers, the shepherd robs the word of its true meaning. Consequently, when the villagers hear that word from the shepherd, they do not associate it with danger.

Communication requires us to agree on what we mean by particular words, gestures, and other symbols. In this lesson you will learn words about communication.

WORD LIST

audible
coherent
digress
eloquent
garble
impromptu
monologue
oratory
proclaim
verbal

DEFINITIONS

After you have studied the definitions and example for each word, write the vocabulary word on the line to the right.

1. **audible** (ô′də-bəl) *adjective*   Capable of being heard. (From the Latin word *audire*, meaning "to hear")

   Related Words **audibly** *adverb*; **audition** *noun*
   Example   Dog whistles are not *audible* to humans because they are too high-pitched.

   1. _____

2. **coherent** (kō-hîr′ənt) *adjective*   Clearly thought out or expressed. (From the Latin word *cohaerere*, meaning "to cling together")

   Related Words **coherence** *noun*; **coherently** *adverb*
   Example   The writer did a good job of making the explanation *coherent* for the reader.

   2. _____

3. **digress** (dī-grĕs′) *verb*   To stray from the main subject when you are writing or speaking. (From the Latin *dis-*, meaning "apart," and *gradi*, meaning "to go")

   Related Word **digression** *noun*
   Example   In his talk about carnivals, the speaker *digressed* by giving impressions of different cities.

   3. _____

4. **eloquent** (ĕl′ə-kwənt) *adjective*   Persuasive and graceful in speaking or writing. (From the Latin word *eloqui*, meaning "to speak out")

   Related Words **eloquence** *noun*; **eloquently** *adverb*
   Example   The speaker at the United Nations made an *eloquent* plea for better relations among nations.

   4. _____

5. **garble** (gär′bəl) *verb*   To mix up or scramble a piece of communication so much that people cannot understand it.

   Example The speaker *garbled* his words to the extent that we could not follow his talk.

5. _____

6. **impromptu** (ĭm-prŏmp′tōō) *adjective*   Presented without preparation or rehearsal.   *adverb*   Without rehearsal or preparation. (From the Latin phrase *in promptu*, meaning "at hand")

   Example At the awards ceremony, the crowd urged the singer to give an *impromptu* performance.

6. _____

7. **monologue** (mŏn′ə-lôg′) *noun*   A long speech made by one person. From the Greek words *monos*, meaning "one," and *logos*, meaning "speech")

   Related Word **monologist** *noun*
   Example The professor started a long *monologue* about the nesting habits of various birds.

7. _____

   USAGE NOTE: Compare *monologue* with *dialogue*, a conversation between two people.

8. **oratory** (ôr′ə-tôr′ē) *noun*   The art of speaking in public. (From the Latin word *oratoria*, meaning "the art of speaking")

   Related Words **orate** *verb;* **oration** *noun;* **orator** *noun;* **oratorical** *adjective*
   Example Daniel Webster was famous for his inspiring *oratory*.

8. _____

9. **proclaim** (prō-klām′) *verb*   **a.** To declare so plainly that there is no doubt as to one's meaning.   **b.** To announce officially and in public. (From the Latin *pro-*, meaning "forward," and *clamare*, meaning "to cry out")

   Related Word **proclamation** *noun*
   Example After she saw that her last experiment had proved her theory, Dr. Bernstein *proclaimed* her success to the world.

9. _____

10. **verbal** (vûr′bəl) *adjective*   Communicated through words. (From the Latin word *verbum*, meaning "word")

    Related Word **verbally** *adverb*
    Example It is wiser to have a written contract rather than just a *verbal* agreement.

10. _____

    USAGE NOTE: *Verbal* usually means "communicated through words." *Oral* has a similar but narrower definition of "spoken."

EXERCISE 1 MATCHING WORDS AND DEFINITIONS

Match the definition in Column B with the word in Column A. Write the
letter of the correct definition on the answer line.

Column A

1. audible
2. digress
3. eloquent
4. garble
5. monologue
6. oratory
7. proclaim
8. verbal
9. coherent
10. impromptu

Column B

a. to mix up or scramble a message
b. to announce or declare plainly
c. capable of being heard
d. presented without rehearsal
e. clearly thought out or expressed
f. to stray from the main subject
g. the art of public speaking
h. persuasive and graceful
i. a long speech by one person
j. expressed through words

1. _____
2. _____
3. _____
4. _____
5. _____
6. _____
7. _____
8. _____
9. _____
10. _____

EXERCISE 2 USING WORDS CORRECTLY

Decide whether the italicized vocabulary word has been used correctly in the
sentence. On the answer line, write *Correct* for correct use and *Incorrect* for
incorrect use.

1. Cassandra whispered in such *audible* tones that several people nearby
   heard her.

2. Alex worked for days preparing his *impromptu* speech.

3. The student's *coherent* essay won the composition prize for clarity.

4. During the Civil War, President Lincoln *proclaimed* the slaves forever free.

5. The debaters *digressed*, sticking closely to the chosen topic.

6. Throughout his *eloquent* speech, the actor stammered and lost his place.

7. The sailor's words were so *garbled* by the wind that the people on the pier
   could not hear him.

8. Henry answered my question with a *monologue* that prevented anyone
   else from speaking.

9. The test required *verbal* answers, such as diagrams and sketches.

10. Willy, who is skilled at *oratory*, has won several public-speaking awards.

1. _____
2. _____
3. _____
4. _____
5. _____
6. _____
7. _____
8. _____
9. _____
10. _____

EXERCISE 3 CHOOSING THE BEST DEFINITION

For each italicized vocabulary word in the following sentences, write the letter of the best definition on the answer line.

1. The distant tree fell with an *audible* crash.
   a. able to be seen b. dangerous c. able to be heard d. silent

   1. _____

2. The performing seal responded to *verbal* commands.
   a. mysterious   c. shouted
   b. consisting of words   d. consisting of gestures

   2. _____

3. During a lesson about the Revolutionary War, our social studies teacher *digressed* by telling stories about George Washington's boyhood.
   a. kept our interest   c. emphasized important points
   b. strayed from the topic   d. added more information

   3. _____

4. After Wilson's dog pulled two children from the river, our town *proclaimed* that the pet was a hero.
   a. denied   c. publicly declared
   b. thought   d. started a rumor

   4. _____

5. Mrs. Collins made an *eloquent* speech in favor of restoring historic buildings.
   a. unfair   b. persuasive   c. poor   d. old-fashioned

   5. _____

6. Action, not *oratory*, was the prizefighter's strong point.
   a. thinking   b. singing   c. arguing   d. public speaking

   6. _____

7. The telegraph operator *garbled* my message.
   a. lost   b. growled   c. threw away   d. mixed up

   7. _____

8. Professor Simons bored everyone with her *monologue* about her vacation.
   a. long speech   b. song   c. photograph album   d. long joke

   8. _____

9. The man gave me *coherent* directions for finding the theater.
   a. boring   b. interesting   c. well-organized   d. complicated

   9. _____

10. When the substitute failed to arrive, the principal made an *impromptu* appearance as our teacher.
    a. unrehearsed   b. entertaining   c. late   d. exciting

    10. _____

EXERCISE 4 USING DIFFERENT FORMS OF WORDS

Decide which form of the vocabulary word in parentheses best completes the sentence. The form given may be correct. Write your answer on the answer line.

1. Her teacher asked Maura to speak more _____. (*audible*)

   1. _____

2. The article was difficult to follow because of its many _____. (*digress*)

   2. _____

3. The senator argued _____ in favor of the bill. (*eloquent*)

   3. _____

4. The sound on the television set was _____. (*garble*)

   4. _____

5. Because Tom had forgotten to prepare a speech, he had to give an _____ one. (*impromptu*)

   5. _____

6. One of the goals of students in a speech class is to speak _____ in front of a group. (*coherent*)

   6. _____

7. The general manager and the player _____ agreed to a new contract. *(verbal)*

7. _____

8. The Declaration of Independence was the _____ by the American colonies that they "ought to be Free and Independent States." *(proclaim)*

8. _____

9. Because of her _____ ability, Katya addressed the assembly. *(oratory)*

9. _____

10. My cousin does not converse; he delivers _____. *(monologue)*

10. _____

READING COMPREHENSION

Each numbered sentence in the following passage contains an italicized word or related form. After you read the passage, you will complete an exercise.

DEMOSTHENES: SELF-MADE SPEAKER

(1) Demosthenes, a Greek citizen who lived in the fourth century B.C. became so famous for his great *oratory* that even today he serves as a model for speech students. One remarkable aspect of Demosthenes' career was the fact that he overcame many obstacles.

(2) As a young man, Demosthenes had an unpleasant voice, and when he attempted to *proclaim* his ideas in public, he stammered and stuttered. (3) To make matters worse, he also *digressed* frequently from his topic. (4) Because he was committed to a political career, he knew that he had to train himself to give *eloquent* speeches.

To improve his speaking ability, Demosthenes went to the shore of the Aegean Sea. He picked up pebbles from the beach, put them into his mouth, and tried to speak. (5) At first, he **garbled** his speech. (6) However, as he practiced, his speech became more **coherent.**

(7) After he had learned to *verbalize* clearly with a mouthful of pebbles, Demosthenes climbed to the top of some nearby cliffs to

work on the volume of his delivery. (8) The roar of the pounding surf made his speech *inaudible* at first. (9) As he continued shouting *monologues* above the noise, though, his voice grew stronger.

(10) To learn to stay on the subject, he also gave *impromptu* speeches on many topics. Demosthenes became the greatest orator in Greece and a famous statesman.

Each of the following statements corresponds to a numbered sentence in the passage. Each statement contains a blank and is followed by four answer choices. Decide which choice fits best in the blank. The word or phrase that you choose must express roughly the same meaning as the italicized word in the passage. Write the letter of your choice on the answer line.

1. Demosthenes is known for his ability as a _____.
   a. speaker   **b.** philosopher   **c.** teacher   **d.** writer

   1. _____

2. Demosthenes had difficulty when he tried to _____ his ideas.
   a. deny   **b.** change   **c.** write   **d.** declare

   2. _____

3. He often _____ the main topic of his speeches.
   a. stressed   **c.** wandered from
   b. became emotional about   **d.** supported

   3. _____

4. Demosthenes knew that to succeed in politics, he must learn to give _____ speeches.
   a. political   **b.** persuasive   **c.** long   **d.** mild

   4. _____

5. When first he put pebbles in his mouth, he _____.
   a. choked   **c.** could not breathe
   b. shouted clearly   **d.** spoke unclearly

   5. _____

6. With more practice, Demosthenes' speeches became _____.
   a. confusing   **b.** clearer   **c.** personal   **d.** shorter

   6. _____

7. Placing pebbles in his mouth helped Demosthenes to _____.
   a. chew   **b.** get elected   **c.** communicate   **d.** stay quiet

   7. _____

8. The pounding surf made Demosthenes' speech _____ at first.
   a. strong   **b.** effective   **c.** faint   **d.** natural

   8. _____

9. Demosthenes strengthened his voice by shouting _____.
   a. speeches   **b.** poems   **c.** prayers   **d.** songs

   9. _____

10. To practice staying on the subject, Demosthenes gave _____ speeches.
    a. long   **b.** unrehearsed   **c.** organized   **d.** meaningless

    10. _____

WRITING ASSIGNMENT

Describe an incident in which two or more people solve a problem by cooperating and communicating clearly with one another. This incident may be from your own experience or from something that you read about, such as a historical event. Besides describing the incident, explain how clear communication contributes to the solution of the problem. In your composition use at least five of the words from this lesson, and underline those words.

DICTIONARY SKILLS

UNDERSTANDING ETYMOLOGIES

The story of a word's origin and how it has passed from one language to another is called its **etymology.** Most dictionaries give etymologies for the words they list. Some dictionaries provide etymologies in the margins near the word entries. A statement in the entry, such as "See Note," refers you to the etymology. Other dictionaries include etymologies in the entries themselves.

An etymology is like a family tree. It lists the ancestors of a modern English word, beginning with the most recent and ending with the oldest. The ancestors are earlier versions of the word in English or in other languages. The following list shows the languages from which many modern English words are derived. The languages are listed according to their dictionary abbreviations.

Abbreviation	Language
Gk.	Greek, spoken by the people of ancient Greece
Lat.	Latin, spoken by the people of ancient Rome
Med. Lat.	Medieval Latin, used in Europe about A.D. 700–1500
OE	Old English, spoken in England about 450–1100
ME	Middle English, spoken in England about 1100–1500
OFr.	Old French, spoken in France about 900–1500
Fr.	French, spoken in modern France

The origins of some words are not known. In such a case the dictionary entry usually states "Orig. unknown."

In the following entry for *lion,* the etymology is given in brackets after the part-of-speech label.

> **li•on** (lī´ən) *n.* [ME< OFr. < Lat. *leo* < Gk. *leōn.*]
> **1.** A large carnivorous feline mammal, *Panthera leo* of Africa and India, with a short tawny coat and a long heavy mane in the male. **2.** A large wildcat, esp. the cougar.
> **3.** A person felt to resemble a lion, as in ferocity or bravery. **4.** A person of extraordinary importance or prestige.

The entry tells you that *lion* is a very old word. The original ancestor was an ancient Greek word. The Greek word was borrowed by the Romans, and it became the Latin word *leo.* As Latin developed into Old French, *leo* became *lion,* the form that came into English. The English word has not changed since Middle English. Etymologies can help you remember the meanings of words. They also provide fascinating information about the words you use. For both of these reasons, this textbook includes the etymologies of many vocabulary words.

EXERCISE UNDERSTANDING ETYMOLOGIES

Etymologies are given in the dictionary entries at the end of this exercise. Use them to answer each of the following questions.

1. How many languages are listed in the etymology of *legacy?*

_____

2. From what language does *sun* come?

_____

3. What was the Middle English word for *sun?*

_____

4. What is the meaning of the French word from which *toupee* comes?

_____

5. According to the etymology of *foil*[1], the Middle English word *foilen* was an alteration of two other words. What were the meanings of the two words?

_____

6. What is the meaning of the Latin word from which *foil*[2] comes?

_____

7. What is the origin of *foil*[3]?

_____

8. What was the meaning of the Greek word *hippopotamos?*

_____

foil[1] (foil) *v.* **foiled, foil•ing, foils.** [ME *foilen,* alteration of *fullen,* to trample, and *filen,* to pollute, defile.] **1.** To prevent from being successful: THWART **2.** To obscure or confuse (a trail or scent) so as to evade pursuers. —*n.* **1.** *Archaic.* A repulse: setback. **2.** An animal's trail or scent.

foil[2] (foil) *n.* [ME < OFr. < Lat. *folium,* leaf.] **1.** A thin, flexible leaf or sheet of metal. **2.** A thin layer of bright metal placed under a displayed gem to lend it brilliance. **3.** One that by strong contrast underscores the distinctive characteristics of another. **4.** The metal coating applied to the back of a plate of glass to form a mirror. **5.** A leaflike design or space worked in stone or glass, found esp. in Gothic window tracery. **6.** *Naut.* A hydrofoil. —*v.* **foiled, foil•ing, foils. 1.** To back or cover with foil. **2.** To set off by contrast.

foil[3] (foil) *n.* [Orig. unknown.] **1.** A fencing sword with a flat guard for the hand and a thin four-sided blade tipped with a blunt point to prevent injury. **2.** *often* **foils.** The art of fencing with foils.

hip•po•pot•a•mus (hǐp'ə-pŏt'ə-məs) *n., pl.* **-mus•es** *or* **-mi** (-mī')[Lat. < LGk. *hippopotamos* :Gk. *hippos,* horse + Gk. *potamos,* river.] **1.** A large, short-legged, chiefly aquatic African mammal, *Hippopotamus amphibius,* with dark, thick, almost hairless skin and a broad wide-mouthed muzzle. **2.** An animal, *Choeropsis liberiensis,* similar to but smaller than the hippopotamus.

leg•a•cy (lĕg'ə-sē) *n., pl.* **-cies.** [ME *legat* < OFr. < Med. Lat. *legantia* < Lat. *legare,* to bequeath as a legacy.] **1.** Money or property bequeathed by a will. **2.** Something handed down from an ancestor or from the past <a strong *legacy* of personal freedom>

sun (sŭn) *n.* [ME *sonne* < OE *sunne.*] **1.** The central star of the solar system, having a mean distance from Earth of 93 million miles or approx. 150 million kilometers, a diameter of 864,000 miles or approx. 1,390,000 kilometers, and a mass about 330,000 times that of Earth. **2.** A star that is the center of a planetary system. **3.** The radiant energy, esp. heat and visible light, emitted by the sun: SUNSHINE. —*v.* **sunned, sun•ning, suns. 1.** To expose to the sun's rays. **2.** To dry, warm, or tan in the sun. **3.** To bask in the sun. —**place in the sun.** A dominant or favorable position or situation. —**under the sun.** On earth: in the world <the best food *under the sun*>.

tou•pee (tŏŏ-pā') *n.* [Fr. *toupet,* tuft of hair < OFr. *toup.*] **1.** A partial wig or hair piece worn to cover a bald spot. **2.** A curl or lock of hair worn during the 18th cent. as a topknot on a periwig.

Jason walked slowly toward home plate, his stomach knotted with fear as he remembered his latest strikeout. Meanwhile, Rachel sat happily in the dugout and thought about the home run she had hit the last time at bat. As she relived that proud moment, she smiled at the memory of her cheering fans.

What do Jason and Rachel have in common? Both are experiencing strong feelings about baseball. Fear of striking out makes Jason quite unhappy, while Rachel is happy at the memory of hitting a home run. In this lesson you will learn words that describe different emotional states ranging from happiness to unhappiness.

WORD LIST
affable
bliss
compassion
depress
dismay
ecstatic
endear
forlorn
socialize
somber

DEFINITIONS

After you have studied the definitions and example for each word, write the vocabulary word on the line to the right.

1. **affable** (ăf′ə-bəl) *adjective*   Easy to speak to; mild-mannered and pleasant; gentle. (From the Latin *ad-*, meaning "to," and *fari*, meaning "to speak")

   Related Word   **affably** *adverb*
   Example   The *affable* counselor made the students feel relaxed.

   1. _____

2. **bliss** (blĭs) *noun*   Extreme joy, leading to contentment.

   Related Words   **blissful** *adjective*; **blissfully** *adverb*
   Example   After two weeks cooking over outdoor campfires, Jeremy's first home-cooked meal was sheer *bliss*.

   2. _____

3. **compassion** (kəm-păsh′ən) *noun*   The feeling of sharing the suffering of another; sympathy or pity. (From the Latin *com-*, meaning "with," and *pati*, meaning "to suffer")

   Related Words   **compassionate** *adjective*; **compassionately** *adverb*
   Example   The hospital nurses felt great *compassion* for the victims of the accident.

   3. _____

4. **depress** (dĭ-prĕs′) *verb*   **a.** To lower in spirits or to sadden.   **b.** To press down something, such as the gas pedal in a car. (From the Latin *de-*, meaning "down," and *premere*, meaning "to press")

   Related Word   **depression** *noun*
   Example   Two weeks of gray skies and frequent rain *depressed* the travelers.

   4. _____

5. **dismay** (dĭs-mā′) *verb*   To fill with great dread or fear; to discourage or trouble greatly.   *noun*   A sudden loss of courage in the face of danger. (From the Old French word *esmaier,* meaning "to frighten")

   Example   The ferocious lion *dismayed* the zookeeper by roaring at him.

5. _____

6. **ecstatic** (ĕk-stăt′ĭk) *adjective*   Overwhelmingly joyful; intensely delighted. (From the Greek word *existanai,* meaning "to drive out of one's senses")

   Related Words   ecstasy *noun;* ecstatically *adverb*
   Example   The contestant was *ecstatic* because she won a trip around the world.

6. _____

7. **endear** (ĕn-dîr′) *verb*   To cause to be well liked; to inspire warm feelings.

   Example   Alice *endeared* herself to her in-laws by remembering their wedding anniversary.

7. _____
USAGE NOTE: *Endear* is used with a pronoun: His kind acts endeared *him* to me; he endeared *himself* to me.

8. **forlorn** (fər-lôrn′) *adjective*   Lonely; abandoned; sad. (From the Old English word *forleosan,* meaning "to abandon")

   Related Word   forlornly *adverb*
   Example   The shipwrecked sailors wore *forlorn* expressions.

8. _____

9. **socialize** (sō′shə-līz′) *verb*   To associate or mix with other people in a friendly way. (From the Latin word *socialis,* meaning "of companionship")

   Related Words   sociable *adjective;* social *adjective*
   Example   The people in our neighborhood often socialize at informal parties.

9. _____

10. **somber** (sŏm′bər) *adjective*   Dark; gloomy.

    Related Words   somberly *adverb;* somberness *noun*
    Example   Ted wore a *somber* expression after losing his wallet.

10. _____

EXERCISE 1 MATCHING WORDS AND DEFINITIONS

Match the definition in Column B with the word in Column A. Write the
letter of the correct definition on the answer line.

Column A	**Column B**	
1. bliss	**a.** easy to speak to	1. _____
2. dismay	**b.** to associate with others in a friendly way	2. _____
3. endear	**c.** extreme happiness that leads to contentment	3. _____
4. somber	**d.** to sadden	4. _____
5. affable	**e.** dark and gloomy	5. _____
6. socialize	**f.** overwhelmingly joyful	6. _____
7. depress	**g.** a feeling of deep sympathy	7. _____
8. ecstatic	**h.** to fill with dread or fear	8. _____
9. forlorn	**i.** lonely or abandoned	9. _____
10. compassion	**j.** to cause to be well-liked	10. _____

EXERCISE 2 USING WORDS CORRECTLY

Each of the following questions contains an italicized vocabulary word.
Decide the answer to the question, and write *Yes* or *No* on the answer line.

1. Is *compassion* a good personality trait for a friend to have?   1. _____

2. Would you *endear* yourself to someone by being rude?   2. _____

3. Might a child who is lost in a department store look *forlorn*?   3. _____

4. Would you expect someone who just won a prize to be *somber*?   4. _____

5. Do people usually *socialize* at a party?   5. _____

6. Could breaking a bone *depress* a skier?   6. _____

7. Is Santa Claus usually portrayed as an *affable* character?   7. _____

8. Would getting a low mark on a test cause most students to feel great *bliss*?   8. _____

9. Does the prospect of a stay in the hospital *dismay* most people?   9. _____

10. Could a trip to an amusement park cause a young child to become *ecstatic*?   10. _____

Decide which vocabulary word or related form best expresses the meaning of the italicized word or phrase in the sentence. On the answer line, write the letter of that word.

1. The sight of rain clouds in the morning *lowered the spirits of* the scouts.
   a. socialized   **b.** endeared   **c.** depressed   **d.** made ecstatic

   1. _____

2. Maria is extremely popular because she is so *easy to talk to.*
   a. ecstatic   **b.** affable   **c.** forlorn   **d.** somber

   2. _____

3. The *gloomy* look on Barry's face told his mother that he had lost the wrestling match.
   a. somber   **b.** ecstatic   **c.** compassionate **d.** affable

   3. _____

4. Keith *earned the liking of* his elderly neighbors by shoveling their sidewalks whenever it snowed.
   a. depressed   **c.** endeared himself to
   b. dismayed   **d.** socialized with

   4. _____

5. The threat of a nuclear war is a source of *dread* to many people.
   a. bliss   **b.** compassion   **c.** dismay   **d.** ecstasy

   5. _____

6. Something that brings *extreme happiness* to one person may not please someone else.
   a. compassion   **b.** dismay   **c.** depression   **d.** bliss

   6. _____

7. Animals can usually sense when a veterinarian has *sympathy for their suffering.*
   a. depression   **b.** dismay   **c.** bliss   **d.** compassion

   7. _____

8. The homeless people in the shelter had *nearly hopeless* looks on their faces.
   a. forlorn   **b.** affable   **c.** endearing   **d.** ecstatic

   8. _____

9. Teresa was *overwhelmingly joyful* when she found out that she had qualified for the Olympics.
   a. depressed   **b.** somber   **c.** affable   **d.** ecstatic

   9. _____

10. Twice a year the company held a large party so that its employees could *get together in a friendly way.*
    a. be depressed **b.** socialize   **c.** dismay   **d.** endear

    10. _____

Decide which form of the vocabulary word in parentheses best completes the sentence. Write your answer on the answer line.

1. The actor's agent smiled _____. *(affable)*

   1. _____

2. Mrs. Gilbert was _____ when the police notified her of the accident. *(dismay)*

   2. _____

3. Laura listened _____ to her favorite singer. *(ecstatic)*

   3. _____

4. People like Anthony because of his _____ nature. *(compassion)*

   4. _____

5. Kittens have many _____ qualities. *(endear)*

   5. _____

6. Having fun is a good way to combat mild _____. *(depress)*

   6. _____

7. Greg waved _____ from his grandmother's porch as his parents left for the weekend. *(forlorn)*

7. _____

8. Vincent soaked _____ in the soothing hot bath. *(bliss)*

8. _____

9. Kristin nodded _____ when asked whether she had heard the disappointing news. *(somber)*

9. _____

10. In our school there is not much _____ between the fifth graders and the eighth graders. *(socialize)*

10. _____

READING COMPREHENSION

Each numbered sentence in the following passage contains an italicized vocabulary word or related form. After you read the passage, you will complete an exercise.

LOUIS PASTEUR: A CHEMIST WHO SAVED LIVES

(1) When scientists do complicated research, they may react **somberly** to their failure to reach an important goal. (2) This mood can easily change to **bliss** if they make a discovery that will aid humanity. Louis Pasteur (1822–1895), the famous French chemist, surely experienced such alternating moods during his long career.

(3) A dedicated scientist, Pasteur had little time to **socialize** with his peers. (4) When **affable** fellow workers encouraged him to spend more time with other people, he said, "Three things fill human existence—will, work, and success. I have to work."

Although Pasteur was involved in many areas of science, he is best remembered for his discoveries in medicine. His attempts to find a cure for rabies attracted much attention. (5) Before 1885, many people died every year from this **dismaying** disease, which was caused by the bite of an infected animal.

Pasteur developed a successful treatment for rabid animals in the early 1880s, but he was not

sure whether the treatment would also work on humans. Pasteur's answer came in the form of nine-year-old Joseph Meister. (6) Looking **forlorn**, Joseph entered Pasteur's laboratory on July 6, 1885. (7) Joseph's **depressed** parents told the sympathetic scientist that their son had been bitten by a rabid dog.

They begged Pasteur to help.

(8) Strong **compassion** for the unfortunate boy made Pasteur decide to administer the treatment. (9) When Joseph made a full recovery, his parents were **ecstatic**. (10) Pasteur's lifesaving research **endeared** him to the Meisters and to people throughout the world.

Happiness and Unhappiness   **65**

Each of the following statements corresponds to a numbered sentence in the passage. Each statement contains a blank and is followed by four answer choices. Decide which choice fits best in the blank. The word or phrase that you choose must express roughly the same meaning as the italicized word in the passage. Write the letter of your choice on the answer line.

1. When their experiments fail, scientists sometimes talk _____ with their associates.
   a. secretly   **b.** angrily   **c.** gloomily   **d.** happily

2. They may experience _____ if they reach an important goal.
   a. accomplishment   **c.** success
   b. fame   **d.** joy

3. Pasteur spent so much time working that he did not have time to _____ with others.
   a. do research   **b.** argue   **c.** associate   **d.** correspond

4. Pasteur's fellow workers were _____.
   a. difficult   **b.** easygoing   **c.** reluctant   **d.** ambitious

5. Rabies was a _____ disease caused by an animal bite.
   a. dreaded   **b.** contagious   **c.** mysterious   **d.** widespread

6. Joseph Meister looked _____ as he entered Pasteur's laboratory.
   a. shy   **b.** sad   **c.** cautious   **d.** sick

7. His parents appeared to be _____.
   a. positive   **b.** curious   **c.** in low spirits   **d.** optimistic

8. Because of his _____, Pasteur tried the treatment on the boy.
   a. selfishness   **b.** sympathy   **c.** curiosity   **d.** anxiety

9. The Meisters were _____ when Joseph recovered.
   a. quiet   **b.** talkative   **c.** joyful   **d.** active

10. Pasteur's lifesaving research _____ people all over the world.
    a. surprised   **c.** made him well liked by
    b. shocked   **d.** made him well known to

1. _____
2. _____
3. _____
4. _____
5. _____
6. _____
7. _____
8. _____
9. _____
10. _____

Imagine that on the morning of your seventeenth birthday you receive a small package. To your amazement it contains a set of keys and a note that reads: "The rest of your present is parked in the driveway." In a paragraph describe this experience. Contrast the feelings that you have before and after receiving the car. Use at least five vocabulary words from the lesson, and underline each word.

The two suffixes -*phile* and -*phobia* are very nearly opposite in meaning. The suffix -*phile* is from the Greek word *philia,* meaning "friendship." A word ending in -*phile* indicates someone having great fondness or preference for something. For example, a *hippophile* (from the Greek *hippos,* meaning "horse," and -*phile*) is someone who is interested in or fond of horses.

In contrast to -*phile,* -*phobia* indicates a strong, unreasonable, or abnormal fear or dislike of something. *Hippophobia* is an intense fear of horses. *Phobia* is also a word in itself, meaning "any strong or irrational fear." In the following lesson, you will learn words ending in -*phile* and -*phobia.*

WORD LIST

acrophobia
agoraphobia
ailurophobia
Anglophile
audiophile
bibliophile
claustrophobia
hydrophobia
xenophobia
zoophobia

DEFINITIONS

After you have studied the definitions and example for each word, write the vocabulary word in the blank to the right.

1. **acrophobia** (ăk′rə-fō′bē-ə) *noun* Intense fear of high places. (From the Greek word *akros,* meaning "high," and -*phobia,* meaning "fear")

   Related Word **acrophobic** *adjective*
   Example Kyle's *acrophobia* prevented him from going up to the observation deck of the skyscraper.

   1. _____
   MEMORY CUE: *Acrobats* would not have *acrophobia.*

2. **agoraphobia** (ăg′ər-ə-fō′bē-ə) *noun* Strong fear of open places. (From the Greek word *agora,* meaning "open space," and -*phobia*)

   Related Word **agoraphobic** *adjective*
   Example People with severe *agoraphobia* may be afraid to leave their houses.

   2. _____
   See *claustrophobia.*

3. **ailurophobia** (ī′loor-ə-fō′bē-ə) *noun* A great fear or hatred of cats. (From the Greek word *ailuros,* meaning "cat," and -*phobia*)

   Related Word **ailurophobic** *adjective*
   Example Even a fluffy little kitten can be cause for alarm to someone who suffers from *ailurophobia.*

   3. _____
   See *zoophobia.*

4. **Anglophile** (ăng′glə-fīl′) *noun* One who has strong admiration or affection for England, the English, or English goods. (From the Medieval Latin word *Angli,* meaning "the English people," and -*phile,* meaning "enthusiast")

   Related Word **Anglophilia** *noun*
   Example Connor is such an *Anglophile* that he speaks with an English accent even though he is an American.

   4. _____

5. **audiophile** (ô'dē-ə-fīl') *noun* One keenly interested in recorded sound. (From the Latin word *audire*, meaning "to hear," and *-phile*)

   Example   Elizabeth was such an *audiophile* that she spent more on her CD player than on the rest of her furniture.

5. _____

6. **bibliophile** (bĭb'lē-ə-fīl') *noun* One devoted to the collection and preservation of books, particularly old and rare books. (From the Greek word *biblion*, meaning "book," and *-phile*)

   Example   Tatiana is a *bibliophile* with a beautiful collection of books, but she does not like to read.

6. _____

7. **claustrophobia** (klô'strə-fō'bē-ə) *noun* Strong fear of small or enclosed places. (From the Latin word *claustrum*, meaning "enclosure," and *-phobia*)

   Related Word   **claustrophobic** *adjective*
   Example   A person with *claustrophobia* would probably fear going into a closet or elevator.

7. _____

   MEMORY CUE: *Agoraphobia* and *claustrophobia* are opposites.

8. **hydrophobia** (hī'drə-fō'bē-ə) *noun* **a.** Intense fear of water. **b.** The disease rabies. (From the Greek *hydro-*, meaning "water," and *-phobia*)

   Related Word   **hydrophobic** *adjective*
   Example   Both Pierre and Lupe refused to travel by boat because they suffered from *hydrophobia*.

8. _____

9. **xenophobia** (zĕn'ə-fō'bē-ə) *noun* Intense fear or hatred of strangers or foreigners. (From the Greek word *xenos*, meaning "stranger," and *-phobia*)

   Related Words   **xenophobe** *noun;* **xenophobic** *adjective*
   Example   People with *xenophobia* might not enjoy traveling abroad or meeting new people.

9. _____

10. **zoophobia** (zō'ə-fō'bē-ə) *noun* A strong fear of animals. (From the Greek word *zōion*, meaning "living being," and *-phobia*)

    Related Word   **zoophobic** *adjective*
    Example   Someone with *zoophobia* would not enjoy having pets.

10. _____

    MEMORY CUE: Someone with *zoophobia* would surely suffer from *ailurophobia*.

EXERCISE 1 COMPLETING DEFINITIONS

On the answer line, write the word from the vocabulary list that best completes each definition.

1. Fear or hatred of strangers or foreigners is _____.

2. Fear of high places is _____.

3. One who loves fine old books is a(n) _____.

4. Fear of open places is _____.

5. A person who strongly admires the English is a(n) _____.

6. Fear or hatred of cats is _____.

7. Fear of small or enclosed places is _____.

8. Fear of water is _____.

9. Fear of animals is _____.

10. A lover of fine recordings is a(n) _____.

1. _____

2. _____

3. _____

4. _____

5. _____

6. _____

7. _____

8. _____

9. _____

10. _____

EXERCISE 2 USING WORDS CORRECTLY

Each of the following questions contains an italicized vocabulary word. Decide the answer to the question, and write *Yes* or *No* on the answer line.

1. Would someone with *acrophobia* be likely to work as a window washer on a skyscraper?

2. Would someone with *hydrophobia* be interested in being a lifeguard?

3. Is an *Anglophile* likely to admire Shakespeare, Churchill, and Queen Victoria?

4. If you had *agoraphobia*, would you enjoy going camping and sleeping out at night under the stars?

5. Would someone with *xenophobia* be likely to welcome new neighbors from a foreign country?

6. Would you expect an animal trainer to suffer from *zoophobia*?

7. If you had *ailurophobia*, would you avoid leopards and panthers?

8. If you were a *bibliophile*, would you collect fine books?

9. Would someone with *claustrophobia* enjoy spending three weeks on a submarine?

10. Do *audiophiles* like sound systems?

1. _____

2. _____

3. _____

4. _____

5. _____

6. _____

7. _____

8. _____

9. _____

10. _____

For each italicized vocabulary word in the following sentences, write the letter of the best definition on the answer line.

1. Because Neal has *hydrophobia,* he has not learned to swim.
   a. fear of darkness   **c.** fear of water
   b. fear of crowds   **d.** fear of drowning

   1. _____

2. Juliana has to avoid some exhibits at the zoo because of her *ailurophobia.*
   a. fear of all animals   **c.** fear of crowds
   b. fear of open spaces   **d.** fear of cats

   2. _____

3. Michael's collection of rare books shows that he is a *bibliophile.*
   a. librarian   **c.** lover of records
   b. lover of fine books   **d.** lover of the theater

   3. _____

4. Loretta turned down a good job offer in the desert town because of the anxiety caused by her *agoraphobia.*
   a. fear of crowds   **c.** fear of air
   b. fear of open places   **d.** fear of disease

   4. _____

5. Douglas did not go to the top of the Empire State Building because of his *acrophobia.*
   a. fear of darkness   **c.** fear of high places
   b. fear of storms   **d.** fear of light

   5. _____

6. Gregory is working hard to overcome his *xenophobia.*
   a. fear of strangers   **c.** fear of animals
   b. fear of conversation   **d.** fear of storms

   6. _____

7. An *Anglophile* would enjoy eating a steak-and-kidney pie.
   a. lover of French cooking   **c.** admirer of the English
   b. one afraid of foreigners   **d.** admirer of the Slavs

   7. _____

8. Tamara's *claustrophobia* kept her from visiting the pharaohs' tombs in Egypt.
   a. fear of the dead   **c.** fear of fields
   b. fear of enclosed spaces   **d.** fear of disease

   8. _____

9. Steven and Sheila wanted a pet, but their father suffered from *zoophobia.*
   a. fear of cats   **c.** fear of happy children
   b. fear of zoos   **d.** fear of animals

   9. _____

10. An *audiophile* might spend more than five thousand dollars for a CD player and speakers.
    a. one interested in CDs   **c.** one interested in spending
    b. one interested in music   **d.** one interested in recorded sound

    10. _____

Decide which vocabulary word or related form best expresses the meaning of each italicized word or phrase. On the answer line, write the letter of that word.

1. Dictators sometimes encourage *hatred of foreigners* among their people.
   a. xenophobia   **b.** Anglophilia   **c.** ailurophobia   **d.** claustrophobia

   1. _____

2. Louis Pasteur developed a successful treatment for *rabies*.
   a. zoophobia   **b.** ailurophobia   **c.** hydrophobia   **d.** xenophobia
   2. _____

3. The Morgan Library in New York is a mecca for *lovers of fine books*.
   a. Anglophiles   **b.** xenophobes   **c.** audiophiles   **d.** bibliophiles
   3. _____

4. The Lorenzinis have ocelots for pets; they have no *fear of animals*.
   a. ailurophobia   **b.** acrophobia   **c.** agoraphobia   **d.** zoophobia
   4. _____

5. I think we shall get *fear of enclosed spaces* in this tiny classroom.
   a. claustrophobia **b.** agoraphobia   **c.** hydrophobia   **d.** xenophobia
   5. _____

6. If an Anglophobe dislikes the English and a Slavophile admires the Slavs, what do you suppose we call an *admirer of the English?*
   a. xenophobe   **b.** Anglophile   **c.** audiophile   **d.** bibliophile
   6. _____

7. Gina never goes shopping because of her *fear of public places*.
   a. acrophobia   **c.** claustrophobia
   b. ailurophobia   **d.** agoraphobia
   7. _____

8. Melanie knows a lot about electronics and acoustics because she is *a person interested in recorded sound*.
   a. agoraphobe   **b.** audiophile   **c.** bibliophile   **d.** Anglophile
   8. _____

9. Winston overcame *a fear of heights* and then climbed Mount Whitney.
   a. agoraphobia   **b.** ailurophobia   **c.** acrophobia   **d.** hydrophobia
   9. _____

10. Rita gets nervous whenever she sees Boots because she has *a fear of cats*.
    a. claustrophobia **b.** hydrophobia   **c.** ailurophobia   **d.** acrophobia
    10. _____

READING COMPREHENSION

Each numbered sentence in the following passage contains an italicized vocabulary word. At the end of the passage, you will complete an exercise.

TRAVEL—NIGHTMARE OR DELIGHT?

For many people, traveling is one of life's most rewarding experiences. (1) Consider, for instance, the *Anglophile* in Albuquerque, New Mexico, who spends every vacation exploring the British countryside. (2) Of course, right next door in Albuquerque there may be a neighbor who, because of *xenophobia,* would not enjoy traveling in Britain.

One appealing aspect of traveling is the change of surroundings it offers. (3) Sooner or later most city dwellers get a touch of *claustrophobia* and wish to escape for a while. (4) Provided they do not have *agoraphobia,* they may find a few weeks in the Arizona desert to be a welcome change. (5) They might also enjoy camping in the Adirondack Mountains of New York if they do not suffer from *acrophobia.*

(6) In contrast, a *bibliophile* from a rural area might travel to a city with notable libraries so that he or she could look at fine books. (7) An *audiophile* would probably choose a vacation with opportunities for listening to recordings. (8) Someone with *hydrophobia* would certainly not choose a boating vacation!

The rewards of traveling are as varied as the tastes of travelers. For some people, photographing animals in Africa or Asia is tremendously exciting. (9) For one with *zoophobia,* however, a safari would be a nightmare. (10) Imagine how a person with *ailurophobia* would react to being awakened by the roar of lions!

Each of the following statements corresponds to a numbered sentence in the passage. Each statement contains a blank and is followed by four answer choices. Decide which choice fits best in the blank. The word or phrase that you choose must express roughly the same meaning as the italicized word in the passage. Write the letter of your choice on the answer line.

1. The _____ in Albuquerque travels abroad.
   a. person fond of the English
   b. person fond of royalty
   c. person afraid of angles
   d. person fond of the French

   1. _____

2. The neighbor suffers from a _____.
   a. fear of foreigners
   b. fear of cats
   c. fear of neighbors
   d. fear of English

   2. _____

3. Eventually, some city dwellers get a slight _____.
   a. fear of traffic jams
   b. fear of enclosed places
   c. fear of heights
   d. fear of neighbors

   3. _____

4. People without a _____ may enjoy the desert.
   a. fear of open spaces
   b. fear of snakes
   c. fear of heat
   d. fear of heights

   4. _____

5. If they do not have a _____, city dwellers may enjoy the mountains.
   a. fear of heights
   b. fear of bears
   c. fear of snow
   d. fear of isolation

   5. _____

6. A person _____ would find museums and libraries interesting.
   a. fond of studying
   b. fond of paintings
   c. fond of books
   d. fond of records

   6. _____

7. A person _____ would choose to vacation where he or she could listen to cassettes and CDs.
   a. interested in recorded sound
   b. interested in open spaces
   c. interested in movies
   d. interested in cats

   7. _____

8. A person with a _____ certainly would not choose sailing for a vacation activity.
   a. fear of boats
   b. fear of swimming
   c. fear of water
   d. fear of open spaces

   8. _____

9. Safaris are not fun for people with a _____.
   a. fear of zoos
   b. fear of cats
   c. fear of animals
   d. fear of cameras

   9. _____

10. The roar of lions would greatly frighten someone with a _____.
    a. fear of animals
    b. fear of the jungle
    c. fear of Africa
    d. fear of cats

    10. _____

WRITING ASSIGNMENT

Anthropophobia, ornithophobia, Francophile, and *Sinophile* are four uncommon words using the suffixes *-phobia* and *-phile*. Choose one of the words, find out more about it in your dictionary or encyclopedia, and write a brief paper reporting your findings to your classmates.

Our hopes and wishes help us to strive for better things. Hoping for better lives, the ancestors of many of us came to North America. At times they wished to escape from persecution. At other times they simply wanted to support themselves and their families. Hopes and wishes also motivated people to move from east to west within North America. Many people from the east coast, in states such as New York and Virginia, went west to California, hoping to become rich in the California Gold Rush of 1848–1849. Later, people moved west in search of gold in Alaska. People sometimes have moved simply hoping to acquire more farmland for their family. All of us hope or wish for something, be it a new place to live, something to own, a career, or a hobby. In this lesson you will study words that refer to hoping and wishing.

WORD LIST

anticipate
aspire
covet
enviable
expectation
inclination
persevere
reluctant
voluntary
wistful

DEFINITIONS

After you have studied the definitions and example for each word, write the vocabulary word on the line to the right.

1. **anticipate** (ăn-tĭs′ə-pāt′) *verb* **a.** To expect or foresee: *to anticipate trouble.* **b.** To look forward to something with pleasure: *to anticipate a holiday.* From the Latin *ante-*, meaning "before," and *capere*, meaning "to take")

   Related Word **anticipation** *noun*
   Example   Based on the reviews she had read, Pam *anticipated* that the movie would be good.

   1. _____

2. **aspire** (ə-spīr′) *verb* To have a great ambition; to desire something strongly. (From the Latin word *aspirare*, meaning "to desire")

   Related Word **aspiration** *noun*
   Example   Robert *aspired* to set a new record at the track meet.

   2. _____

3. **covet** (kŭv′ĭt) *verb* **a.** To wish for longingly. **b.** To desire something that belongs to another. (From the Latin word *cupere*, meaning "to desire")

   Example   Hypnotized by the toy store's display window, the child *coveted* the giant stuffed animal.

   3. _____

4. **enviable** (ĕn′vē-ə-bəl) *adjective* Admirable or desirable enough to be wanted.

   Related Words **envious** *adjective;* **envy** *noun;* **envy** *verb*
   Example   The baseball pitcher established an *enviable* record of five no-hit games.

   4. _____

5. **expectation** (ĕk'spĕk-tā'shən) *noun* **a.** The act or state of believing that a certain thing will occur. **b.** (Usually plural) Hopes; prospects. (From the Latin *ex-*, meaning "out," and *spectare*, meaning "to look at")

Related Word   expect *verb*
Example   She took the job with the *expectation* that she would soon be promoted.

5. _____

6. **inclination** (ĭn'klə-nā'shən) *noun*   A tendency or an attitude toward something; a preference or desire. (From the Latin *in-*, meaning "toward," and *clinare*, meaning "to lean")

Related Word   incline *verb*
Example   After climbing six flights of stairs, Gerald's *inclination* was to take the elevator to the nineteenth floor.

6. _____

7. **persevere** (pûr'sə-vîr') *verb*   To continue to do something in spite of obstacles or discouragement. (From the Latin word *perseverus*, meaning "very serious")

Related Word   perseverance *noun*
Example   The book was very difficult to understand, but Jason *persevered*.

7. _____

MEMORY CUE: Don't put an *r* in the second syllable of *persevere*; it's a "severe" word.

8. **reluctant** (rĭ-lŭk'tənt) *adjective*   Unwilling or not wanting to do something; offering resistance. (From the Latin *re-*, meaning "against," and *luctari*, meaning "to struggle")

Related Words   reluctance *noun;* reluctantly *adverb*
Example   On the chilly afternoon, Marlene was *reluctant* to dive into the swimming pool.

8. _____

9. **voluntary** (vŏl'ən-tĕr'ē) *adjective*   Acting out of one's own free will. (From the Latin word *voluntas*, meaning "choice")

Related Words   voluntarily *adverb;* volunteer *noun*
Example   Sergio's decision to rake leaves for his grandmother was a *voluntary* one.

9. _____

10. **wistful** (wĭst'fəl) *adjective*   Full of a sad yearning or longing; wishful.

Related Words   wistfully *adverb;* wistfulness *noun*
Example   Marianne's *wistful* expression could be explained by her recent cross-country move.

10. _____

EXERCISE 1 WRITING CORRECT WORDS

On the answer line, write the word from the vocabulary list that fits
each definition.

1. A tendency to act in a certain way

2. The state of believing that a certain thing will happen

3. Admirable enough to be wanted

4. Acting out of free choice

5. To have great ambition

6. To long for something that belongs to someone else

7. To continue in spite of difficulties

8. Unwilling

9. Full of sad longing or yearning; wishful

10. To foresee; look forward to something with pleasure

1. _____
2. _____
3. _____
4. _____
5. _____
6. _____
7. _____
8. _____
9. _____
10. _____

EXERCISE 2 USING WORDS CORRECTLY

Decide whether the italicized vocabulary word has been used correctly in the
sentence. On the answer line, write *Correct* for correct use and *Incorrect* for
incorrect use.

1. The catcher *anticipated* the steal and threw the runner out at second base.

2. Meredith was forced to accept the *voluntary* assignment.

3. Because he *covets* power, Macbeth kills King Duncan.

4. During an attempt to climb Mount Everest, some people on the
   expedition *persevere*, giving up after going only part way.

5. "If you are *reluctant* to work hard," said the coach, "you belong on the
   team. Rowing is hard work!"

6. After years of preparation, the astronauts had every *expectation* of success.

7. Because Sophia *aspired* to be a concert violinist, she gave up her violin
   lessons after two years.

8. "It is my *inclination* to order the daily special," Ann-Marie told the
   waitress.

9. Emil's cousin is in the *enviable* position of having been accepted at five
   universities.

10. Cathy was in a *wistful* mood after she had parted with her good friend.

1. _____
2. _____
3. _____
4. _____
5. _____
6. _____
7. _____
8. _____
9. _____
10. _____

For each italicized vocabulary word in the following sentences, write the letter of the best definition on the answer line.

1. "There is an *inclination* toward baldness in my family," said Mike.
   a. preference   b. absence   c. tendency   d. hatred

   1. _____

2. Because of a generous tax refund, Sarah could *anticipate* taking a three-week cruise to South America.
   a. give up   c. stop worrying about
   b. dread   d. look forward to

   2. _____

3. People with a fear of heights are *reluctant* to climb mountains.
   a. slow   b. unwilling   c. eager   d. careful

   3. _____

4. Kai's decision to become a blood donor was *voluntary*.
   a. forced upon him   c. demanded by others
   b. his own choice   d. important to him

   4. _____

5. Nancy Astor *persevered* in her campaign and became the first woman elected to the British House of Commons.
   a. regrouped   b. continued   c. hesitated   d. failed

   5. _____

6. Many *aspire* to be famous, but few are able to achieve that goal.
   a. desire strongly   c. work steadfastly
   b. pretend desperately   d. eagerly expect

   6. _____

7. At the restaurant the dieter *coveted* his neighbor's seven-course meal.
   a. ignored   b. noticed   c. criticized   d. desired

   7. _____

8. After many trades Jo has an *enviable* collection of baseball cards.
   a. worthy of being admired   c. worthy of being sold
   b. worthy of being protected   d. worthy of being traded

   8. _____

9. Seeing the kitten filled Kirsten's mind with *wistful* memories of her own lost cat.
   a. joyful   b. amusing   c. sad and longing   d. meaningful

   9. _____

10. Tyesha trained with the *expectation* of making the gymnastics team.
    a. prospect   c. unlikely fantasy
    b. foolish idea   d. grim reality

    10. _____

Each sentence contains an italicized vocabulary word in a form that does not fit the sentence. On the answer line, write the form of that word that does fit the sentence.

1. Two-year-old children often show great *reluctant* to do what their parents tell them.

   1. _____

2. "If you keep practicing," promised Chris's piano teacher, "your *persevere* will pay off."

   2. _____

3. Andrea was filled with *wistful* at the thought of missing her reunion.

   3. _____

4. Jerome *voluntary* worked five hours a week at the animal shelter.

   4. _____

5. As the day for the rafting trip neared, Carla's *anticipate* was high.

   5. _____

6. Bruce *covet* his cousin's collection of rare coins.   6. _____

7. Judy was *envy* of her sister's athletic ability.   7. _____

8. Benjamin Disraeli said, "What we anticipate seldom occurs; what we least   8. _____
    expectation generally happens."

9. Jack was *inclination* to take an airplane rather than drive two thousand   9. _____
    miles.

10. "My sole *aspire* for the next half-hour," explained Ellie, "is to finish my   10. _____
    homework."

READING COMPREHENSION

Each numbered sentence in the following passage contains an
italicized vocabulary word or related form. After you read the
passage, you will complete an exercise.

A SKATER'S DREAM: FELICIA'S STORY

For as long as I can remember, the
alarm clock has been jarring me
awake at the unmentionable hour
of 4:30 A.M. **(1)** My first *inclination*
is to turn over and ignore its per-
sistent ring. **(2)** Still hoping to
catch a few more minutes of
sleep, I'm *reluctant* to throw off
the covers and prepare for
another hectic but rewarding day.

There's only one other person
I know who gets up as early as I
do. That's my dad, who is also
my ice-skating coach and owner
of the Wolverine Skating Rink.
By 5:30 A.M., Dad and I are at the
rink, bleary-eyed but ready to
begin my three hours of skating
practice before school. After
attending classes, I return to the
rink for three more hours of figure skating. My evenings are
devoted to homework and frequent ballet classes.

People who don't know me
very well are baffled by my
exhausting schedule. "Why are
you doing all this?" they ask.
(3) My answer is always the same:
"I am a dedicated ice skater who
aspires to be a champion."

(4) While juggling the hours of
my tightly packed schedule, I
often think of professional skating stars who have achieved
enviable success. **(5)** Like them,
I decided *voluntarily* to skate
competitively.

Living with this decision has
not been easy. **(6)** Many of my

friends have already dropped out
of competitive skating because
they do not have the physical or
mental *perseverance* demanded
by this exhausting sport.

What makes me go on? I simply can't give up on a dream that
I've had since I was seven years
old. **(7)** My friends tell me that
I'm asking for too much from
life, but I have very high *expectations.* I hope to qualify for the
Olympics and, someday, to skate
professionally in an ice show.

Sometimes I'll admit that I
have my doubts. I'll feel as if I'm
missing out on things or that I'm
too ambitious. **(8)** "We miss you,"
my friends complain *wistfully*
when I turn down their invitations. **(9)** Often, though, I'll attend
an ice show and catch myself
coveting the lead skater's starring
role. Dad tells me that this is the
way all athletes feel if they really
want to accomplish something.

According to Dad, a positive
mental attitude is very important. **(10)** "You have to *anticipate*
success, not failure," he is fond of
saying. I'm going to listen to him.

Each of the following statements corresponds to a numbered sentence in the passage. Each statement contains a blank and is followed by four answer choices. Decide which choice fits best in the blank. The word or phrase that you choose must express roughly the same meaning as the italicized word in the passage. Write the letter of your choice on the answer line.

1. When the alarm goes off, Felicia has the _____ to go back to sleep.
   a. courage   b. desire   c. nerve   d. ambition

   1. _____

2. She is _____ to throw off her covers.
   a. happy   b. sad   c. unwilling   d. quick

   2. _____

3. Felicia _____ to become a champion ice skater.
   a. greatly desires   c. boldly asks
   b. strictly exercises   d. sternly refuses

   3. _____

4. Many of Felicia's idols have achieved success that is _____.
   a. unimportant   b. critical   c. admirable   d. honorable

   4. _____

5. Felicia's choice to skate competitively has been _____.
   a. her mother's   c. her friends'
   b. her coach's   d. her own

   5. _____

6. Competitive ice-skating takes great mental and physical _____.
   a. practice   b. endurance   c. talent   d. energy

   6. _____

7. Felicia has _____.
   a. much stamina   c. great hopes
   b. great fears   d. great abilities

   7. _____

8. Her friends complain _____ when Felicia refuses their invitations.
   a. sadly and longingly   c. happily
   b. angrily   d. nervously

   8. _____

9. At an ice show, Felicia will sometimes _____ the starring role.
   a. memorize   b. criticize   c. desire   d. learn

   9. _____

10. Felicia's coach tells her to _____ success.
    a. find   b. reject   c. disguise   d. expect

    10. _____

PRACTICE WITH ANALOGIES

Strategy   Express to yourself the relationship between the given words and eliminate answer choices that are obviously incorrect.

Directions   On the answer line, write the vocabulary word or a form of it that completes each analogy.

1. Detour is to route as _____ is to subject. *(Lesson 9)*

   1. _____

2. Blur is to image as _____ is to word. *(Lesson 9)*

   2. _____

3. Forlorn is to hope as merciless is to _____. *(Lesson 10)*

   3. _____

4. Hydrophobia is to water as _____ is to strangers. *(Lesson 11)*

   4. _____

5. Request is to demand as _____ is to require. *(Lesson 12)*

   5. _____

TEST-TAKING SKILLS

SENTENCE-COMPLETION TESTS

Many tests include sentence-completion items. These items require you to complete a sentence by filling in a blank with the word or phrase that makes the best sense. Here is a procedure for answering sentence-completion test items.

PROCEDURE

1. *Read the directions carefully.* Sometimes students lose credit for test items because they do not follow the correct procedure for answering the test questions. The best way to avoid this mistake is to read the directions carefully.

2. *Look for the key word or phrase.* Test sentences contain key words or phrases that will help you determine the missing word.

   The play's organization is _____; that is, each scene is presented in the order of its occurrence.
   a. confusing   **b.** controversial   **c.** interesting   **d.** chronological

   In the test item above, "presented in the order of its occurrence" is the key phrase. It tells that the play's organization must be chronological.

3. *The key word or phrase can be a definition.* In definitional sentences, the key word or phrase is a definition or explanation. In the test item above, the phrase "presented in the order of its occurrence" is a definition of *chronological*.

4. *Insert the word or phrase in the blank, and read the sentence again to make sure that it makes sense.* Try this with the following test item.

   Serge checked the books out of the library because he is _____ about sailing.
   a. interested   **b.** willing   **c.** seasick   **d.** curious

   The correct answer is *d. Curious* is the only choice that can be followed by the preposition *about*. If you had not inserted your answer in the sentence, you might have selected *interested*. It has a similar meaning but cannot be used with *about*.

EXERCISE ANSWERING SENTENCE-COMPLETION TEST ITEMS

Choose the word that best completes each of the following sentences. Write the letter of your choice on the answer line. Use your dictionary as needed.

1. Lilly's distinguishing trait is her _____; she always seems to be full of energy and spirit.
   a. compassion   b. fanaticism   c. depression   d. vivacity

   1. _____

2. The investigators promised to _____ new evidence that would solve the mystery.
   a. confide   b. destroy   c. conceal   d. disclose

   2. _____

3. Buddha is often called _____ because of his reputation for great wisdom and sound judgment.
   a. a sage   b. an orator   c. a calligrapher   d. an actor

   3. _____

4. Daryl is _____ person who enjoys socializing with his friends.
   a. a somber   b. a forlorn   c. an affable   d. a wistful

   4. _____

5. Nathan is admired for being a _____ who enjoys shopping in used book stores.
   a. zoologist   b. bibliophile   c. xenophobe   d. botanist

   5. _____

6. Like a true _____, Sean dedicated his life to working for a cause.
   a. orator   b. pest   c. fanatic   d. mimic

   6. _____

7. Theresa was a _____ person who felt great sympathy for those less fortunate than her.
   a. compassionate   c. covetous
   b. bigoted   d. jealous

   7. _____

8. Stubborn by nature, Ken became even more _____ when asked to complete a task he didn't enjoy.
   a. alluring   b. jubilant   c. reluctant   d. vivacious

   8. _____

9. Lexa demonstrated the _____ that one would expect from a zealot.
   a. clarity   c. cultivation
   b. enlightenment   d. fervor

   9. _____

10. Daniel Webster's speeches are often praised as models of _____ because his ideas were well organized and clearly presented.
    a. digression   b. texture   c. allusion   d. coherence

    10. _____

Just as things may be built, born, or grown, they can also be spoiled or destroyed. Some destruction actually has a positive effect. For example, certain medicines kill germs that cause disease. Destruction also can have a negative effect. Heavy rains or flooding may wash away the soil needed for planting crops.

Each word in this lesson deals with a slightly different sense of destruction. By learning the definitions, you will increase your ability to understand many aspects of this topic.

DEFINITIONS

After you have studied the definitions and example for each word, write the vocabulary word on the line to the right.

1. **annihilate** (ə-nī′ə-lāt′) *verb*   To destroy completely; to abolish. (From the Latin *ad-,* meaning "to," and *nihil,* meaning "nothing")

   Related Word   **annihilation** *noun*
   Example   A volcanic eruption *annihilated* the population of ancient Pompeii.

   1. _____

2. **contaminate** (kən-tăm′ə-nāt′) *verb*   To make impure by contact or mixture; to taint or pollute.

   Related Word   **contamination** *noun*
   Example   Bacteria *contaminated* the medicine, making it dangerous to use.

   2. _____

3. **corrode** (kə-rōd′) *verb*   **a.** To wear away or dissolve through chemical action.   **b.** To be eaten away or worn away: *Iron corrodes and produces rust.* (From the Latin word *corrodere,* meaning "to gnaw away")

   Related Words **corrosion** *noun;* **corrosive** *adjective*
   Example   Acid will *corrode* brass.

   3. _____

4. **deplete** (dĭ-plēt′) *verb*   To use up or reduce in quantity or amount. (From the Latin word *deplere,* meaning "to empty")

   Related Word   **depletion** *noun*
   Example   Too many expensive activities have *depleted* our club's treasury.

   4. _____
   USAGE NOTE: A related adjective is *replete,* which means "abundantly supplied"—filled to overflowing, in other words. See also *deteriorate.*

5. **deteriorate** (dĭ-tîr'ē-ə-rāt') *verb*   To become worse; to decrease in quality or value. (From the Latin word *deterior*, meaning "worse")

   Related Word   **deterioration** *noun*
   Example   Dancers' flexibility and agility may *deteriorate* unless they exercise regularly.

5. _____
MEMORY CUE: Note that *deteriorate* involves decreasing quality but *deplete* involves reducing quantity.

6. **dismantle** (dĭs-măn'tl) *verb*   To take apart or tear down; to reduce to pieces.

   Example   Alex purchased a special bicycle that he could *dismantle* and store easily.

6. _____
USAGE NOTE: *Mantle* is not an antonym for *dismantle*; *mantle* means "to cover or conceal."

7. **extinct** (ĭk-stĭngkt') *adjective*   No longer existing or living: *an extinct plant species.* (From the Latin word *extinctus*, meaning "extinguished")

   Related Word   **extinction** *noun*
   Example   Short-eared owls may soon become *extinct* unless steps are taken to protect them.

7. _____

8. **negate** (nĭ-gāt') *verb*   **a.** To make ineffective or worthless.   **b.** To rule out or deny. (From the Latin word *negare*, meaning "to deny")

   Related Word   **negation** *noun*
   Example   His smile *negated* the effect of the scolding he gave his son.

8. _____

9. **rancid** (răn'sĭd) *adjective*   Smelling or tasting like spoiled oils or fats. (From the Latin word *rancere*, meaning "to stink")

   Related Word   **rancidness** *noun*
   Example   Before refrigeration, people used salt to prevent meat from becoming *rancid*.

9. _____

10. **squander** (skwŏn'dər) *verb*   To waste; to spend uselessly.

   Related Word   **squanderer** *noun*
   Example   Jed *squandered* his money on comic books.

10. _____

EXERCISE 1 COMPLETING DEFINITIONS

On the answer line, write the word from the vocabulary list that best
completes each definition.

1. To waste or spend uselessly is to _____.

2. To destroy completely is to _____.

3. Something that smells or tastes like spoiled oils or fats is probably _____.

4. To make impure by contact or mixture is to _____.

5. To make ineffective or to deny is to _____.

6. To wear away or dissolve through chemical action is to _____.

7. To be no longer existing or living is to be _____.

8. To use up or reduce in quantity is to _____.

9. To take apart or tear down is to _____.

10. To become worse or to decline in quality is to _____.

1. _____

2. _____

3. _____

4. _____

5. _____

6. _____

7. _____

8. _____

9. _____

10. _____

EXERCISE 2 USING WORDS CORRECTLY

Each of the following statements contains an italicized vocabulary word.
Decide the answer to the question, and write *Yes* or *No* on the answer line.

1. Would *contaminated* milk be good to drink?

2. If you *dismantled* a piece of furniture to move it, would you completely
destroy it?

3. Would most parents want their children to *squander* money?

4. Would a restaurant whose service has *deteriorated* probably lose
customers?

5. If a refrigerator has a *rancid* odor, should someone clean it out quickly?

6. Has a disaster ever *annihilated* a whole town?

7. If animals and plants are in danger of *extinction*, might they cease to exist?

8. Will careful watering and weeding *negate* a person's attempts to grow
vegetables?

9. If the stock in a supermarket has been *depleted*, are the shelves filled to
capacity?

10. If the fender of a car has *corroded*, has it begun to show signs of rust?

1. _____

2. _____

3. _____

4. _____

5. _____

6. _____

7. _____

8. _____

9. _____

10. _____

Decide which vocabulary word best completes the sentence, and write the letter of that word on the answer line.

1. If you leave an iron object out in the rain, it will _____.
   a. corrode   **b.** deplete   **c.** negate   **d.** dismantle

   1. _____

2. In *Poor Richard's Almanac*, Benjamin Franklin advised his readers not to _____ time, "for that's the stuff life is made of."
   a. dismantle   **b.** corrode   **c.** squander   **d.** negate

   2. _____

3. Even though their supplies were quickly _____, the Texans holding the Alamo refused to surrender.
   a. depleted   **b.** dismantled   **c.** extinct   **d.** deteriorated

   3. _____

4. Such materials as cloth and leather can _____ so much over time that they fall apart.
   a. contaminate   **b.** negate   **c.** deteriorate   **d.** extinct

   4. _____

5. Thousands of species of plants have become _____ through the ages.
   a. corroded   **b.** rancid   **c.** negated   **d.** extinct

   5. _____

6. Meat should be refrigerated so that it will not become _____.
   a. extinct   **b.** rancid   **c.** corroded   **d.** negated

   6. _____

7. Chemical sprays may help to _____ mosquitoes in swampy areas.
   a. corrode   **b.** dismantle   **c.** squander   **d.** annihilate

   7. _____

8. Laws have been passed to prevent the chemical dumping that has _____ our water.
   a. corroded   **b.** contaminated   **c.** negated   **d.** dismantled

   8. _____

9. An antidote is something that can _____ the effects of a poison and thus save the victim.
   a. contaminate   **b.** deplete   **c.** negate   **d.** corrode

   9. _____

10. London Bridge once crossed the Thames River, but in 1968 it was _____ and moved to Lake Havasu City in Arizona.
    a. corroded   **b.** depleted   **c.** dismantled   **d.** deteriorated

    10. _____

EXERCISE 4 USING DIFFERENT FORMS OF WORDS

Decide which form of the vocabulary word in parentheses best completes the sentence. The form given may be correct. Write your answer on the answer line.

1. Air pollution has a _____ effect on buildings and statues. (*corrode*)

   1. _____

2. "My opponent, if elected, will be a _____ of city funds," declared the mayoral candidate. (*squander*)

   2. _____

3. _____ may result if foods are not properly refrigerated. (*rancid*)

   3. _____

4. Rob was reading a science-fiction book about a space colony that escaped _____ by a band of warriors. (*annihilate*)

   4. _____

5. A decrease in the number of American bald eagles has increased the concern about their _____. (*extinct*)

   5. _____

6. The _____ of natural resources like coal and gas may cause an increase in some home-fuel costs. *(deplete)*

    6. _____

7. Last year's budget cuts resulted in the _____ of our school's athletic program. *(dismantle)*

    7. _____

8. The discovery that some students unknowingly had voted twice caused the _____ of the school election results. *(negate)*

    8. _____

9. Red tide, which is an overabundance of tiny plantlike animals in the ocean, caused the _____ of shellfish. *(contaminate)*

    9. _____

10. Many museums have climate-controlled rooms to prevent _____ of their art treasures. *(deteriorate)*

    10. _____

READING COMPREHENSION

Each numbered sentence in the following passage contains an italicized vocabulary word or related form. After you have read the passage, you will complete an exercise.

POLLUTION AND PROGRESS

Advances in science and industry have dramatically improved the quality of modern living. (1) Before modern means of refrigeration were developed, for example, fresh meat became *rancid* within a few days. Today, meat stored properly in electric refrigerators and freezers remains edible for months.

Unfortunately, some modern inventions also have had the negative effect of adding to the pollution of our environment. (2) The air quality of many of our cities has *deteriorated* because of the fumes from cars. Industrial plants may also produce air pollution. (3) In heavily industrial areas, the metal surfaces of cars and buildings *corrode* rapidly.

(4) Pollution has affected our water supply, some of which has been *contaminated* by chemical waste. (5) Chemicals have *depleted* the amount of oxygen in water. (6) As a result, plants and animals in some ponds have been *annihilated.*

Pollution may even be affecting the temperature of the earth's atmosphere. Some scientists warn that a "greenhouse effect" could warm the entire world. This condition would melt glaciers and cause widespread flooding. (7) Many types of plants and animals would not be able to adjust to a changed environment and would become *extinct.*

In response to these dangers, government and industry have taken many steps to reduce pollution. Legislators have passed laws to protect air and water quality. (8) Industrial firms have *dismantled* machinery that once polluted the air and have replaced it with less harmful equipment. Many automobiles now carry pollution-control devices. (9) Government, industry, and private citizens want to make certain that the benefits of healthful surroundings will not be *negated* by the harmful effects of pollution. (10) People are determined not to *squander* the precious resources of the environment.

Each of the following statements corresponds to a numbered sentence in the passage. Each statement contains a blank and is followed by four answer choices. Decide which choice fits best in the blank. The word or phrase that you choose must express roughly the same meaning as the italicized word in the passage. Write the letter of your choice on the answer line.

1. Meat often turned _____ before modern refrigeration was invented.
   a. brown   **b.** foul   **c.** tasty   **d.** smooth

   1. _____

2. Because of automobile pollution, the air quality in many cities has _____.
   a. worsened   **b.** developed   **c.** improved   **d.** changed

   2. _____

3. Metal surfaces often _____ when they are exposed to industrial pollution.
   a. become smooth   **c.** topple
   b. change direction   **d.** wear away

   3. _____

4. Our water supply has been _____ by chemical waste.
   a. used up   **b.** stopped   **c.** polluted   **d.** renewed

   4. _____

5. The amount of oxygen in water has been _____ by chemicals.
   a. reduced   **b.** provided   **c.** located   **d.** helped

   5. _____

6. Without the oxygen in pond water, some plants and animals have been _____.
   a. saved   **b.** destroyed   **c.** analyzed   **d.** absorbed

   6. _____

7. Animals that cannot adjust to changes in the environment _____.
   a. get healthier   **c.** are replaced
   b. move away   **d.** cease to exist

   7. _____

8. Industries have _____ machinery that harms the environment.
   a. invented   **b.** slowed down   **c.** taken apart   **d.** acquired

   8. _____

9. Responsible people want to be sure that the benefits of some environments will not be _____ by pollution.
   a. made worthless   **c.** encouraged
   b. made valuable   **d.** created

   9. _____

10. People do not want to _____ environmental resources.
   a. trade   **b.** waste   **c.** forget   **d.** complicate

   10. _____

Weather can be a destructive force. Tornadoes can uproot trees and flatten buildings. Lack of rain can cause crops to die. Flooding can destroy entire areas. Choose one type of destructive weather, and write a short composition about the negative effects that it can have. End with an explanation of the steps that people can take to minimize the effects of poor weather conditions. Use at least four of the words from this lesson in your composition, and underline each word that you use.

Today's books and magazines are filled with self-help strategies. Do any of these titles look familiar?

"How to Get Organized and Stay That Way!"
"A Fabulous New Diet for a Fabulous New You!"
"Twenty Ways to Feel Good About Yourself!"

All how-to articles and books revolve around some area of self-improvement, physical or psychological. Some of the words in this lesson are useful for describing self-help processes, while others are suitable for describing the physical improvement of places and things.

WORD LIST

compensate
conserve
constructive
enhance
enrichment
idealize
neutralize
preservation
redeem
restore

DEFINITIONS

After you have studied the definitions and example for each word, write the vocabulary word in the blank to the right.

1. **compensate** (kŏm′pən-sāt′) *verb*   **a.** To make up for or offset; counterbalance.   **b.** To pay or reimburse. (From the Latin *com-*, meaning "together," and *pensare*, meaning "to pay out")

   Related Words compensation *noun*; **compensatory** *adjective*
   Example   The basketball player *compensated* for his low scoring by becoming an excellent defensive player.

   1. _____

2. **conserve** (kən-sûrv′) *verb*   **a.** To protect from loss or from being totally used up: *to conserve natural resources*.   **b.** To use carefully without waste. (From the Latin word *conservare*, meaning "to preserve")

   Related Word   conservation *noun*
   Example   The town council agreed on a rationing system to *conserve* water.

   2. _____
   See *preservation*.

3. **constructive** (kən-strŭk′tĭv) *adjective*   Serving a useful purpose or helping to improve conditions. (From the Latin *com-*, meaning "together," and *struere*, meaning "to pile up")

   Related Words constructively *adverb*; **constructiveness** *noun*
   Example   The teacher's *constructive* criticism helped Robert to improve his piano playing.

   3. _____
   USAGE NOTE: An antonym of *constructive* is *destructive*, meaning "ruinous" or "designed to disprove or discredit."

4. **enhance** (ĕn-hăns′) *verb*   To add to or increase in value, cost, or beauty.

   Related Word   enhancement *noun*
   Example   Vanessa *enhanced* the appearance of the yard by putting in new shrubbery.

   4. _____

5. **enrichment** (ĕn-rĭch'mənt) *noun*   The act of making something more meaningful, fulfilling, or rewarding.

> **Related Word**   **enrich** *verb*
> **Example**   An art museum is a good environment for cultural *enrichment*.

5. _____

6. **idealize** (ī-dē'ə-līz') *verb*   To set someone or something up as a model or standard of excellence.

> **Related Words**   **ideal** *noun;* **idealist** *noun;* **idealistic** *adjective*
> **Example**   People around the world have *idealized* George Washington as a great leader.

6. _____

7. **neutralize** (noo'trə-līz') *verb*   To cancel or counteract the effect of something.

> **Related Word**   **neutral** *adjective*
> **Example**   An apology can *neutralize* someone's anger.

7. _____

8. **preservation** (prĕz'ər-vā'shən) *noun*   The act of guarding something from injury, danger, or deterioration; maintenance of the original condition of something. (From the Latin *prae-*, meaning "before," and *servare*, meaning "to guard")

> **Related Words**   **preservative** *noun;* **preserve** *verb*
> **Example**   A city may require the *preservation* of historical buildings.

8. _____
USAGE NOTE: *Conserve* implies protection (of things) from depletion or waste; *preserve* implies protection (of things, people) from injury or change. See also *restore*.

9. **redeem** (rĭ-dēm') *verb*   **a.** To turn in coupons or stock certificates in exchange for an item or money.   **b.** To recover ownership by paying a sum.   **c.** To make up for. (From the Latin *red-*, meaning "back," and *emere*, meaning "to buy")

> **Related Words**   **redeemable** *adjective;* **redemption** *noun*
> **Example**   At the supermarket John *redeemed* ten coupons and saved $3.75 on his grocery bill.

9. _____

10. **restore** (rĭ-stôr') *verb*   **a.** To bring back into existence: *to restore one's faith in humanity.*   **b.** To return to original condition. (From the Latin word *restaurare*, meaning "to repair")

> **Related Words**   **restoration** *noun;* **restorative** *adjective*
> **Example**   A cool glass of water *restored* the hiker's energy.

10. _____
USAGE NOTE: If you *preserve* something, you *keep* it in its original condition; if you *restore* something you *return* it to its original condition.

EXERCISE I COMPLETING DEFINITIONS

On the answer line, write the word from the vocabulary list that best completes each definition.

1. To cancel or counteract something is to _____ it.

2. If you view something as perfect, you _____ it.

3. To protect something from loss or waste is to _____ it.

4. The act of making an activity more meaningful or rewarding is the process of _____ .

5. To regain something through monetary payment is to _____ it.

6. To bring something back to its original condition is to _____ it.

7. To increase the value, cost, or beauty of something is to _____ it.

8. To make up for or offset is to _____ .

9. Something that has a useful purpose is _____ .

10. The act of saving something from injury, harm, or deterioration is called _____ .

1. _____
2. _____
3. _____
4. _____
5. _____
6. _____
7. _____
8. _____
9. _____
10. _____

EXERCISE 2 USING WORDS CORRECTLY

Each of the following statements contains an italicized vocabulary word. Decide whether the sentence is true or false, and write *True* or *False* on the answer line.

1. A student might *compensate* for a poor grade on a test by studying hard for the next exam.

2. Watching educational television can provide *enrichment.*

3. Calling someone ridiculous is a good example of *constructive* criticism.

4. One way to *conserve* energy is to leave the lights on all night.

5. People often *idealize* movie stars by overlooking their idols' negative qualities.

6. One who attempts to *restore* old paintings tries to make them look as they did when they were first painted.

7. Game wardens are concerned with the *preservation* of birds and animals.

8. Sunscreen lotion helps to *neutralize* the negative effects of the sun.

9. A cook can *enhance* the flavor of the meal by overcooking it.

10. You can sometimes *redeem* cereal box labels for special merchandise.

1. _____
2. _____
3. _____
4. _____
5. _____
6. _____
7. _____
8. _____
9. _____
10. _____

Help and Improvement **89**

EXERCISE 3 CHOOSING THE BEST DEFINITION

For each italicized vocabulary word in the following sentences, write the
letter of the best definition on the answer line.

1. A substance such as bicarbonate of soda can *neutralize* the effect of an acid
   like lemon juice.
   a. accelerate   **b.** cancel   **c.** intensify   **d.** equal

   1. _____

2. After two days without exercise, the jogger *compensated* by running five
   extra miles.
   a. injured himself   **c.** made up for it
   b. ignored the problem   **d.** exerted himself

   2. _____

3. Lindy planned her weekend around such *constructive* activities as playing
   tennis and studying.
   a. busy   **b.** useful   **c.** wasteful   **d.** necessary

   3. _____

4. Reading a novel a week contributed to Jeremy's personal *enrichment*.
   a. reading ability **b.** problems   **c.** diary   **d.** improvement

   4. _____

5. Cosmetic manufacturers claim that customers can *enhance* their looks with
   make-up.
   a. improve   **b.** enjoy   **c.** spoil   **d.** hide

   5. _____

6. Jessica had *idealized* London so much that she was disappointed when she
   arrived there.
   a. dreamed of   **c.** imagined to be perfect
   b. worried about   **d.** looked forward to

   6. _____

7. The movie star purchased two hundred garment bags for the *preservation*
   of her wardrobe.
   a. reconstruction **b.** safekeeping   **c.** destruction   **d.** celebration

   7. _____

8. Winning a close game *restored* the team's spirit.
   a. increased   **b.** decreased   **c.** brought back **d.** added to

   8. _____

9. To *conserve* their food supplies, the pioneers ate only two small meals
   a day.
   a. build up   **b.** weaken   **c.** save   **d.** eliminate

   9. _____

10. Sharon *redeemed* the trading stamps and received an electric frying pan.
    a. sacrificed   **b.** collected   **c.** threw away   **d.** turned in

    10. _____

EXERCISE 4 USING DIFFERENT FORMS OF WORDS

Decide which form of the vocabulary word in parentheses best completes the
sentence. Write your answer on the answer line.

1. The pawnbroker told Marian that her antique necklace was no longer
   _____ . *(redeem)*

   1. _____

2. The small salad offered little _____ to the hungry dieter. *(compensate)*

   2. _____

3. Members of the writing club commented _____ on one another's
   compositions. *(constructive)*

   3. _____

4. "We are trying to _____ wildlife here, not destroy it," the ranger informed
   the hunters. *(preservation)*

   4. _____

5. The creation of parks and gardens can result in the _____ of an entire city. (*enhance*)

5. _____

6. Patrick wants to paint the living room beige or some other _____ color. (*neutralize*)

6. _____

7. Susan hoped to _____ her life by buying some good paintings. (*enrichment*)

7. _____

8. _____ of run-down houses is Patrick's favorite hobby. (*restore*)

8. _____

9. Attending a Broadway show is an _____ way to spend an evening in New York City. (*idealize*)

9. _____

10. One way the United States government has encouraged _____ is by creating national parks. (*conserve*)

10. _____

READING COMPREHENSION

Each numbered sentence in the following passage contains an italicized vocabulary word or related form. After you read the passage, you will complete an exercise.

A CLASS DEBATE

Several years ago, members of a graduating class gathered in an auditorium to discuss a farewell gift to their school.

As usual, Mike, the class comedian, had a great deal to contribute. (1) "I don't see why we need to *enhance* the school's appearance," he began. "The place looks fine to me. (2) Think of all the aluminum cans we had to *redeem* to raise funds. I vote to use the money for a class trip to the beach."

Samantha, the next speaker, gave Mike a disgusted look. (3) "Some of us would like to make the school a more *enriching* place for students. We could buy books for the school library."

"What for?" Mike groaned. "The library already has enough books."

"Of course, you would say that!" Samantha accused. "The only thing you ever read are the directions to video games."

(4) Before Mike could reply, Jennifer, the class president, spoke up to *neutralize* the negative mood created by the argument. (5) "Why don't we donate our money to a *constructive* project that would beautify the city? (6) I think we should make a donation in the school's name to the city park *restoration* project so that this important open area can be returned to its original condition."

"I second the motion!" said Amy Wright, Jennifer's best friend.

"Wait a minute!" Mike protested. "That was not a motion. It was a suggestion and a worthless one at that. I played in that park in the fourth grade, and it was perfect, stupendous, outstanding! Nothing could be more magnificent! I wouldn't change a thing."

(7) "That visit was a long time ago, and that's the first time I've ever heard you describe anything as *ideal*," Samantha pointed out. (8) "You're just trying to *compensate* for an advanced case of selfishness. You think that if you praise the park, we won't notice that you want to spend the class money on having fun."

"I don't know how you can say the park is in good condition," Amy said with an accusing stare at Mike. "The fountain is so damaged that it's been turned off for years, and the wrought iron fences are all covered with rust. (9) It really needs *preservation!*"

"Okay, okay. I give in. Donate all our hard-earned money to the park. What do I care?" Mike said, finally abandoning his position.

"Good," Jennifer smiled. (10) "I move that we donate our money to *conserve* the city park." The response was overwhelmingly positive. "The ayes have it," Jennifer concluded.

READING COMPREHENSION EXERCISE

Each of the following statements corresponds to a numbered sentence in the passage. Each statement contains a blank and is followed by four answer choices. Decide which choice fits best in the blank. The word or phrase that you choose must express roughly the same meaning as the italicized word in the passage. Write the letter of your choice on the answer line.

1. Mike did not want to _____ the school's decor.
   a. judge   **b.** improve   **c.** talk about   **d.** think about

2. He reminded the class of all the aluminum cans they had _____.
   a. sold   **c.** turned in for money
   b. destroyed   **d.** thrown away

3. Samantha felt that buying library books would be a(n) _____ addition to the school.
   a. rewarding   **b.** entertaining   **c.** popular   **d.** useful

4. Jennifer tried to _____ the negative mood.
   a. reinforce   **b.** cancel out   **c.** add to   **d.** create

5. The class president wanted to donate the money to a _____ project.
   a. serious   **b.** gigantic   **c.** long-term   **d.** useful

6. The project was the _____ of the city park.
   a. total destruction   **c.** viewing
   b. returning to its original condition   **d.** decoration

7. It was unusual for Mike to view something as _____.
   a. serious   **b.** interesting   **c.** perfect   **d.** attractive

8. Samantha accused Mike of attempting to _____ for a selfish attitude.
   a. win encouragement   **c.** get help
   b. get credit   **d.** make up

9. Amy said that the park really needed _____.
   a. alteration   **b.** destruction   **c.** protection   **d.** decoration

10. The class wanted to _____ the city park.
    a. save   **b.** move   **c.** change   **d.** destroy

1. _____
2. _____
3. _____
4. _____
5. _____
6. _____
7. _____
8. _____
9. _____
10. _____

WRITING ASSIGNMENT

Think of an area in your life that needs help or improvement. You might consider an area of self-help, such as gaining more control of your time or improving your physical stamina. You might also consider a place that needs improvement, such as your own room or a local playground. In a paragraph, describe the condition as it is now, and then explain how it could be improved. Include at least five of the words from this lesson, and underline each word.

The word *appearance* refers to the way that somebody or something looks to others. When something presents an attractive appearance, it is often judged in a positive way. Appearances, however, can be misleading. Two traditional sayings that warn against judging something only by its appearance are "You can't tell a book by its cover" and "All that glitters is not gold." The words in this lesson describe many ways in which people and things can appear.

WORD LIST

becoming
chic
debonair
disheveled
dowdy
drab
garb
rumpled
unsightly
veneer

DEFINITIONS

After you have studied the definitions and example for each word, write the vocabulary word on the line to the right.

1. **becoming** (bĭ-kŭm′ĭng) *adjective*   Attractive; suitable; pleasing to the eye.

   Related Word   **becomingly** *adverb*
   Example   People like to wear colors that are *becoming*.

   1. _____

2. **chic** (shēk) *adjective*   **a.** Stylish; fashionable.   **b.** Fashionably dressed. *noun*   Elegance; sophistication.

   Related Word   **chicly** *adverb*
   Example   The *chic* restaurant attracted the most sophisticated people in town.

   2. _____

3. **debonair** (dĕb′ə-nâr′) *adjective*   Sophisticated in a lively, gracious manner. (From the Old French phrase *de bonne aire*, meaning "of good disposition")

   Example   The *debonair* guide took us to the most famous sites in Europe.

   3. _____

4. **disheveled** (dĭ-shĕv′əld) *adjective*   Untidy, messy. (From the Old French word *descheveler*, meaning "to disarrange the hair")

   Related Word   **dishevelment** *noun*
   Example   The child's clothes became *disheveled* while he played on the gym equipment.

   4. _____
   See *rumpled*.

5. **dowdy** (dou′dē) *adjective*   Shabby and lacking in style.

   Related Words   **dowdily** *adverb;* **dowdiness** *noun*
   Example   *Dowdy* clothes are out of place at elegant parties.

5. _____

6. **drab** (drăb) *adjective*   Faded and dull in appearance; uninteresting.

   Related Words   **drably** *adverb;* **drabness** *noun*
   Example   The gray clouds and cold drizzle made the day seem *drab.*

6. _____

7. **garb** (gärb) *noun*   Clothing, especially clothing for a particular job or occasion.

   Example   People in many countries have distinctive national *garb.*

7. _____

8. **rumpled** (rum′pəld) *adjective*   Wrinkled or creased.

   Related Word   **rumple** *verb*
   Example   Clothing that is not carefully folded or hung on hangers becomes *rumpled.*

8. _____

USAGE NOTE: *Rumpled* means wrinkled or creased; *disheveled* means in disorder or wind-blown.

9. **unsightly** (ŭn-sīt′lē) *adjective*   Ugly; unpleasant to look at.

   Related Word   **unsightliness** *noun*
   Example   The essay was well written, but Terri crossed out so many words that the pages were *unsightly.*

9. _____

10. **veneer** (və-nîr′) *noun*   **a.** An appearance that gives a favorable, though false, impression: *a veneer of friendliness.*   **b.** A layer of material, such as wood, covering another, usually inferior, material.

    Example   He hid his unhappiness beneath a cheerful *veneer.*

10. _____

EXERCISE 1 WRITING CORRECT WORDS

On the answer line, write the word from the vocabulary list that fits
each definition.

1. Faded and dull in appearance

2. Wrinkled or creased

3. An appearance giving a favorable but false impression

4. Untidy; messy

5. Old-fashioned in appearance; unstylish

6. Sophisticated in a lively manner

7. Unpleasant to look at

8. Stylish

9. Clothing for a particular job or occasion

10. Pleasant to look at; suitable

1. _____

2. _____

3. _____

4. _____

5. _____

6. _____

7. _____

8. _____

9. _____

10. _____

EXERCISE 2 USING WORDS CORRECTLY

Each of the following statements contains an italicized vocabulary word.
Decide whether the sentence is true or false, and write *True* or *False* on the
answer line.

1. A *debonair* person is ill at ease with other people.

2. A cheerful *veneer* might disguise unhappiness.

3. A *chic* woman does not keep up with the latest fashion trends.

4. A *becoming* suit adds to one's appearance.

5. *Rumpled* sheets should be smoothed and straightened when a bed
   is made.

6. A person with untidy hair and rumpled clothing looks *disheveled*.

7. A well-tended garden is *unsightly* all summer long.

8. Violet, bright yellow, and scarlet are all *drab* colors.

9. The *garb* of a ballerina includes a leotard and toe shoes.

10. Someone wearing an old moth-eaten sweater, torn stockings, and worn-
    out shoes would look *dowdy*.

1. _____

2. _____

3. _____

4. _____

5. _____

6. _____

7. _____

8. _____

9. _____

10. _____

EXERCISE 3 CHOOSING THE BEST DEFINITION

For each italicized vocabulary word in the following sentences, write the
letter of the best definition on the answer line.

1. The spilled paint left an *unsightly* splotch on the rug.
   a. indelible   **b.** indistinct   **c.** dark   **d.** ugly

   1. _____

2. The campers looked *disheveled* after hiking through the underbrush.
   a. dirty   **b.** exhausted   **c.** messy   **d.** confused

   2. _____

3. The hospital corridors were painted a *drab* green.
   a. dull   **b.** bright   **c.** dark   **d.** ugly

   3. _____

4. The acrobat hid his fear beneath a *veneer* of calm.
   a. feeling   **b.** reaction   **c.** pretense   **d.** performance

   4. _____

5. Kim's blue dress is *becoming* because it emphasizes her beautiful eyes.
   a. attractive   **b.** sensible   **c.** striking   **d.** dull

   5. _____

6. Louise looked very trim in her fire-fighting *garb*.
   a. helmet   **b.** clothes   **c.** boots   **d.** truck

   6. _____

7. The hotel had *dowdy* old sofas in the lobby.
   a. soft   **b.** big   **c.** antique   **d.** unfashionable

   7. _____

8. Many *debonair* young men and women attended the movie star's garden
   party.
   a. hopeful   **b.** sophisticated   **c.** rich   **d.** happy

   8. _____

9. Nick's clothes were so *rumpled* that we thought he had slept in them.
   a. wrinkled   **b.** messy   **c.** torn   **d.** unsightly

   9. _____

10. Cristobal Balenciaga made very *chic* clothes.
    a. lovely   **b.** short   **c.** bizarre   **d.** stylish

    10. _____

EXERCISE 4 USING DIFFERENT FORMS OF WORDS

Each sentence contains an italicized vocabulary word in a form that does not
fit the sentence. On the answer line, write the form of that word that does fit
the sentence.

1. The *dowdy* of the apartment made it very unpleasant to live in.

   1. _____

2. The *unsightly* of the school yard led the students to sponsor a
   clean-up day.

   2. _____

3. Though it belonged to her sister, the child's dress fit her quite *becoming*.

   3. _____

4. A bright wall hanging can sometimes lessen the *drab* of a room.

   4. _____

5. Catherine is always very *chic* dressed.

   5. _____

6. The clown's clothes were in a permanent state of *disheveled*.

   6. _____

7. One should not dress *drab* when planning to dance the tango.

   7. _____

8. Roman likes to *rumpled* his pillows when he goes to sleep.

   8. _____

9. My uncle was dressed *dowdy* in an old bathrobe when we arrived.

   9. _____

10. By *rumpled* paper, you can throw it farther.

    10. _____

READING COMPREHENSION

Each numbered sentence in the following passage contains an italicized vocabulary word. After you read the passage, you will complete an exercise.

FASHIONS OF THE PAST

Can you imagine wearing shoes with five-inch pointed toes or a hair style rising eighteen inches above your head? People of the past did such things just to appear fashionable.

(1) In the 1300s pointed shoes were considered essential to the *debonair* gentleman. The points were often so long that the toe of the shoe had to be stuffed or tied to the knee. **(2)** Because bright colors and gold decorations were in style, few people looked *drab*. Some people even wore a shoe of a different color on each foot. **(3)** Despite the attempt at elegance, the total effect must have been *unsightly*.

In the 1700s hair styles rose to new heights at the court of Louis XVI. **(4)** A woman was considered *dowdy* unless she piled her hair far above her head in an elaborate creation. Hairdos contained fake fruit, miniature houses, and models of ships. **(5)** One *chic* woman celebrated the American Revolution with the "hairdo of liberty." **(6)** Fashionable ladies tried hard to prevent their hair from becoming *disheveled.* They often knelt in carriages to protect their high hairdos from the low tops.

(7) Their clothes, however, sometimes became *rumpled* in the process. **(8)** Not everyone found the new hair styles *becoming.* **(9)** Some people commented that a fashionable *veneer* could not hide the silliness of some of the men and women at court.

(10) Even soldiers have worn strange *garb* in the past. In the 1800s the bright red uniforms of British soldiers looked wonderful in parades. Unfortunately, they were also highly visible targets for enemy fire.

Some people today still wear uncomfortable and unusual fashions. Most modern fashions, however, are easier to wear than those of the past.

Each of the following statements corresponds to a numbered sentence in the passage. Each statement contains a blank and is followed by four answer choices. Decide which choice fits best in the blank. The word or phrase that you choose must express roughly the same meaning as the italicized word in the passage. Write the letter of your choice on the answer line.

1. In the 1300s people considered pointed shoes necessary for the _____ gentleman.
   a. wealthy **b.** noble **c.** sophisticated **d.** up-to-date

   1. _____

2. Bright colors and gold decorations made a _____ appearance a rarity.
   a. dark **b.** dreary **c.** special **d.** lively

   2. _____

3. Even though the effect was meant to be elegant, the appearance must have been _____.
   a. poor **b.** overdressed **c.** pleasing **d.** ugly

   3. _____

4. A woman without an elaborate hair style was considered _____.
   a. shabby **b.** lazy **c.** ugly **d.** poor

   4. _____

5. One _____ hairdo celebrated the American Revolution.
   a. tasteful **b.** dull **c.** attractive **d.** stylish

   5. _____

6. Fashionable ladies attempted to keep their hairdos from looking _____.
   a. untidy **b.** ugly **c.** silly **d.** dirty

   6. _____

7. Frequently their clothes became _____.
   a. dirty **b.** torn **c.** sticky **d.** creased

   7. _____

8. Some did not find the new hair styles _____.
   a. flattering **b.** easy **c.** cheap **d.** comfortable

   8. _____

9. Some noted that a stylish _____ did not conceal the silliness.
   a. wardrobe **b.** exterior **c.** wit **d.** personality

   9. _____

10. The _____ of the British soldier in the 1800s was another strange fashion.
    a. hat **b.** greeting **c.** gun **d.** uniform

    10. _____

PRACTICE WITH ANALOGIES

See pages 26, 52, and 78 for some other strategies to use with analogies.

Strategy Examine all answer choices to make sure that you have selected the best one. A choice may be close but not the best.

Directions On the answer line, write the vocabulary word or a form of it that completes each analogy.

1. Depreciate is to value as _____ is to quality. (*Lesson 13*)

   1. _____

2. Brackish is to water as _____ is to butter. (*Lesson 13*)

   2. _____

3. Rumpled is to clothing as _____ is to hair. (*Lesson 15*)

   3. _____

4. Gilt is to gold as _____ is to wood. (*Lesson 15*)

   4. _____

5. Dull is to personality as _____ is to appearance. (*Lesson 15*)

   5. _____

6. Abrasive is to skin as _____ is to iron. (*Lesson 13*)

   6. _____

READING SKILLS
CONTEXT CLUES: DEFINITION IN THE SENTENCE

A sentence containing an unfamiliar word often provides clues to the meaning of that word. Words that provide these hints are known as **context clues.**

Context clues can suggest the general meaning of an unfamiliar word. Sometimes they actually define the word. Suppose that you don't know the meaning of the italicized word in the following sentence.

> The *surfeit* of food for the holiday dinner meant that the family would be eating leftovers for days.

To use context clues in figuring out the meaning of *surfeit,* and other unfamiliar words, follow this procedure.

PROCEDURE

1. *Read the sentence carefully for clues to the meaning of the word.* In the example sentence, you will find two clues to the meaning of *surfeit.* First, there were leftovers from the holiday meal. Second, there must have been a large amount of leftover food because the family would be eating it for days.

2. *Decide on the meaning of the word, and reread the sentence to see if your definition makes sense.* Using the clues just given, you can conclude that a *surfeit* is an oversupply of something. This definition makes sense in the sentence.

3. *Check the meaning of the word in your dictionary.* To confirm your definition, find the word in your dictionary. One dictionary definition of *surfeit* is "too much of something; an excess." This is close to the definition drawn from the context clues.

EXERCISE USING CONTEXT CLUES

Use context clues to figure out the meaning of the italicized word in each sentence. *Step 1:* Write the clues contained in the sentence. There may be one or several clues. *Step 2:* Write your definition of the word. *Step 3:* Write the dictionary definition of the word. Choose the definition that best fits the way the word is used in the sentence.

1. People call John *waspish* because he often seems irritated.

   Clue(s) _____

   Your Definition _____

   Dictionary Definition _____

2. The *suave* young man's good manners and charm made him quite popular.

   Clue(s) _____

   Your Definition _____

   Dictionary Definition _____

3. He showed his *solicitude* by visiting me in the hospital twice a day.

   Clue(s) _____

   Your Definition _____

   Dictionary Definition _____

4. Kara's *gullible* friend believed anything we told her.

   Clue(s) _____

   Your Definition _____

   Dictionary Definition _____

5. Ed was a *hindrance* to the rest of the band because he played off-key.

   Clue(s) _____

   Your Definition _____

   Dictionary Definition _____

6. The plant-nibbling giraffe, which never eats meat, is a good example of a *herbivore*.

   Clue(s) _____

   Your Definition _____

   Dictionary Definition _____

7. The gymnast risked serious injury throughout the *perilous* routine.

   Clue(s) _____

   Your Definition _____

   Dictionary Definition _____

8. The *capricious* child changed her dinner order twice for no reason.

   Clue(s) _____

   Your Definition _____

   Dictionary Definition _____

9. The *maladroit* gymnast fell repeatedly from the balance beam.

   Clue(s) _____

   Your Definition _____

   Dictionary Definition _____

You probably think that you are sitting relatively still in your chair as you begin this lesson. Because of the earth's rotation, however, you and everything around you are actually moving. In the same way, constant change is occurring even though you may not realize it. Each day you get a bit older and more knowledgeable. Each day weather wears away mountains or changes the size of islands.

The words in this lesson describe different kinds of movement and different degrees of change. Learning the words may help you be more aware of the activity going on around you.

DEFINITIONS

After you have studied the definitions and example for each word, write the vocabulary word on the line to the right.

1. **amble** (ăm′bəl) *verb*   To walk slowly or leisurely; to saunter or stroll. (From the Latin word *ambulare*, meaning "to walk")

   Example   During the warm spring days, we *ambled* through the woods and picked wildflowers.

   1. _____

2. **convert** (kən-vûrt′) *verb*   **a.** To change in form, substance, character, or function: *Freezing converts water into ice.*   **b.** To persuade someone to adopt a particular religion or belief.   **c.** To undergo a change.   *noun* (kŏn′vûrt′) One who has been converted, especially from one religion or belief to another. (From the Latin word *convertere*, meaning "to turn completely around")

   Related Words   **conversion** *noun;* **convertible** *adjective*
   Example   Lee has *converted* a rusty old vehicle into an elegant antique car.

   2. _____
   See *modification.*

3. **dawdle** (dôd′l) *verb*   **a.** To move aimlessly; to take more time than necessary: *to dawdle in the sun.*   **b.** To waste by idling: *to dawdle away the afternoon.*

   Related Word   **dawdler** *noun*
   Example   The children *dawdled* as they approached the door.

   3. _____

4. **distort** (dĭ-stôrt′) *verb* **a.** To change in shape by twisting, pulling, or exaggerating certain parts. **b.** To change from the truth; to misrepresent or falsify. (From the Latin *dis-*, meaning "apart," and *torquere*, meaning "to twist")

    Related Word   **distortion** *noun*
    Example   A good reporter does not *distort* the news.

4. _____

5. **itinerary** (ī-tĭn′ə-rĕr′ē) *noun* An outline or detailed plan for a proposed journey. (From the Latin word *iter*, meaning "journey")

    Related Word   **itinerant** *adjective*
    Example   Their *itinerary* included visits to national parks in Utah and Colorado.

5. _____

6. **mobilize** (mō′bə-līz′) *verb* **a.** To assemble or bring into readiness for a particular purpose. **b.** To become organized and ready.

    Related Word   **mobilization** *noun*
    Example   The student council *mobilized* committees to prepare for the state conference.

6. _____

7. **modification** (mŏd′ə-fĭ-kā′shən) *noun* A change or adjustment. (From the Latin words *modus*, meaning "measure," and *facere*, meaning "to make")

    Related Word   **modify** *verb*
    Example   The Senate committee made several *modifications* in the tax bill.

7. _____
USAGE NOTE: *Convert* and *modify* both mean "to change in form or character." *Convert* implies a transformation; *modify* implies alteration, a milder change.

8. **quiver** (kwĭv′ər) *verb* To shake with a slight but rapid motion; to tremble or shiver.

    Example   The whole room *quivered* during the earthquake.

8. _____

9. **recede** (rĭ-sēd′) *verb* **a.** To move back or away from a point or mark. (From the Latin *re-*, meaning "back," and *cedere*, meaning "to go away")

    Example   The flood waters *receded* slowly.

9. _____
USAGE NOTE: An antonym of *recede* is *proceed*, which means "to go forward or onward."

10. **traverse** (trə-vûrs′) *verb* **a.** To travel across, over, or through. **b.** To extend across; to cross. (From the Latin *trans-*, meaning "across," and *vertere*, meaning "to turn")

    Example   A narrow footbridge *traversed* the valley between the two mountains.

10. _____
USAGE NOTE: The adjective *transverse* is formed from the same two Latin roots and means "situated or lying across."

EXERCISE 1 COMPLETING DEFINITIONS

On the answer line, write the word from the vocabulary list that best
completes each definition.

1. When a person takes more time than necessary, he or she _____.

2. A change or adjustment is a(n) _____.

3. To walk leisurely is to _____.

4. If a person travels across a place, he or she _____ it.

5. To change the form of something is to _____ it.

6. A plan indicating the route that you want to follow on a trip is a(n) _____.

7. When something draws back or away from where it was, it _____.

8. To change the shape of something by twisting is to _____ it.

9. To assemble a group for a particular purpose is to _____ it.

10. When an object shakes with a slight but rapid movement, it _____.

1. _____

2. _____

3. _____

4. _____

5. _____

6. _____

7. _____

8. _____

9. _____

10. _____

EXERCISE 2 USING WORDS CORRECTLY

Decide whether the italicized vocabulary word has been used correctly in the
sentence. On the answer line, write *Correct* for correct use and *Incorrect* for
incorrect use.

1. Mirrors in an amusement park's fun house *distort* the appearance of a
person's body.

2. The salesclerk looked up the price of the stove in the store *itinerary*.

3. Pony Express riders rode horses that *ambled* between stations.

4. After the floods destroyed the wheat crop, the farmer had to *recede* his
fields.

5. The developer *converted* the old mansion into an apartment house.

6. Spot is eating his dinner in huge gulps; I've never seen a dog *dawdle* like
that over his food.

7. The ranger told us not to *traverse* the mountain pass without a four-
wheel-drive vehicle.

8. After a slight *modification* of the sleeves, Kelly's jacket fit perfectly.

9. When Martha finished mowing the lawn, she *mobilized* the mower into
the garage.

10. The smell of pine trees and the chirp of crickets sent a *quiver* of delight
through Carlos.

1. _____

2. _____

3. _____

4. _____

5. _____

6. _____

7. _____

8. _____

9. _____

10. _____

Decide which vocabulary word or related form best completes the sentence, and write the letter of your choice on the answer line.

1. Our family likes to _____ along the banks of the river.
   a. convert   **b.** recede   **c.** amble   **d.** distort

   1. _____

2. As patrol leader, George knew that he must _____ our club's snow shovel brigade.
   a. mobilize   **b.** dawdle   **c.** traverse   **d.** amble

   2. _____

3. Michelle claims to have a secret formula to _____ water into gasoline.
   a. traverse   **b.** recede   **c.** amble   **d.** convert

   3. _____

4. In Rick's unusual science project, he measured how much a cube of gelatin can _____.
   a. amble   **b.** quiver   **c.** dawdle   **d.** mobilize

   4. _____

5. "You'll miss the bus if you _____ any longer," Mother reminded us.
   a. recede   **b.** convert   **c.** distort   **d.** dawdle

   5. _____

6. Neon lights can _____ your perception of color.
   a. mobilize   **b.** amble   **c.** distort   **d.** dawdle

   6. _____

7. Karen plans to _____ the entire United States on foot.
   a. quiver   **b.** traverse   **c.** convert   **d.** recede

   7. _____

8. Jeff's _____ called for a three-hour layover in the Gunnison airport.
   a. modification   **b.** mobilization   **c.** distortion   **d.** itinerary

   8. _____

9. Alexis watched the darkness _____ before her candle as she tiptoed down the corridor.
   a. recede   **b.** dawdle   **c.** traverse   **d.** distort

   9. _____

10. Everybody in the family helped with the _____ of our family room.
    a. mobilization   **b.** modification   **c.** itinerary   **d.** distortion

    10. _____

Decide which form of the vocabulary word in parentheses completes the sentence. The form given may be correct. Write your answer on the answer line.

1. Thor Heyerdahl is known for _____ much of the Pacific Ocean in a small boat. (*traverse*)

   1. _____

2. When I got my new glasses, I found that they _____ everything. (*distort*)

   2. _____

3. The _____ of carbon into diamonds requires intense pressure. (*convert*)

   3. _____

4. The _____ mule was a favorite of gold prospectors. (*amble*)

   4. _____

5. Heidi _____ her kitchen cabinets enough to install her new dishwasher. (*modification*)

   5. _____

6. The _____ of the two families were the same. (*itinerary*)

   6. _____

7. The _____ puppy whined feebly. (*quiver*)

   7. _____

8. The _____ of political-action committees occurs well before election time. *(mobilize)*

8. _____

9. No one ever became successful by _____. *(dawdle)*

9. _____

10. The tiny crabs hurried after the _____ waves. *(recede)*

10. _____

READING COMPREHENSION

Each numbered sentence in the following passage contains an italicized vocabulary word or related form. After you read the passage you will complete an exercise.

WAGONS WEST

The people who pushed the frontier westward across the United States probably never thought of themselves as brave pioneers. They simply wanted to improve their lives, and the West offered an opportunity to do so. In overcoming the hardships they encountered on the way, though, they displayed great courage and determination.

Individuals and families who planned to travel west usually met in St. Louis, Missouri. (1) There experienced scouts who knew the best routes and places to camp *mobilized* approximately one hundred covered wagons into wagon trains. The wagons were pulled by mules or oxen, sure-footed and strong animals that could handle the heavy loads and navigate the narrow trails.

Because these cross-country journeys took between four and five months, all wagon trains left in the spring. (2) It was essential to *traverse* the Rocky Mountains before snow blocked the mountain passes. (3) There was no time for *ambling,* and the pioneers traveled fifteen to twenty miles each day. (4) Although their *itineraries* included brief stops at forts or settlements to repair equipment and buy supplies, no one relaxed until after the trip.

Geography and weather conditions often made travel difficult and dangerous. As the pioneers crossed the Great Plains, they encountered two extremes. Either they faced miles of hot, dry, treeless land or they had to cross wide, muddy rivers. (5) For such crossings, they would have liked to *convert* their "prairie schooners" into real schooners.

The desert, too, presented many hardships. (6) The intensity of the sun *distorted* the travelers' vision so that they saw mirages of cool water. (7) The distant horizon seemed to *quiver* under the intense heat. (8) The foothills of the cool mountains appeared to *recede* instead of drawing closer. (9) In order to survive, the settlers had to make certain *modifications* in their wagons, such as throwing away unnecessary items. Often, the pioneers traveled all night. (10) To *dawdle* in the desert meant certain death.

Each of the following statements corresponds to a numbered sentence in the passage. Each statement contains a blank and is followed by four answer choices. Decide which choice fits best in the blank. The word or phrase that you choose must express roughly the same meaning as the italicized word in the passage. Write the letter of your choice on the answer line.

1. Experienced scouts _____ caravans of one hundred covered wagons.
   a. considered   **b.** led   **c.** organized   **d.** abandoned

   1. _____

2. It was essential for the settlers to _____ the Rocky Mountains before winter.
   a. travel over   **b.** avoid   **c.** think about   **d.** admire

   2. _____

3. There was no time for _____.
   a. eating   **c.** stopping
   b. careful thinking   **d.** walking leisurely

   3. _____

4. The _____ of the pioneers included brief stops at forts or settlements.
   a. repairs   **b.** supplies   **c.** secret wishes   **d.** travel plans

   4. _____

5. Thinking of ships, the travelers would have liked to _____ their wagons.
   a. abandon   **b.** alter   **c.** improve   **d.** stop

   5. _____

6. The intensity of the sun _____ the travelers' vision so that they saw mirages.
   a. changed   **b.** emphasized   **c.** helped   **d.** harmed

   6. _____

7. The distant horizon seemed to _____ in the heat.
   a. drop suddenly   **c.** shake slightly
   b. bounce dramatically   **d.** rise slowly

   7. _____

8. The foothills of the mountains appeared to _____ rather than draw closer.
   a. disappear   **b.** move back   **c.** come closer   **d.** rise

   8. _____

9. Settlers had to make _____ their wagons.
   a. additions to   **b.** plans for   **c.** adjustments to   **d.** harnesses for

   9. _____

10. The pioneers faced death if they _____ in the desert.
    a. wasted time   **b.** drank water   **c.** slept   **d.** visited

    10. _____

WRITING ASSIGNMENT

Travel articles in magazines and newspapers describe interesting places to visit. These articles often provide details about places and highlights for visitors. Write a one-paragraph travel article about your city or community. Describe what it looks like, and advise potential tourists about the specific places they should visit and activities that they might find interesting. Use at least five of the vocabulary words from this lesson in your travel article, and underline each word.

Many English words come from the Latin roots -*flect*- and -*flu*-. The root -*flect*- is from the Latin word *flectere*, meaning "to bend," while -*flu*- is from *fluere*, meaning "to flow." In this lesson you will study ten words that are derived from these roots. You will also be able to see how prefixes change the meanings of the words.

<table>
<tr><td>WORD LIST</td></tr>
<tr><td>affluent
deflect
flex
fluctuate
fluid
flume
inflexible
influential
influx
reflex</td></tr>
</table>

DEFINITIONS

After you have studied the definitions and example for each word, write the vocabulary word on the line to the right.

1. **affluent** (ăf′lōō-ənt) *adjective*   Rich; wealthy. (From the Latin *ad-*, meaning "to," and *fluere*, meaning "to flow")

   Related Word   **affluence** *noun*
   Example   Because of a large inheritance, the Dawsons were the most *affluent* people in Cactus Gulch.

   1. _____

2. **deflect** (dĭ-flĕkt′) *verb*   To turn aside or cause to turn aside. (From the Latin *de-*, meaning "away," and *flectere*, meaning "to bend")

   Example   The tip of the cape *deflects* the ocean current.

   2. _____

   USAGE NOTE: Compare *deflect* with *reflect*, which means "to throw or bend back (light, for example) from a surface."

3. **flex** (flĕks) *verb*   To bend or contract. (From the Latin word *flectere*)

   Related Words   **flexibility** *noun;* **flexible** *adjective*
   Example   The weight lifter's arms rippled as he *flexed* his muscles.

   3. _____

   See *inflexible.*

4. **fluctuate** (flŭk′chōō-āt′) *verb*   To change back and forth or vary greatly. (From the Latin word *fluere*)

   Related Word   **fluctuation** *noun*
   Example   The threat of war caused prices on the stock market to *fluctuate* wildly.

   4. _____

5. **fluid** (flōō′ĭd) *noun*   A substance, such as air or water, that flows easily and takes on the shape of its container.   *adjective*   Graceful; capable of flowing. (From the Latin word *fluere*)

   Example   Someone with a sore throat usually finds fruit juice an easy *fluid* to swallow.

   5. _____

6. **flume** (flo͞om) *noun* A gap, gorge, or narrow channel through which a stream of water flows. (From the Latin word *flumen,* meaning "river")

    Example The icy water roared through the *flume* on its way to the river.

    6. _____

7. **inflexible** (ĭn-flĕk′sə-bəl) *adjective* **a.** Not able to bend. **b.** Not able to change or be persuaded. (From the Latin *in-,* meaning "not," and *flectere*)

    Related Words **inflexibility** *noun;* **inflexibly** *adverb*

    Example The *inflexible* general refused to remove the troops from the village.

    7. _____
    USAGE NOTE: An antonym of *inflexible* is *flexible.*

8. **influential** (ĭn′flo͞o-ĕn′shəl) *adjective* **a.** Having power or importance. **b.** Producing a lasting change or effect. (From the Latin *in-,* meaning "in," and *fluere*)

    Related Words **influence** *noun;* **influence** *verb*

    Example Her grandfather was *influential* in Sarah's choice of career.

    8. _____

9. **influx** (ĭn′flŭks′) *noun* A steady stream of people or things flowing or pouring in. (From the Latin *in-,* meaning "in," and *fluxus,* meaning "flowing")

    Example An *influx* of locusts destroyed the wheat crops.

    9. _____
    USAGE NOTE: An antonym of *influx* is *out-flow,* a word from Old English rather than Latin.

10. **reflex** (rē′flĕks′) *noun* An instinctive or automatic physical response, as a hiccup. (From the Latin *re-,* meaning "back," and *flectere*)

    Example A race-car driver must have excellent *reflexes.*

    10. _____

108   The Roots *-flect-* and *-flu-*

© Great Source DO NOT COPY

EXERCISE 1 WRITING CORRECT WORDS

On the answer line, write the word from the vocabulary list that fits
each definition.

1. Powerful or important

2. An easily flowing substance, such as air or water

3. An instinctive response

4. Incapable of change

5. To vary considerably

6. To bend or contract

7. A steady stream of people or things flowing in

8. To cause a moving object to turn

9. A channel through which water flows

10. Having great wealth

1. _____

2. _____

3. _____

4. _____

5. _____

6. _____

7. _____

8. _____

9. _____

10. _____

EXERCISE 2 USING WORDS CORRECTLY

Each of the following questions contains an italicized vocabulary word.
Decide the answer to the question, and write *Yes* or *No* on the answer line.

1. Would the temperature be likely to *fluctuate* dramatically during a heat
   wave?

2. Is an *inflexible* person easily persuaded?

3. Would a successful movie star probably be *affluent*?

4. Would a popular football player consider two fan letters an *influx* of mail?

5. Might a shield be used to *deflect* an arrow?

6. Would an *influential* person be able to change the lives of others?

7. Do people often *flex* their muscles while exercising?

8. During a flood, would a *flume* hold back the water?

9. Is dialing a telephone number a *reflex*?

10. Do *fluids* fit more easily than solid objects into narrow glass jars?

1. _____

2. _____

3. _____

4. _____

5. _____

6. _____

7. _____

8. _____

9. _____

10. _____

EXERCISE 3 CHOOSING THE BEST WORD

Decide which vocabulary word or related form best completes the sentence, and write the letter of your choice on the answer line.

1. The pond's water level _____ because heavy rain was followed by a long dry spell.
   a. flexed   **b.** deflected   **c.** fluctuated   **d.** was inflexible

2. The Sabins were a(n) _____ family in the community.
   a. flexible   **b.** inflexible   **c.** fluctuating   **d.** influential

3. The doctor advised Jane to take plenty of _____ while she was ill.
   a. fluids   **b.** fluctuations   **c.** flumes   **d.** reflexes

4. My friend with the _____ political beliefs was annoyed by my opposing viewpoint.
   a. deflecting   **b.** affluent   **c.** inflexible   **d.** flexing

5. Water moved through the narrow _____ at an amazing rate.
   a. affluence   **b.** flume   **c.** influx   **d.** fluid

6. The doctor asked Kirk to _____ his toes.
   a. influx   **b.** fluctuate   **c.** deflect   **d.** flex

7. An unexpected _____ of bananas into the market caused a sharp drop in their prices.
   a. affluence   **b.** influx   **c.** flume   **d.** flexibility

8. The _____ restaurant owner explained the secrets of her great financial success.
   a. fluctuating   **b.** flexible   **c.** inflexible   **d.** affluent

9. Looking over his shoulder was a(n) _____ for the lion tamer.
   a. reflex   **b.** affluence   **c.** influx   **d.** influence

10. The outfielder's glove _____ the baseball.
   a. fluctuated   **b.** flexed   **c.** deflected   **d.** made fluid

1. _____
2. _____
3. _____
4. _____
5. _____
6. _____
7. _____
8. _____
9. _____
10. _____

EXERCISE 4 USING DIFFERENT FORMS OF WORDS

Decide which form of the vocabulary word in parentheses best completes the sentence. The form given may be correct. Write your answer on the answer line.

1. The lumberjack threw the log into the _____. *(flume)*

2. Albert Einstein was a major _____ in the development of modern theories of physics. *(influential)*

3. Ralph's _____ about working hours infuriated Janet. *(inflexible)*

4. The gust of wind _____ the pitched ball. *(deflect)*

5. An unexpected _____ of ants forced us to move our picnic to another spot. *(influx)*

6. The economists could not explain the sudden _____ in food prices. *(fluctuate)*

7. A sneeze is a common _____. *(reflex)*

1. _____
2. _____
3. _____
4. _____
5. _____
6. _____
7. _____

110   The Roots *-flect-* and *-flu-*

8. The _____ movements of the gymnast were exciting to watch. *(fluid)*

9. The expensively furnished home indicated the family's _____. *(affluent)*

10. Everyone admired the ballet dancer's great _____. *(flex)*

8. _____

9. _____

10. _____

READING COMPREHENSION

Each numbered sentence in the following passage contains an italicized vocabulary word or related form. After you read the passage, you will complete an exercise.

BRINGING WATER TO ROME

One of the Romans' chief contributions to western culture was in the area of engineering. (1) City engineers were *inflexible* in their determination to improve living conditions. A good example of that determination is the Roman system of aqueducts, which are large pipes designed to transport water from distant sources.

(2) Today, it is almost a *reflex* to turn on the faucet and take as much water as we need. Roman citizens, however, had to go to city wells for water. So long as Rome was not heavily populated, the wells could supply enough water. (3) With the *influx* of thousands of people into Rome, though, the need for increased amounts of water became acute. (4) In addition, *affluent* Romans wanted luxurious bathhouses, which required extra gallons of water.

(5) Faced with these growing needs, Roman engineers searched for water sources that would not *fluctuate.* (6) Among the engineers who *flexed* their mental muscles was Sextus Julius Frontinus, who thought of using the water in the mountains sur-

rounding Rome. He noticed that the spring thaw transformed the snow and ice on the slopes into water. (7) Afterwards, gallons of water traveled through the *flumes* that eroded the mountainsides.

(8) To bring this precious *fluid* to Rome, Frontinus designed a series of stone aqueducts. The greatest challenge came in getting the water across the valleys.

To do so, Frontinus built rows of arches that supported the aqueducts. (9) No obstacle *deflected* the water from its destination in Rome. By A.D. 97, Rome had nine aqueducts, which brought millions of gallons of water into the city every day. Visitors to Rome can see the aqueducts even today. (10) The work of Frontinus was *influential* in the design of aqueducts for many centuries.

Each of the following statements corresponds to a numbered sentence in the passage. Each statement contains a blank and is followed by four answer choices. Decide which choice fits best in the blank. The word or phrase that you choose must express the same meaning as the italicized word in the passage. Write the letter of your choice on the answer line.

1. Roman engineers were _____ in their determination to upgrade city life.
   a. enthusiastic   **b.** unselfish   **c.** unchanging   **d.** lively

2. Using water freely is almost a(n) _____ for many people.
   a. invitation
   b. automatic response
   c. selfish act
   d. problem

3. The Romans needed more water after a(n) _____ of thousands of people.
   a. decrease   **b.** census   **c.** exit   **d.** large movement

4. _____ Romans wanted to build bathhouses, which required even more water.
   a. Greedy
   b. Fun-loving
   c. Community-minded
   d. Wealthy

5. The Romans saw a need for a water supply that would not _____.
   a. turn sour   **b.** increase   **c.** vary greatly   **d.** evaporate

6. Engineers _____ their mental muscles over the city's water problem.
   a. exercised   **b.** slowed   **c.** accelerated   **d.** stopped

7. Water moved down the mountainside through _____.
   a. channels   **b.** rocks   **c.** waterfalls   **d.** caves

8. Frontinus designed a way to bring this _____ to Rome.
   a. slush   **b.** mud   **c.** liquid   **d.** vapor

9. The water could not be _____ from its path.
   a. stopped   **b.** collected   **c.** observed   **d.** turned away

10. Frontinus was _____ in the history of engineering.
   a. unknown   **b.** interested   **c.** important   **d.** unusual

1. _____

2. _____

3. _____

4. _____

5. _____

6. _____

7. _____

8. _____

9. _____

10. _____

WRITING ASSIGNMENT

Imagine visiting an amusement park that features such attractions as a log flume, a tube shoot, and a variety of water slides. Pick one of these attractions and describe it in a paragraph or two. You might want to picture this ride from a distance or create a dramatic, first-person account of your experiences with it. Include at least five of the vocabulary words, and underline each word.

Every day you encounter thousands of forms and boundaries. For example, in a city you can see the rectangular forms of buildings and the billowing forms of smoke pouring from chimneys. You can see many boundaries—for example, the boundary between land and water on a beach. Some boundaries, however, cannot be seen. For instance, there is usually no line to show the boundary between two cities. In this lesson you will learn words to describe many types of forms and boundaries.

WORD LIST
adjacent
align
brink
contour
dimension
engulf
indent
solidify
symmetry
tangible

DEFINITIONS

After you have studied the definitions and example for each word, write the vocabulary word on the line to the right.

1. **adjacent** (ə-jā′sənt) *adjective*   Next to or close to; adjoining. (From the Latin word *adjacere*, meaning "to lie near")

   Example Because my room is *adjacent* to my brother's room, I often hear his radio through the wall.

   1. _____

2. **align** (ə-līn′) *verb*   To place in line. (From the Old French *a-*, meaning "to," and *ligne*, meaning "line")

   Related Word **alignment** *noun*
   Example A mechanic *aligns* the wheels of an automobile so that the front and back wheels head in precisely the same direction.

   2. _____

3. **brink** (brĭngk) *noun*   An edge or border.

   Example The captain, by spotting the iceberg, pulled the ship back from the *brink* of disaster.

   3. _____

4. **contour** (kŏn′toor′) *noun*   The outline of a shape or figure. (From the Italian word *contornare*, meaning "to draw in outline")

   Example The *contours* of trees and buildings are often clearest at sunset.

   4. _____

5. **dimension** (dĭ-mĕn′shən) *noun*   **a.** A measure of width, height, or length. **b.** Size or extent. (From the Latin word *dimetiri*, meaning "to measure")

   Related Word **dimensional** *adjective*
   Example The *dimensions* of the room were ten feet by twelve feet.

   5. _____

6. **engulf** (ĕn-gŭlf′) *verb*   To surround or enclose; swallow up; overwhelm.

    Example   Water will *engulf* the land during a major flood.

6. _____

7. **indent** (ĭn-dĕnt′) *verb*   **a.** To make dents or impressions in.   **b.** To set something inward from a given line.

    Related Word   **indentation** *noun*
    Example   Artisans in the Middle East *indent* brass to make beautiful objects.

7. _____

    ETYMOLOGY NOTE: *Indent* comes from the Latin words for "in" and "tooth"; perhaps an indent was originally a tooth mark.

8. **solidify** (sə-lĭd′ə-fī′) *verb*   To make or become hard or compact.

    Related Words   **solid** *adjective;* **solid** *noun*
    Example   Foods containing gelatin *solidify* when they are refrigerated.

8. _____

9. **symmetry** (sĭm′ĭ-trē) *noun*   A relationship of balance between different objects or different parts of the same object. (From the Greek *syn-,* meaning "like," and *metron,* meaning "measure")

    Related Words   **symmetrical** *adjective;* **symmetrically** *adverb*
    Example   Some trees exhibit *symmetry* because they have the same number of branches on each side of the trunk.

9. _____

10. **tangible** (tăn′jə-bəl) *adjective*   Capable of being touched; existing physically. (From the Latin word *tangere,* meaning "to touch")

    Related Word   **tangibly** *adverb*
    Example   The statues of ancient Greece are *tangible* reminders of its artistic achievement.

10. _____

    USAGE NOTE: An antonym for *tangible* is *intangible,* "incapable of being perceived by the senses"; it is often used to refer to ideas and concepts.

EXERCISE 1 WRITING CORRECT WORDS

On the answer line, write the word from the vocabulary list that fits
each definition.

1. A measure of width, height, or length

2. To make hard, strong, or compact

3. Next to; adjoining

4. To surround, enclose, overwhelm

5. An edge or margin

6. To set inward; make impressions in

7. To arrange in a line

8. Capable of being touched; existing physically

9. A balanced, harmonious relationship

10. The outline of a shape or figure

1. _____

2. _____

3. _____

4. _____

5. _____

6. _____

7. _____

8. _____

9. _____

10. _____

EXERCISE 2 USING WORDS CORRECTLY

Each of the following statements contains an italicized vocabulary word or
related form. Decide whether the sentence is true or false, and write *True* or
False on the answer line.

1. The first line of a paragraph is usually *indented.*

2. The Fongs' house is *adjacent* to the Winstons' house, which is a block
   away.

3. In drawing a face, an artist has to pay close attention to the *contours* of the
   forehead, nose, and chin.

4. When people feel overwhelmed by problems, they may say that they are
   engulfed by them.

5. You should not walk on wet concrete until it has had a chance to *solidify.*

6. The fragrance of a certain cologne is *tangible* evidence that can be used in
   court.

7. A composer would sit down at the piano to *align* a new song for her
   upcoming album.

8. A basketball team that is losing by four points with three seconds left on
   the clock is on the *brink* of defeat.

9. Before buying a large piece of furniture, you should compare its
   dimensions with those of the doorways through which it has to fit.

10. A house with two windows on one side and four on the other side shows
    symmetry.

1. _____

2. _____

3. _____

4. _____

5. _____

6. _____

7. _____

8. _____

9. _____

10. _____

Decide which vocabulary word or related form best expresses the meaning of the italicized word or phrase in the sentence. On the answer line, write the letter of that word.

1. The diamond ring was the *physical* evidence that the police needed.
   a. adjacent   b. tangible   c. contour   d. indent

   1. _____

2. We could see the *outline* of the peaks and valleys on the map.
   a. dimension   b. brink   c. symmetry   d. contour

   2. _____

3. Mr. Long put the vegetable garden *next* to the strawberry patch.
   a. tangible   b. align   c. adjacent   d. indent

   3. _____

4. The flames quickly *swallowed up* the building.
   a. solidified   b. indented   c. engulfed   d. aligned

   4. _____

5. I need to know the *measurements* of the rooms.
   a. dimensions   b. symmetry   c. contours   d. brink

   5. _____

6. The grease in the frying pan had *hardened* enough so that it could be scraped out with a spatula.
   a. indented   b. solidified   c. aligned   d. engulfed

   6. _____

7. Naghib produced designs in the metal by *making dents in* it with a pointed instrument and a small hammer.
   a. engulfing   b. aligning   c. indenting   d. solidifying

   7. _____

8. There is a guardrail at the *edge* of the lookout on the mountain.
   a. adjacent   b. contour   c. dimension   d. brink

   8. _____

9. At the amusement-park shooting gallery, Jane *lined up* the target and the gunsight.
   a. engulfed   b. aligned   c. indented   d. solidified

   9. _____

10. The child's face was attractively *balanced and well proportioned*.
    a. aligned   b. indented   c. adjacent   d. symmetrical

    10. _____

Decide which form of the vocabulary word in parentheses best completes the sentence. The form given may be correct. Write your answer on the answer line.

1. In Norway the deep _____ where the sea cuts into the land are called fjords. *(indent)*

   1. _____

2. Mrs. Morrow valued most of all things that are not _____: friendship, kindness, honor, and dignity. *(tangible)*

   2. _____

3. For each of his sons, Mr. Nicholas built a house _____ to his own property. *(adjacent)*

   3. _____

4. More than one child who has forgotten to put away clay has returned to find that it has dried into an unworkable _____. *(solidify)*

   4. _____

5. A tsunami, or tidal wave, may _____ an entire island. *(engulf)*

   5. _____

6. If a car steers poorly, one should check the wheel _____. *(align)*

   6. _____

7. Although paintings have flat surfaces, they sometimes appear three-_____. (*dimension*)

    7. _____

8. Solid geometric figures such as cubes are _____. (*symmetry*)

    8. _____

9. The candidate has many different people working toward _____ his base of voter support. (*solidify*)

    9. _____

10. The _____ on the map show a mountainous area. (*contour*)

    10. _____

READING COMPREHENSION

Each numbered sentence in the following passage contains an italicized vocabulary word or related form. After you read the passage, you will complete an exercise.

THE NETHERLANDS: CONQUEST OF THE SEA

The Netherlands is one of the most remarkable countries in the world, for it has been created in large part by its people. Most of the Netherlands lies beneath sea level. (1) In its natural state, it would be *engulfed* by water. Through cleverness and hard work, though, the Dutch have made cities and countryside where formerly there was nothing but the sea. (2) They have changed the *contour* of their land. (3) By doing so, they have greatly increased the *dimensions* of their country.

(4) The story of the Netherlands begins two thousand years ago, when people living at the *brink* of the sea built high mounds to protect their houses. (5) These mounds served as dikes, which are walls built *adjacent* to the sea. Dikes prevent the sea from flooding the land.

Some time afterward, the Dutch started building dikes of sand and clay. (6) Layers of rock *solidified* these structures. (7) The layers were carefully *aligned* and fitted together. Using the dikes, the Dutch started to take land from the sea by building "polders." First they built dikes to enclose an area. Then they drained off the water. Windmills provided the power to pump the water back into the sea. (8) The polders provided rich farmland where, among other things, the Dutch raise tulips in neat, *symmetrical* plots.

In 1900 the Dutch faced another problem. (9) For several centuries sea water had been making *indentations* into two sides of the Netherlands and threatening to divide the country. Only thirty-seven miles of land connected the two parts of the country. The Dutch decided to act. They built a dike that held off the approaching sea. The dike also created a lake of salt water next to the piece of land that had been disappearing. By making polders, the Dutch have gradually been turning this lake into farmland. (10) This rich farmland is *tangible* evidence of the determination of the Dutch people to build their homeland.

READING COMPREHENSION EXERCISE

Each of the following statements corresponds to a numbered sentence in the passage. Each statement contains a blank and is followed by four answer choices. Decide which choice fits best in the blank. The word or phrase that you choose must express roughly the same meaning as the italicized word in the passage. Write the letter of your choice on the answer line.

1. In its natural state, water would _____ most of the Netherlands.
   a. dry out   **b.** swallow up   **c.** go under   **d.** supply

   1. _____

2. The Dutch have changed the _____ of their land.
   a. height   **b.** temperature   **c.** solidness   **d.** shape

   2. _____

3. The Dutch have increased the _____ of their country.
   a. farmland   **b.** size   **c.** shape   **d.** sea

   3. _____

4. People who lived at the _____ of the sea protected their houses.
   a. top   **b.** crossroads   **c.** edge   **d.** bottom

   4. _____

5. The dikes and the sea are _____ .
   a. next to each other   **c.** surrounded
   b. the same thing   **d.** distant from each other

   5. _____

6. Layers of rock _____ the dikes.
   a. strengthen   **b.** raise up   **c.** weaken   **d.** pull down

   6. _____

7. The rocks were carefully _____ .
   a. pushed aside   **b.** torn down   **c.** lined up   **d.** moistened

   7. _____

8. Tulips are grown in orderly, _____ plots.
   a. fertile   **b.** long   **c.** unmeasured   **d.** balanced

   8. _____

9. Sea water has been making _____ into the land.
   a. incidents   **b.** deposits   **c.** layers   **d.** inroads

   9. _____

10. Rich farmland is _____ evidence of the will of the Dutch to build their homeland.
    a. amazing   **b.** physical   **c.** exciting   **d.** good

    10. _____

PRACTICE WITH ANALOGIES

Directions   On the answer line, write the vocabulary word or a form of it that completes each analogy.

See pages 26, 52, 78, and 98 for some strategies to use with analogies.

1. Chat is to talk as _____ is to walk. *(Lesson 16)*

   1. _____

2. Agenda is to meeting as _____ is to journey. *(Lesson 16)*

   2. _____

3. Visible is to seen as _____ is to touched. *(Lesson 18)*

   3. _____

4. Dexterity is to juggler as _____ is to acrobat. *(Lesson 17)*

   4. _____

READING SKILLS

THE PREFIX *DIS-*

A **prefix** is a letter or group of letters that is added to the beginning of a root. A **root** is the part of a word that contains its basic meaning. A root can also be a complete word. The addition of a prefix changes the meaning of the root.

If you know the meanings of prefixes, you can use them to determine the meanings of unfamiliar words. The prefix *dis-* has two common meanings, "not" and "reverse of."

Prefix Meaning	Word	Definition
1. not	disorderly	not orderly
2. reverse of	dislodge	reverse of "to lodge" = force out

Use the following procedure to determine the meanings of words that begin with the prefix *dis-*.

PROCEDURE

1. *Substitute the meaning of the prefix for the prefix itself.* For example, suppose that you do not know the meaning of *discomfort.*

   discomfort = "not" or "reverse of" + *comfort*

2. *Think of possible meanings of the entire word.* Add the meaning of the prefix to the meaning of the root.

   discomfort = "reverse of comfort" = "lack of comfort"

3. *Check the meaning of the word in your dictionary.* Analyzing the meanings of the prefix and the root gives you an approximate definition of the entire word. Look up the word in your dictionary to be sure of its meaning.

   discomfort = "The condition of being uncomfortable in body or mind"

EXERCISE USING THE PREFIX *DIS-*

Step 1: Write your definition of the italicized word in each of the sentences that follow. *Step 2:* Write the dictionary definition of the word. Choose the definition that best fits the way the word is used in the sentence.
Step 3: Write a sentence of your own in which you use the word correctly.

1. Why did we *disregard* the instructions?

   Your Definition _____

   Dictionary Definition _____

   Sentence _____

2. The child *disobeyed* the crossing guard.

Your Definition _____

Dictionary Definition _____

Sentence _____

3. The runner was *disqualified* from the race.

Your Definition _____

Dictionary Definition _____

Sentence _____

4. Connie did not allow her handicap to be a *disadvantage*.

Your Definition _____

Dictionary Definition _____

Sentence _____

5. Tad was disturbed by his friend's *dishonest* answer.

Your Definition _____

Dictionary Definition _____

Sentence _____

6. Kim and her mother *disagreed* about the music of her favorite group.

Your Definition _____

Dictionary Definition _____

Sentence _____

7. Edgar could accomplish more if he weren't *disorganized*.

Your Definition _____

Dictionary Definition _____

Sentence _____

8. The failure of the experiment *disheartened* the scientist.

Your Definition _____

Dictionary Definition _____

Sentence _____

Galileo, Isaac Newton, and Thomas Edison would have envied the equipment of the modern science laboratory. Many new tools and devices have increased scientists' powers of observation and investigation. In this lesson you will learn about some of the instruments that chemists, biologists, physicists, and other scientists use. Some of the equipment you are already familiar with; other devices will become more important to you in the future.

<table>
<tr><td>

WORD LIST

aperture
apparatus
centrifuge
component
gauge
generator
laser
mechanism
prism
treadmill

</td></tr>
</table>

DEFINITIONS

After you have studied the definitions and example for each word, write the vocabulary word on the line to the right.

1. **aperture** (ăp′ər-chər) *noun*   A hole, gap, slit, or other opening. (From the Latin word *apertus*, meaning "open")

   Example   The *aperture* of a camera lens should be narrowed when you take photographs in bright sun.

   1. _____

2. **apparatus** (ăp′ə-rā′təs) *noun*   Tools or other equipment that is put to a specific use; a group of parts used together for a particular job or function. (From the Latin *ad-*, meaning "to," and *parare*, meaning "to prepare")

   Example   Test tubes, beakers, and Bunsen burners are examples of *apparatus* used in a chemistry laboratory.

   2. _____
   See *component.*

3. **centrifuge** (sĕn′trə-fyo͞oj′) *noun*   A rapidly spinning machine used to separate two substances that have different weights and densities. (From the Latin words *centrum*, meaning "center," and *fugere*, meaning "to flee")

   Related Word   **centrifugal** *adjective*
   Example   One type of *centrifuge* can be used to test the effects of high speed and rapid acceleration on the human body.

   3. _____

4. **component** (kəm-pō′nənt) *noun*   Any of the parts that together make up a whole. (From the Latin *com-*, meaning "together," and *ponere*, meaning "to put")

   Example   A computer engineer must understand all the *components* of a computer.

   4. _____
   MEMORY CUE: An *apparatus* may consist of separate components.

5. **gauge** (gāj) *noun*   A tool used to measure pressure, temperature, water level, thickness, speed, and so forth.   *verb*   **a.** To measure precisely. **b.** To evaluate or judge.

   Example   A scuba diver must use a depth *gauge*.

   5. _____

6. **generator** (jĕn'ə-rā'tər) *noun*   A machine that changes mechanical energy into electrical energy. (From the Latin word *generare,* meaning "to produce")

   Related Words   generate *verb;* generation *noun*
   Example   The *generator* could supply only a few hours of electricity to the apartment complex.

   6. _____

7. **laser** (lā'zər) *noun*   An electronic device that sends out an intense beam of energy in the form of light waves. Lasers are used to perform delicate surgery, to weld or cut metals, and to carry television, radio, and telephone messages. (From the first letters of the words *light amplification* by *stimulated emission* of *radiation*)

   Example   Photographers use *lasers* to create three-dimensional pictures called holograms.

   7. _____

8. **mechanism** (mĕk'ə-nĭz'əm) *noun*   **a.** The arrangement of connected parts in a machine.   **b.** A machine.

   Related Words   mechanic *noun;* mechanical *adjective*
   Example   The gears of a car are an important part of its *mechanism*.

   8. _____

9. **prism** (prĭz'əm) *noun*   **a.** A piece of transparent material that bends light and separates it into the colors of the rainbow.   **b.** An object made of cut glass. (From the Greek word *prizein,* meaning "to saw")

   Example   Isaac Newton used a *prism* to discover that white light is actually composed of numerous colors.

   9. _____

10. **treadmill** (trĕd'mĭl') *noun*   A machine consisting of a wheel or a revolving belt on which a person or animal walks.

    Example   Doctors have patients walk on *treadmills* to measure their heart and lung performance.

    10. _____

EXERCISE 1 MATCHING WORDS AND DEFINITIONS

Make the definition in Column B with the word in Column A. Write the letter
of the correct definition on the answer line.

Column A

1. treadmill
2. aperture
3. laser
4. component
5. mechanism
6. apparatus
7. prism
8. gauge
9. centrifuge
10. generator

Column B

a. a tool for measuring; to measure
b. a piece of transparent material that bends and
   spreads out light
c. tools or equipment for a specific use
d. a machine that changes mechanical energy into
   electrical energy
e. a device that produces an intense beam of light
f. a gap, slit, or other opening
g. a machine with a wheel or a revolving belt
h. the arrangement of connected parts in a machine
i. any of the parts that together make up a whole
j. a machine that spins and separates a substance

1. _____
2. _____
3. _____
4. _____
5. _____
6. _____
7. _____
8. _____
9. _____
10. _____

EXERCISE 2 USING WORDS CORRECTLY

Decide whether the italicized vocabulary word has been used correctly in the
sentence. On the answer line, write *Correct* for correct use or *Incorrect* for
incorrect use.

1. An *aperture* in the cave wall admitted a narrow beam of light.

2. A *laser* works by sending out sound waves and measuring the echoes.

3. Ms. Oakley gathered the *apparatus* for the experiments.

4. As part of his physical examination, Mr. Coe walked on a *treadmill*.

5. Joanie used a *gauge* to cut and style her hair.

6. They tied the newspapers together in *components* and took them to the
   recycling center.

7. The emergency *generator* goes on automatically.

8. Ann rinsed the fruit in a *centrifuge*.

9. The Briners bought sun-blocking *prisms* to cut down on the amount of
   heat entering the house.

10. The *mechanism* of the fan required frequent maintenance.

1. _____
2. _____
3. _____
4. _____
5. _____
6. _____
7. _____
8. _____
9. _____
10. _____

EXERCISE 3 CHOOSING THE BEST WORD

Decide which vocabulary word best expresses the meaning of the italicized
word or phrase in the sentence. On the answer line, write the letter of
that word.

1. When you are dealing with explosive gases, you must use an accurate
   pressure *object for measuring*.
   a. apparatus   **b.** generator   **c.** treadmill   **d.** gauge

1. _____

2. The *opening* of the camera lens is adjusted automatically.
   a. laser **b.** aperture **c.** apparatus **d.** prism

2. _____

3. The *intense light wave* once existed only in science fiction.
   a. prism **b.** generator **c.** laser **d.** treadmill

3. _____

4. The astronauts were tested in a *rapidly spinning machine*.
   a. centrifuge **b.** prism **c.** treadmill **d.** generator

4. _____

5. Many people buy stereo *parts* made by different companies.
   a. prisms **b.** apertures **c.** components **d.** mechanisms

5. _____

6. A high-speed *arrangement of connected parts* operates a dentist's drill.
   a. aperture **b.** mechanism **c.** gauge **d.** generator

6. _____

7. The chandelier was made of hundreds of *cut-glass objects*.
   a. centrifuges **b.** lasers **c.** apparatus **d.** prisms

7. _____

8. Janine's white mice get exercise by running on their *wheel*.
   a. component **b.** prism **c.** treadmill **d.** generator

8. _____

9. To operate the electrical appliances, we need a *machine that changes mechanical energy into electrical energy*.
   a. generator **b.** centrifuge **c.** prism **d.** component

9. _____

10. Setting up the *equipment* for a trapeze act has to be done carefully.
    a. treadmill **b.** gauges **c.** laser **d.** apparatus

10. _____

EXERCISE 4 CHOOSING THE BEST WORD

Decide which vocabulary word best completes the sentence, and write the letter of your choice on the answer line.

1. Mr. Doherty exercises every morning by walking on a _____.
   a. component **b.** gauge **c.** treadmill **d.** centrifuge

1. _____

2. The eye surgeon used a _____ to seal the patient's blood vessels.
   a. gauge **b.** prism **c.** generator **d.** laser

2. _____

3. Consistent hitting, accurate fielding, and alert base running are the _____ of winning baseball.
   a. apertures **b.** components **c.** apparatus **d.** mechanisms

3. _____

4. As the sunlight fell on the _____, rainbows of color filled the room.
   a. aperture **b.** laser **c.** gauge **d.** prism

4. _____

5. Most public buildings have a(n) _____ for use in emergencies.
   a. aperture **b.** treadmill **c.** generator **d.** laser

5. _____

6. A Dutch boy used his thumb to plug a(n) _____ in a leaking dike.
   a. aperture **b.** component **c.** gauge **d.** apparatus

6. _____

7. The balance beam is one type of gymnastic _____.
   a. treadmill **b.** apparatus **c.** aperture **d.** component

7. _____

8. We mistakenly thought that separating cream from milk in a _____ was the same as pasteurizing it.
   a. generator **b.** laser **c.** prism **d.** centrifuge

8. _____

9. Thread jammed the _____ of the sewing machine.
   a. mechanism **b.** prism **c.** generator **d.** laser

9. _____

10. We ran out of gasoline even though the fuel _____ read "Full."
    a. prism **b.** laser **c.** treadmill **d.** gauge

10. _____

READING COMPREHENSION

Each numbered sentence in the following passage contains an italicized vocabulary word. After you read the passage, you will complete an exercise.

FIELD TRIP TO THE SCIENCE MUSEUM

Dear Aunt Sara,

I hope you're not getting bored with my letters about the field trips we take in Mr. Evans's science class. Our recent visit to the Science Museum was the best trip so far.

(1) Our tour began with a slide show on what happens to light when it travels through a *prism.* We were able to see how light is bent, creating a range of colors. (2) The *laser* exhibit provided more information about light. We saw how a laser can be used to cut holes through steel or to perform delicate eye surgery.

A series of energy exhibits was fascinating. (3) I saw how coal produces steam to run a *generator* and supply electricity. (4) I was surprised to learn that at one time *treadmills* were used to produce electricity. (5) Of course, the *mechanisms* of the treadmills were simple in comparison with those in today's generators. (6) We also saw a large model of the *components* of an atom. This exhibit explained how atomic energy is produced.

A number of the exhibits helped us to understand machines by comparing them to parts of the body. (7) For example, one exhibit compared the *apparatus* of a camera to that of the human eye. (8) I think I'll be able to take better photographs now that I know how the *aperture* of a camera lens resembles the pupil of my eye.

(9) My favorite hands-on display was the *centrifuge,* which we were able to control. We could actually watch the machine separate oil from water and cream from milk. (10) *Gauges* on the centrifuge showed the relative weights of each substance.

As you can see, I learned a great deal from our trip and am more interested than ever in becoming a scientist like you. Please say hello to Uncle Archie for me.

Your niece,
Leslie

READING COMPREHENSION EXERCISE

Each of the following statements corresponds to a numbered sentence in the passage. Each statement contains a blank and is followed by four answer choices. Decide which choice fits best in the blank. The word or phrase that you choose must express roughly the same meaning as the italicized word in the passage. Write the letter of your choice on the answer line.

1. The device that bends light to produce colors was a(n) _____.
   a. piece of transparent material   c. magnifying glass
   b. intense beam of light   d. color wheel

   1. _____

2. The exhibit with a _____ provided more information about light.
   a. radio wave
   b. device producing atomic energy
   c. device producing an intense beam of light
   d. machine producing electricity

   2. _____

3. Steam powered _____.
   a. a device used for delicate eye surgery
   b. the slowly rotating wheel of a clock
   c. specialized measuring tools
   d. a machine that produced electricity

   3. _____

4. At one time _____ also produced electricity.

    a. spinning cylinders   **c.** bursts of energy

    b. revolving belts   **d.** beams of sunlight

4. _____

5. The _____ treadmills were simple in comparison with those of generators.

    a. arrangement of connected parts in

    b. necessary elements of

    c. tools of

    d. light waves in

5. _____

6. A model helped the students to understand the _____ of the atom.

    a. openings   **c.** energy charges

    b. light rays   **d.** parts

6. _____

7. The _____ in a camera lens work much like the pupil of the eye.

    a. magnifier   **c.** parts used together

    b. glass   **d.** electronic devices

7. _____

8. People can take better photographs if they understand how the _____ of the camera works.

    a. opening   **c.** measuring device

    b. chemistry   **d.** magnifier

8. _____

9. Leslie's favorite hands-on exhibit was the _____.

    a. wheel or continuous belt

    b. machine that produces electricity

    c. rapidly spinning machine

    d. computer

9. _____

10. _____ showed the relative weights of oil and water.

    a. Graphs   **c.** Diagrams

    b. Measuring instruments   **d.** Computers

10. _____

WRITING ASSIGNMENT

Imagine that you are a scientist who has been working on an important laboratory experiment, such as testing the acidity level of rainfall. In one paragraph, write a report that you will share with fellow scientists, explaining the progress and the results of your experiment. Use at least five of the vocabulary words in your paragraph, and underline each one.

VOCABULARY ENRICHMENT

Words like *laser* are known as *acronyms*. An acronym is a special kind of abbreviation formed from the first letter, or sometimes the first two letters, of each main word in a phrase. The word *acronym* comes from the Greek words *akros,* meaning "topmost" or "extreme," and *onyma,* meaning "name." *Laser* is an acronym for the descriptive phrase *light amplification by stimulated emission of radiation.* The names of many organizations are acronyms. Examples are NATO (North Atlantic Treaty Organization) and NASA (National Aeronautics and Space Administration).

Activity   Look up the following acronyms in your dictionary and see what words their letters stand for. Define each acronym.

1. BASIC   2. CAT scan   3. flak   4. hi-fi   5. radar

Throughout history, humanity has progressed by learning to use the materials available in the environment. We use water for cooking, for washing our clothes, and for making electricity. We use the earth for growing food and for obtaining the minerals needed for industrial progress. In deciding how to use something, we ask ourselves how appropriate or suitable it is. Is it the right size? Can it be handled easily? Will it last a long time? The words in this lesson will help you to answer such questions in more specific ways.

<table>
<tr><td>

WORD LIST

applicable
expedient
extraneous
functional
futile
obsolete
opportune
pragmatic
relevant
utilitarian
</td></tr>
</table>

DEFINITIONS

After you have studied the definitions and example for each word, write the vocabulary word on the line to the right.

1. **applicable** (ăp'lĭ-kə-bəl) *adjective*   Appropriate; suitable; capable of being used for a particular purpose.

   Related Words **application** *noun;* **apply** *verb*
   Example   The new requirements for graduation are *applicable* only to students now in the seventh grade.

   1. _____

2. **expedient** (ĭk-spē'dē-ənt) *adjective*   **a.** In one's own interest: *an expedient decision.*   **b.** Convenient; appropriate for a certain purpose.   *noun* Something that answers a particular purpose.

   Related Words **expediency** *noun;* **expediently** *adverb*
   Example   Representative Smith found it *expedient* to oppose the bill because most people in her district were against it.

   2. _____

3. **extraneous** (ĭk-strā'nē-əs) *adjective*   Not essential or related; not to the point: *extraneous comments.* (From the Latin word *extra*, meaning "outside")

   Related Word **extraneously** *adverb*
   Example   The debater lost points for using *extraneous* facts.

   3. _____
   MEMORY CUE: If something is *extraneous*, it's *extra*, not needed.

4. **functional** (fŭngk'shə-nəl) *adjective*   **a.** Able to operate or work. **b.** Designed for a particular purpose. (From the Latin word *functio*, meaning "performance")

   Related Words **function** *noun;* **function** *verb;* **functionally** *adverb*
   Example   Our twenty-year-old typewriter is still *functional.*

   4. _____
   See *utilitarian.*

5. **futile** (fyo͞ot'l) *adjective*   Not successful; without result or effect: *a futile attempt.*

   Related Words   **futilely** *adverb;* **futility** *noun*
   Example   In the 1500s, Ponce de Leon led a *futile* search in Florida for a "fountain of youth."

5. _____

6. **obsolete** (ŏb'sə-lēt') *adjective*   Not used anymore; outmoded or old-fashioned. (From the Latin word *obsolescere*, meaning "to wear out")

   Example   Hoop skirts were once popular but are now *obsolete.*

6. _____

7. **opportune** (ŏp'ər-to͞on') *adjective*   Well timed; occurring at an appropriate or fitting time.

   Related Words   **opportunely** *adverb;* **opportunity** *noun*
   Example   The job offer came at an *opportune* time, because Charlotte needed money for school.

7. _____

   USAGE NOTE: Don't confuse *opportune* with *importune*, which means "to beset with repeated and insistent requests."

8. **pragmatic** (prăg-măt'ĭk) *adjective*   Concerned with needs and results rather than theories. (From the Greek word *prattein*, meaning "to do")

   Related Words   **pragmatically** *adverb;* **pragmatism** *noun;* **pragmatist** *noun*
   Example   *Pragmatic* people want to get things done efficiently.

8. _____

9. **relevant** (rĕl'ə-vənt) *adjective*   Related to the matter at hand; connected or associated. (From the Latin verb *relevare*, meaning "to relieve")

   Related Word   **relevance** *noun*
   Example   Mark's comments at the hearing were *relevant* because they addressed the problem of bus safety.

9. _____

   MEMORY CUE: Be sure not to switch the *l* and the *v* in *relevant.*

10. **utilitarian** (yo͞o-tĭl'ĭ-târ'ē-ən) *adjective*   Useful; emphasizing the value of practical qualities. (From the Latin word *uti*, meaning "to use")

    Related Word   **utility** *noun*
    Example   Although a factory may not be beautiful, it has *utilitarian* value because products are manufactured in it.

10. _____

    USAGE NOTE: *Functional* means "fulfilling a specific purpose." *Utilitarian* simply means "practical."

EXERCISE 1 WRITING CORRECT WORDS

On the answer line, write the word from the vocabulary list that fits
each definition.

1. Not to the point; not essential

2. No longer in use

3. Appropriate for a particular purpose

4. Without result or effect

5. Well timed

6. In one's own interest

7. Concerned with results rather than theories

8. Able to operate or work

9. Useful in a practical way

10. Related to the matter at hand

1. _____

2. _____

3. _____

4. _____

5. _____

6. _____

7. _____

8. _____

9. _____

10. _____

EXERCISE 2 USING WORDS CORRECTLY

Each of the following statements contains an italicized vocabulary word.
Decide whether the statement is true or false, and write *True* or *False* on the
answer line

1. If a snowmobile is *functional*, it will not work.

2. One would probably give up a search that seems *futile*.

3. An *extraneous* remark is on the subject.

4. People who daydream so frequently that they forget important tasks are
   pragmatic.

5. To equip a workshop, a person would go to a hardware store and buy
   obsolete tools.

6. If three solutions to a problem seem *applicable*, you probably would not
   use any of them.

7. If your car needed new brakes, a new transmission, and a new engine,
   you might decide that it was an *opportune* time to buy a new car.

8. To save time, it may be *expedient* to take a ferry across a lake rather than
   drive around it.

9. The president's knowledge of rock music was *relevant* to his handling of
   world affairs.

10. A book on bicycle repair is probably *utilitarian*.

1. _____

2. _____

3. _____

4. _____

5. _____

6. _____

7. _____

8. _____

9. _____

10. _____

Decide which vocabulary word best completes the sentence, and write the letter of your choice on the answer line.

1. In revising her report, Lisa eliminated all the _____ material.
   a. functional   b. pragmatic   c. applicable   d. extraneous

   1. _____

2. Mr. Starr decided to buy a new computer while the lower prices were still _____.
   a. futile   b. applicable   c. obsolete   d. extraneous

   2. _____

3. Words that people no longer use are _____.
   a. obsolete   b. functional   c. opportune   d. relevant

   3. _____

4. Dean didn't need an expensive car; he simply needed one that was _____ enough to drive across the country.
   a. relevant   b. futile   c. obsolete   d. functional

   4. _____

5. The pencil is a(n) _____ tool.
   a. futile   b. obsolete   c. utilitarian   d. extraneous

   5. _____

6. Livia, who has a good deal of common sense, makes _____ suggestions.
   a. extraneous   b. obsolete   c. pragmatic   d. futile

   6. _____

7. Christina waited for a(n) _____ moment to ask her employer for a raise.
   a. obsolete   b. opportune   c. futile   d. extraneous

   7. _____

8. The first attempt to rescue the victims was _____, but the second attempt succeeded.
   a. futile   b. expedient   c. functional   d. applicable

   8. _____

9. Brian found it more _____ to hire someone to type the report than to type it himself.
   a. extraneous   b. obsolete   c. expedient   d. futile

   9. _____

10. The attorney asked the witnesses for information that was _____ to the crime.
    a. opportune   b. pragmatic   c. extraneous   d. relevant

    10. _____

Decide which form of the vocabulary word in parentheses best completes the sentence. The form given may be correct. Write your answer on the answer line.

1. Our work stopped when the copy machine would not _____. (functional)

   1. _____

2. Patricia relied on personal _____ in making her decision. (expedient)

   2. _____

3. The defense attorney found a court decision that _____ to the case. (applicable)

   3. _____

4. The players felt a sense of _____ after falling far behind. (futile)

   4. _____

5. Most of what Calvin said was _____ to the topic. (extraneous)

   5. _____

6. The band's concert tour was _____ timed for the same month as the release of the new album. (opportune)

   6. _____

7. Jan is successful in her job because she deals _____ with problems. *(pragmatic)*

7. _____

8. Although the computer has made some jobs _____, it has created others. *(obsolete)*

8. _____

9. The witness's remarks had no _____ to the case being tried. *(relevant)*

9. _____

10. The _____ of the pump is to keep the basement dry during storms. *(functional)*

10. _____

READING COMPREHENSION

Each numbered sentence in the following passage contains an italicized vocabulary word. After you read the passage, you will complete an exercise.

STEAM-POWERED AUTOMOBILES

When inventors first tried making automobiles, they experimented with steam power because it had worked successfully in factories and for railroads. (1) As long ago as 1769, a *functional* steam-powered car was built in France, but it could travel only three miles per hour.

By the 1820s the English were using steam-powered carriages that resembled the buses we ride today. The carriages traveled up to fifteen miles per hour. However, some people considered these vehicles noisy, dirty, and dangerous. (2) In 1865 the English Parliament passed two laws that were *applicable* to steam carriages. One prevented the carriages from going more than four miles per hour. The other required that a person carrying a flag walk in front of the carriage to signal its approach. (3) Under such limiting laws further development of the steam carriage seemed *futile,* and the railroad soon replaced it. (4) Perhaps investors in railroads found it *expedient* to support laws that hurt the rival steam carriage.

In spite of these setbacks in England, engineers in the United States continued to develop steam-powered automobiles. (5) The Stanley steamer, developed by Francis and Freelan Stanley, was a *utilitarian* car. It could reach speeds of more than 120 miles per hour and go backward as well as forward.

(6) A *pragmatic* American, Henry Ford, believed that gasoline, not steam, was the best way to power automobiles. (7) Consequently, he developed a gasoline-powered car, stripped it of all *extraneous* features, and sold it at a low price. (8) Ford's automobile, the Model T, soon made steam cars *obsolete.*

Recently, experts have been trying once again to design a steam-powered car because steam engines produce less pollution than do gasoline engines. (9) In addition, the rising cost of oil has made steam power *relevant* to the search for more efficient automobiles. (10) Perhaps we have reached the *opportune* point for a modern steam automobile. Soon we may be filling our cars at the water faucet rather than the gasoline pump.

Each of the following statements corresponds to a numbered sentence in the passage. Each statement contains a blank and is followed by four answer choices. Decide which choice fits best in the blank. The word or phrase that you choose must express roughly the same meaning as the italicized word in the passage. Write the letter of your choice on the answer line.

1. A steam-powered vehicle built in France in 1769 _____.
   a. succeeded in running
   b. excited crowds
   c. caused numerous accidents
   d. failed to run

   1. _____

2. Two laws passed by the English Parliament _____ steam-powered carriages.
   a. made things easier for
   b. allowed the export of
   c. rewarded the inventors of
   d. applied to

   2. _____

3. Because of limiting laws, future development of the steam carriage seemed _____.
   a. difficult   b. necessary   c. rewarding   d. useless

   3. _____

4. Railroad investors may have found it _____ to support laws limiting steam-powered carriages.
   a. unfair   b. difficult   c. convenient   d. fair

   4. _____

5. The Stanley steamer was _____.
   a. useful   b. complicated   c. fast   d. dangerous

   5. _____

6. Henry Ford was _____.
   a. greedy   b. practical   c. intelligent   d. well-organized

   6. _____

7. Henry Ford stripped his gasoline-powered cars of all _____ features.
   a. unnecessary   b. rich   c. beautiful   d. foreign

   7. _____

8. Steam-powered autos became _____.
   a. expensive   b. more popular   c. old-fashioned   d. dangerous

   8. _____

9. Because of high oil prices, the use of steam power in cars _____.
   a. is timely importance once again
   b. is totally unrealistic
   c. hurts the nation
   d. benefits oil companies

   9. _____

10. Perhaps now is the _____ time for a modern steam-powered automobile.
    a. worst   b. final   c. first   d. right

    10. _____

WRITING ASSIGNMENT

In our daily lives, we use many appliances and machines, including stoves, refrigerators, washing machines, dryers, saws, drills, radios, televisions, cars, buses, boats, and tractors. Choose one of the appliances or machines that you or members of your family use, and write a description of what it looks like and how it functions. The description is for people in the future who wish to read about life in our time. Use at least five words from this lesson in your composition, and underline the words.

LESSON 21 BUSINESS

Because business involves the production and sale of goods and services, it influences all parts of our lives. We depend on factories and stores to produce and distribute most of the things we need. Business provides jobs and influences the economy. It is little wonder, then, that business terms occur so frequently on television and in newspapers and magazines. This lesson introduces vocabulary words that will help you to understand more about the world of business.

WORD LIST

backlog
barter
commerce
franchise
inflation
inventory
merger
monopoly
transaction
vender

DEFINITIONS

After you have studied the definitions and example for each word, write the vocabulary word on the line to the right.

1. **backlog** (băk′lŏg′) *noun*   A quantity of unfinished work or unfilled orders.

   Example   Because of the *backlog* of work in the office, the entire staff was asked to work overtime.

   1. _____

2. **barter** (bär′tər) *verb*   To trade goods or services without exchanging money.   *noun*   The act of trading without money.

   Example   Before the use of money, people *bartered* goods that they had, such as crops, for goods that they needed, such as tools.

   2. _____

3. **commerce** (kŏm′ərs) *noun*   The buying and selling of merchandise, especially in large amounts, between different places. (From the Latin *com-*, meaning "together," and *merces*, meaning "merchandise")

   Related Word   **commercial** *adjective*
   Example   Throughout the nineteenth century, there was a growing amount of *commerce* among the states.

   3. _____

4. **franchise** (frăn′chīz′) *noun*   The right granted to an individual or a group to sell a product or service.   *verb*   To grant the right to sell a product or service. (From the French word *franche*, meaning "free")

   Example   Simone hopes eventually to purchase a natural-foods *franchise*.

   4. _____

5. **inflation** (ĭn-flā'shən) *noun*   **a.** An expansion or increase.   **b.** An increase in the prices of goods and services. (From the Latin word *inflatus*, meaning "blown into")

   Related Words   inflate *verb;* **inflationary** *adjective*
   Example   Because of *inflation,* the price of butter rose to two dollars a pound.

5. _____

6. **inventory** (ĭn'vən-tôr´ē) *noun*   **a.** A quantity of articles in stock.   **b.** A detailed list of the available articles.   *verb* To make a list of the articles on hand. (From the Latin word *invenire,* meaning "to find")

   Example   The *inventory* in the warehouse has increased since last year because the number of orders has decreased.

6. _____

7. **merger** (mûr'jər) *noun*   A process by which two or more businesses or organizations join to make one. (From the Latin word *mergere,* meaning "to plunge")

   Related Word   **merge** *verb*
   Example   Wright Oil Corporation was the result of the *merger* of several small companies.

7. _____

8. **monopoly** (mə-nŏp'ə-lē) *noun*   **a.** Complete control by one group of the means of producing or selling a product or service.   **b.** A company having such complete control. (From the Greek words *monos,* meaning "one," and *pōlein,* meaning "to sell")

   Related Word   **monopolize** *verb*
   Example   Their *monopoly* on ticket sales allowed them to charge high prices.

8. _____

9. **transaction** (trăn-săk'shən) *noun*   A business activity that is carried out, performed, managed, or conducted: *a cash transaction.* (From the Latin *trans-,* meaning "through," and *agere,* meaning "to drive")

   Related Word   **transact** *verb*
   Example   She relied on the clerk to record each sales *transaction.*

9. _____

10. **vender** also **vendor** (vĕn'dər) *noun*   A person or company whose business is selling a product or service. (From the Latin word *vendere,* meaning "to sell")

    Related Word   **vend** *verb*
    Example   Street *venders* usually must obtain licenses to display and sell their goods.

10. _____

MEMORY CUE: a *vending* machine is one that sells products.

EXERCISE I WRITING CORRECT WORDS

On the answer line, write the word from the vocabulary list that fits
each definition.

1. To trade one object for another

2. A person or company whose business is selling a product or service

3. A quantity of articles in stock; a detailed list of available articles

4. The joining of two or more businesses

5. A quantity of unfinished work

6. An expansion; an increase in prices

7. The right to sell a product or service

8. A business activity that is carried out, managed, or conducted

9. Complete control by one group of the means of producing or selling a
   product or service

10. The large-scale buying and selling of goods and services

1. _____

2. _____

3. _____

4. _____

5. _____

6. _____

7. _____

8. _____

9. _____

10. _____

EXERCISE 2 USING WORDS CORRECTLY

Each of the following statements contains an italicized vocabulary word.
Decide whether the sentence is true or false, and write *True* or *False* on the
answer line.

1. The Department of *Commerce* of the federal government deals mainly
   with educational institutions.

2. You may be able to *barter* a service rather than pay money for the things
   you need.

3. If you are absent from school, you may have a *backlog* of assignments
   when you return.

4. The aim of most companies is to make a profit from their business
   transactions.

5. When many companies compete by selling similar services or products, a
   monopoly exists.

6. If a business allows its *inventory* to get too low, it may not be able to fill all
   the orders that it receives.

7. During a period of *inflation*, prices fall and great quantities of goods are
   sold.

8. Some companies sell their products to the public through *franchises*.

9. In a business deal, the person who buys the product is the *vender*.

10. When a company fails, a *merger* has occurred.

1. _____

2. _____

3. _____

4. _____

5. _____

6. _____

7. _____

8. _____

9. _____

10. _____

Decide which vocabulary word or related form best completes the sentence, and write the letter of your choice on the answer line.

1. Mrs. Gorski wanted to _____ several pieces of her jewelry in return for repairs to her porch.
   a. transact   **b.** barter   **c.** monopolize   **d.** merge

   1. _____

2. Many fast-food companies sell their products through _____ owned by individuals.
   a. inflations   **b.** mergers   **c.** monopolies   **d.** franchises

   2. _____

3. A child's first _____ may consist of selling fruit juice to neighbors.
   a. transaction   **b.** backlog   **c.** merger   **d.** monopoly

   3. _____

4. A company with a _____ on a product or service can charge whatever it wants because there is no competition.
   a. merger   **b.** vender   **c.** backlog   **d.** monopoly

   4. _____

5. _____ between two countries can be difficult if they have severe political differences.
   a. Inventories   **b.** Venders   **c.** Commerce   **d.** Backlogs

   5. _____

6. The federal government might try to prevent _____ by limiting wage and price increases.
   a. inventory   **b.** monopoly   **c.** inflation   **d.** backlog

   6. _____

7. The computer exhibit attracted more than one hundred _____ of hardware and software.
   a. mergers   **b.** venders   **c.** monopolies   **d.** backlogs

   7. _____

8. Many stores hold special sales to decrease their _____.
   a. inventories   **b.** inflations   **c.** franchises   **d.** monopolies

   8. _____

9. The two small companies hoped that a(n) _____ would give them a better chance of success.
   a. inventory   **b.** inflation   **c.** vender   **d.** merger

   9. _____

10. Frustration and stress on the job can occur if there is a constant _____ of work.
    a. transaction   **b.** franchise   **c.** backlog   **d.** inventory

    10. _____

Decide which form of the vocabulary word in parentheses best completes the sentence. The form given may be correct. Write your answer on the answer line.

1. Jeff and Maureen _____ their lawn-mowing businesses. (*merger*)

   1. _____

2. They agreed to use only cash when _____ business. (*transaction*)

   2. _____

3. Alicia says that the price increase is not _____. (*inflation*)

   3. _____

4. Children often _____ toys they don't want for ones they do want. (*barter*)

   4. _____

5. She is interested in pursuing a _____ career. (*commerce*)

   5. _____

6. Ms. Tahari purchased a sporting goods _____. (*franchise*)

   6. _____

7. Jake dropped his coins into the fruit-juice _____ machine. (*vender*)

   7. _____

8. Dellum's Department Store is closed for _____. *(inventory)*   8. _____

9. Acme Trucking Company once _____ the transport of goods throughout   9. _____
the Southwest. *(monopoly)*

10. Mr. David postponed his vacation until he had reduced his _____ of   10. _____
paperwork. *(backlog)*

READING COMPREHENSION

Each numbered sentence in the following passage contains an
italicized vocabulary word or related form. After you read the
passage, you will complete an exercise.

A BRIEF HISTORY OF BUSINESS IN THE UNITED STATES

Calvin Coolidge said that the business of America is business, but this hasn't always been so. (1) Early colonists found it difficult to *transact* business because they lived so far apart. As settlements grew larger, however, trade became easier. (2) Colonists *bartered* candles for fabric, for example, or dairy products for lumber. (3) As time passed, people specialized and became shoemakers, weavers, blacksmiths, or *venders* of other products and services.

The colonists could not produce everything that they needed, however. (4) To get manufactured articles, people entered into *commerce* with other countries. They bought ships, loaded them with household products made in the colonies, and set sail for Europe and the West Indies. (5) There they traded their *inventories* for sugar, furniture, and machinery.

In the early nineteenth century, Americans began to manufacture products that they had previously obtained from other countries. (6) In 1798, for example, the government granted Eli Whitney a *franchise* to make muskets for American soldiers.

(7) By 1860 small textile and machinery factories could not produce goods fast enough to keep up with their *backlog* of orders. (8) Therefore, a number of small companies *merged* to form larger ones. With progress came abuse, unfortunately. (9) Often the power of the large companies reduced competition, and *monopolies* resulted. (10) This development led, in turn, to a period of highly *inflated* prices.

The threat posed by monopolies and inflation caused great concern throughout the country. In 1890 the government passed the Sherman Anti-Trust Act, which prevented any business from gaining a monopoly over a product or service. Other measures taken by the federal government also helped to reduce inflation. These reforms set the stage for the continued growth of business in the twentieth century.

READING COMPREHENSION EXERCISE

Each of the following statements corresponds to a numbered sentence in the
passage. Each statement contains a blank and is followed by four answer
choices. Decide which choice fits best in the blank. The word or phrase that
you choose must express roughly the same meaning as the italicized word in
the passage. Write the letter of your choice on the answer line.

1. Early colonists were too widely scattered to _____ much business.   1. _____
   a. conduct   c. fight
   b. be interested in   d. expect

2. People _____ candles for fabric.
   a. dropped   b. replaced   c. advertised   d. traded

2. _____

3. People specialized and became _____ of products or services.
   a. buyers   b. makers   c. sellers   d. users

3. _____

4. The need for manufactured articles led people to engage in _____.
   a. factory building   c. large-scale buying and selling
   b. strong competition   d. small-scale service organizations

4. _____

5. Merchants traded their _____ for the products they needed.
   a. crews   c. services
   b. available articles   d. sellers

5. _____

6. The government gave Eli Whitney _____ to manufacture muskets.
   a. an idea   b. a job   c. a factory   d. the right

6. _____

7. Small factories could not produce articles fast enough to keep up with their _____.
   a. unfilled orders   c. quotas
   b. unexpected shortages   d. money

7. _____

8. A number of small companies _____ to form larger ones.
   a. decided   b. joined   c. declined   d. ceased

8. _____

9. The large companies reduced competition and developed _____.
   a. new manufacturing techniques
   b. manufacturing networks
   c. complete control of products
   d. good reputations

9. _____

10. Monopolies led to a period of highly _____ prices.
    a. increased   b. decreased   c. unusual   d. desirable

10. _____

WRITING ASSIGNMENT

Choose one of your hobbies, talents, or special interests, and write a paragraph in which you explain how you might develop your interest into a business. For example, you might explain how your interest in records and music could help you run a record store. Use at least five of the vocabulary words from this lesson in your paragraph and underline each word that you use.

VOCABULARY ENRICHMENT

The word *merger* comes from the Latin verb *mergere,* which means "to plunge, dip, or bury." In a business merger, one business is absorbed by another; in a sense, one business "plunges into" the other. Similarly, when two lanes of traffic *merge,* one lane joins the other lane.

Activity   The Latin word *mergere* is the source of several English words in addition to *merge* and *merger.* Four such words follow. Using a high school or college dictionary, write the etymology of each of the words. Then write a sentence using each word.

1. emerge   2. emergency   3. immersion   4. submerge

The **Test** for Lessons 19, 20, and 21 is on page T23.

READING SKILLS

THE PREFIX *RE-*

You can increase your vocabulary if you know the meanings of common prefixes. By combining the definition of a prefix with the definition of the root, you can determine the meaning of an unfamiliar word.

The prefix *re-* has two common meanings, "back" and "again."

Prefix Meaning	Word	Definition
1. back	regain	to gain back
	replace	to put back
2. again	replay	to play again
	rebuild	to build again

EXERCISE USING THE PREFIX *RE-*

Step 1: Write your definition of the italicized word in each of the following sentences. *Step 2:* Write the dictionary definition of the word. Choose the definition that best fits the word as it is used in the sentence. *Step 3:* Write a sentence of your own in which you use the word correctly.

1. Judy deserves to be *reelected* to the student council.

   Your Definition _____

   Dictionary Definition _____

   Sentence _____

2. Melinda caught the basketball as it *rebounded* off the backboard.

   Your Definition _____

   Dictionary Definition _____

   Sentence _____

3. Geraldine sent the boots back for a *refund*.

   Your Definition _____

   Dictionary Definition _____

   Sentence _____

4. Some greeting cards are made of *recycled* paper.

   Your Definition _____

   Dictionary Definition _____

   Sentence _____

5. The hotel was *redesigned* to include more rooms.

   Your Definition _____

   Dictionary Definition _____

   Sentence _____

6. Mando *reconsidered* his decision not to go to the dance.

   Your Definition _____

   Dictionary Definition _____

   Sentence _____

7. The trail sign *reassured* the lost scouts.

   Your Definition _____

   Dictionary Definition _____

   Sentence _____

8. Rachel *reacted* badly to the medicine.

   Your Definition _____

   Dictionary Definition _____

   Sentence _____

9. The presidential candidates *reexamined* their positions on taxes.

   Your Definition _____

   Dictionary Definition _____

   Sentence _____

10. The garage mechanic *realigned* the automobile tires.

    Your Definition _____

    Dictionary Definition _____

    Sentence _____

11. Janet *reassembled* the broken plate with strong glue.

    Your Definition _____

    Dictionary Definition _____

    Sentence _____

12. After a long separation, John was *reunited* with his family.

    Your Definition _____

    Dictionary Definition _____

    Sentence _____

When people cooperate, they work together in a helpful way. Many activities require cooperation. Making a film requires cooperation among actors, the director, the producer, and the technicians. All these people must work together as a group to make the film successful. In the same way, a football team or political campaign requires cooperation to be successful.

The words in this lesson describe different aspects of cooperation. By learning them, you will enhance your ability to describe cooperative activity.

WORD LIST

alliance
collaborate
colleague
conspire
federation
harmony
interact
populous
unanimous
uniform

DEFINITIONS

After you have studied the definitions and example for each word, write the vocabulary word on the line to the right.

1. **alliance** (ə-līʹəns) *noun*   A formal agreement or union between nations, organizations, or individuals. (From the Latin word *alligare*, meaning "to bind to")

   Related Words   **allied** *adjective*; **ally** *noun*; **ally** *verb*
   Example   Britain, France, and the United States formed an *alliance* in World War I.

   1. _____
   See *federation*.

2. **collaborate** (kə-lăbʹə-rātʹ) *verb*   To work together on a project. (From the Latin word *collaborare*, meaning "to work together")

   Related Words   **collaboration** *noun*; **collaborative** *adjective*; **collaborator** *noun*
   Example   The composer and the lyricist *collaborated* to write the musical score for the movie.

   2. _____

3. **colleague** (kŏlʹēgʹ) *noun*   A fellow member of a profession, staff, or organization; an associate.

   Example   A doctor sometimes seeks the advice of a *colleague* in order to confirm a diagnosis.

   3. _____

4. **conspire** (kən-spīrʹ) *verb*   To plan together secretly, especially to commit an illegal act. (From the Latin *com-*, meaning "together," and *spirare*, meaning "to breathe")

   Related Words   **conspiracy** *noun*; **conspirator** *noun*; **conspiratorial** *adjective*
   Example   Roman senators *conspired* to murder Julius Caesar.

   4. _____

5. **federation** (fĕd´ə-rā´shən) *noun* A league or association formed by people or groups joining together. (From the Latin word *foedus*, meaning "league")

   Related Word   **federal** *adjective*
   Example   A *federation* of dairy workers held their annual convention in Michigan.

5. _____

USAGE NOTE: A *federation* is usually a permanent association. An *alliance* is often a temporary union.

6. **harmony** (här´mə-nē) *noun* **a.** Agreement in feeling or opinion; good will. **b.** The study of the forms and relationships of chords in music. **c.** A pleasing combination of musical sounds.

   Related Words   **harmonious** *adjective;* **harmonize** *verb*
   Example   The growing *harmony* between the two countries resulted in increased trade.

6. _____

7. **interact** (ĭn´tər-ăkt´) *verb* To act on or affect one another: *people who interact peacefully.*

   Related Word   **interaction** *noun*
   Example   Tony *interacted* with his computer by answering questions that appeared on the computer screen.

7. _____

8. **populous** (pŏp´yə-ləs) *adjective* Having many inhabitants; heavily populated. (From the Latin word *populus*, meaning "the people")

   Related Words   **populace** *noun;* **populate** *verb;* **population** *noun*
   Example   With more than one billion people living there, China is a very *populous* country.

8. _____

9. **unanimous** (yōō-năn´ə-məs) *adjective* Sharing the same opinion: *a unanimous vote.* (From the Latin words *unus*, meaning "one," and *animus*, meaning "mind")

   Related Words   **unanimity** *noun;* **unanimously** *adverb*
   Example   In a *unanimous* decision, all members of the student council voted to hold the dance.

9. _____

10. **uniform** (yōō´nə-fôrm´) *adjective* Of the same kind; having the same characteristics: *uniform products.* *noun* A suit of clothing intended to identify the person who wears it as a member of a specific group or organization. (From the Latin words *unus,* meaning "one," and *forma,* meaning "shape" or "form")

    Related Words   **uniformity** *noun;* **uniformly** *adverb*
    Example   Home-baked cookies are rarely of *uniform* size.

10. _____

EXERCISE I WRITING CORRECT WORDS

On the answer line, write the word from the vocabulary list that fits
each definition.

1. To work together

2. An association or organization

3. Agreement of opinion or feeling

4. To affect one another

5. A formal union or agreement

6. Having the same characteristics; of the same kind

7. A fellow worker

8. Agreed to by everyone

9. Heavily populated

10. To plan together secretly

1. _____

2. _____

3. _____

4. _____

5. _____

6. _____

7. _____

8. _____

9. _____

10. _____

EXERCISE 2 USING WORDS CORRECTLY

Each of the following questions contains an italicized vocabulary word.
Decide the answer to the question, and write *Yes* or *No* on the answer line.

1. If two countries are bitter enemies, would they be likely to form an
   alliance?

2. Is it easier to buy clothes when sizes are *uniform?*

3. Is music pleasing when the performers sing in *harmony?*

4. Does the proverb "Two heads are better than one" illustrate the meaning
   of *collaborate?*

5. If you wanted peace and quiet and open spaces, would you be likely to
   move to a *populous* area?

6. If six people vote for one candidate and six people vote for the other
   candidate, is the vote *unanimous?*

7. Do your parents *conspire* with you to do your homework?

8. Would a guidance counselor and a student try to *interact* in a positive
   way?

9. Would one person acting alone be a *federation?*

10. Are dancers and bricklayers likely to be *colleagues?*

1. _____

2. _____

3. _____

4. _____

5. _____

6. _____

7. _____

8. _____

9. _____

10. _____

EXERCISE 3 CHOOSING THE BEST WORD

Decide which vocabulary word or related form best completes the sentence, and write the letter of your choice on the answer line.

1. Urban areas are usually very _____; rural areas are not thickly settled.
   a. unanimous   b. harmonious   c. populous   d. uniform

   1. _____

2. Did the shoplifter act alone, or did he _____ with others?
   a. conspire   b. interact   c. harmonize   d. populate

   2. _____

3. The three small countries formed a(n) _____ to strengthen their defenses.
   a. colleague   b. population   c. alliance   d. interaction

   3. _____

4. Henry Ford's assembly line made possible the production of _____, interchangeable parts.
   a. populous   b. harmonious   c. unanimous   d. uniform

   4. _____

5. Chemistry is the study of substances and how they _____ to form new substances.
   a. collaborate   b. conspire   c. harmonize   d. interact

   5. _____

6. Paul McCartney and John Lennon of the Beatles were two of the most successful songwriters ever to _____.
   a. ally   b. collaborate   c. colleague   d. conspire

   6. _____

7. Organizations may band together in a(n) _____ to work together.
   a. federation   b. interaction   c. uniformity   d. harmony

   7. _____

8. The heart specialist and two _____ wrote a lengthy article for the medical journal.
   a. allies   b. conspirators   c. colleagues   d. uniformities

   8. _____

9. If a Supreme Court decision is not _____, those who disagree write a minority opinion.
   a. populous   b. unanimous   c. conspiratorial   d. interactive

   9. _____

10. Getting along well with others brings _____ into our lives.
    a. uniformity   b. federation   c. conspiracy   d. harmony

    10. _____

EXERCISE 4 USING DIFFERENT FORMS OF WORDS

Decide which form of the vocabulary word in parentheses best completes the sentence. The form given may be correct. Write your answer on the answer line.

1. Our _____ fought with us in World War II. *(alliance)*

   1. _____

2. Certain laws make it illegal to take part in a _____. *(conspire)*

   2. _____

3. It is important to apply fertilizer _____ to your lawn. *(uniform)*

   3. _____

4. The _____ of the United States is more concentrated in the East than in the West. *(populous)*

   4. _____

5. The _____ settlement of a rental dispute pleased the tenants. *(harmony)*

   5. _____

6. The new trees planted in the downtown area are the result of the _____ of several groups. *(collaborate)*

   6. _____

7. When the president brought up her proposal, Veronica was hoping for _____ among the board members. *(unanimous)*

7. _____

8. Postal service workers are not employees of the _____ government. *(federation)*

8. _____

9. Scientists are studying the _____ of newborn babies and their mothers. *(interact)*

9. _____

10. On April Fools' Day, one can hear people speaking in _____ whispers. *(conspire)*

10. _____

READING COMPREHENSION

Each numbered sentence in the following passage contains an italicized vocabulary word. After you read the passage, you will complete an exercise.

THE MARSHALL PLAN

The Marshall Plan (or European Recovery Program) has been hailed as one of the greatest acts of generosity in history. Through the plan, the United States gave billions of dollars to help Western Europe rebuild after World War II.

(1) When the war ended, several countries that had formed an *alliance* with the United States faced severe economic problems. (2) The *populous* nation of Great Britain, for instance, could not produce enough food for its citizens. British industry was at a standstill. Workers could make little steel, so British steel could not be used in payment for food from other countries.

The situation was even worse in France and Germany. In the winter of 1946–47, two hundred people froze to death in Berlin.

(3) European leaders were afraid some people might *conspire* to overthrow their governments.

The United States decided to help. President Truman asked Secretary of State George Marshall to draw up a proposal for action. (4) Marshall and his *colleagues* planned carefully for success.

(5) First, the United States government asked Western European countries to *interact* more cooperatively with one another than they had in the past. (6) This *harmony* would serve to promote trade among these nations. Previously, if a French firm wanted to import goods from a German company, it had to pay a tariff to the German government. (7) The United States asked the countries of Western Europe to *collaborate*

to eliminate these tariffs. European countries formed a planning organization called the Organization for European Economic Cooperation (OEEC). (8) The succeeding *federation*, now called the European Union (or Common Market), is still active and expanding.

After European countries agreed to cooperate, the United States started to give them aid. Twelve billion dollars was granted in total. (9) The United States did not require all the countries to spend the loans in a *uniform* manner.

The effects of the Marshall Plan were dramatic. Within five years most of Europe had recovered completely. (10) Historians are nearly *unanimous* in praising this effort to help the people of Europe.

Each of the following statements corresponds to a numbered sentence in the passage. Each statement contains a blank and is followed by four answer choices. Decide which choice fits best in the blank. The word or phrase that you choose must express roughly the same meaning as the italicized word in the passage. Write the letter of your choice on the answer line.

1. Several countries that had formed a(n) _____ with the United States faced severe economic problems.
   a. army   **b.** friendship   **c.** closeness   **d.** agreement

   1. _____

2. The _____ nation of Great Britain could not produce enough food.
   a. friendly   **b.** thickly settled   **c.** starving   **d.** well-liked

   2. _____

3. European leaders were afraid that some might _____ to overthrow governments.
   a. plot   **b.** want   **c.** try   **d.** strike

   3. _____

4. Marshall and his _____ planned carefully for success.
   a. good friends   **c.** fellow workers
   b. hated enemies   **d.** superior officers

   4. _____

5. The United States government asked European countries to _____ .
   a. celebrate together   **c.** deal with one another
   b. fight together   **d.** speak to one another

   5. _____

6. This _____ could serve to promote trade.
   a. agreement   **c.** honesty
   b. increased wealth   **d.** equality

   6. _____

7. The United States asked the countries of Europe to _____ to eliminate these tariffs.
   a. work together   **b.** plot   **c.** plan   **d.** begin

   7. _____

8. The European Economic Community (or Common Market) is a(n) _____ that still exists.
   a. mall   **b.** place   **c.** club   **d.** association

   8. _____

9. The United States did not require all the countries to spend loans in a(n) _____ manner.
   a. similar   **b.** worse   **c.** rich   **d.** unpleasant

   9. _____

10. Historians are _____ in praising the effort.
    a. correct   **b.** in agreement   **c.** in error   **d.** in place

    10. _____

PRACTICE WITH ANALOGIES

Directions   On the answer line, write the vocabulary word or a form of it that completes each analogy.

See pages 26, 52, 78, and 98 for some strategies to use with analogies.

1. Odometer is to distance as _____ is to pressure. (*Lesson 19*)

   1. _____

2. Irrelevant is to idea as _____ is to information. (*Lesson 20*)

   2. _____

3. Marriage is to persons as _____ is to business. (*Lesson 21*)

   The **Bonus activity** for Lessons 21 and 22 is on page T25.

   3. _____

4. Union is to workers as _____ is to nations. (*Lesson 22*)

   4. _____

5. Relevant is to extraneous as _____ is to romantic. (*Lesson 20*)

   5. _____

LESSON 23 REMOVAL AND DISPOSAL

23

Think of all the times you have to remove things or throw them out. At the end of the school year, you clean out your folders by throwing away old papers. When your clothes no longer fit, you take them out of your closet. Before you paint a room, you may remove the old paint. Sometimes you must remove things forcefully, and other times, gently. This lesson will provide you with words to cover a great variety of situations in which you must perform the action of forcing out or removing.

WORD LIST
discard
dispel
disperse
displace
disqualify
evict
excise
exile
extinguish
purge

DEFINITIONS

After you have studied the definitions and example for each word, write the vocabulary word on the line to the right.

1. **discard** (dĭs-kärd') *verb* To throw away; reject; get rid of. *noun* The act of throwing away.

   Example   As Philip cleaned out his desk drawer, he *discarded* many items.

1. _____

2. **dispel** (dĭ-spĕl') *verb* To drive away; rid one's mind of a notion or idea. (From the Latin *dis-*, meaning "apart," and *pellere*, meaning "to drive")

   Example   Susan managed to *dispel* her fears about riding the roller coaster.

2. _____
See *disperse*.

3. **disperse** (dĭ-spûrs') *verb* **a.** To move or distribute in different directions; scatter. **b.** To cause to vanish or disappear. (From the Latin *dis-*, meaning "apart," and *sparger*, meaning "to scatter")

   Related Word dispersal *noun*
   Example   The police *dispersed* the crowds outside the burning building.

3. _____
USAGE NOTE: *Dispel* most often refers to a mental activity. *Disperse* refers to a physical activity.

4. **displace** (dĭs-plās') *verb* **a.** To remove or put out of the usual place; change the position of. **b.** To take the place of.

   Related Word displacement *noun*
   Example   Many residents of the small coastal town were *displaced* after an unexpected hurricane swept through the area.

4. _____
See *evict*.

© Great Source DO NOT COPY

Removal and Disposal **147**

5. **disqualify** (dĭs-kwŏl'ə-fī') *verb*   To make or declare unable or unfit to participate in an activity.

    Related Word   **disqualification** *noun*
    Example   After the runner took an unauthorized shortcut, he was *disqualified* from the race.

5. _____

6. **evict** (ĭ-vĭkt') *verb*   **a.** To force out; eject.   **b.** To put out (a tenant) by legal process. (From the Latin word *evincere*, meaning "to conquer")

    Related Word   **eviction** *noun*
    Example   The librarian *evicted* the dedicated students at closing time.

6. _____

USAGE NOTE: A person can be *displaced* through *eviction*.

7. **excise** (ĭk-sīz') *verb*   To remove or cut off. (From the Latin *ex-*, meaning "out," and *caedere*, meaning "to cut")

    Related Word   **excision** *noun*
    Example   The editor *excised* the unnecessary parts of the newspaper article.

7. _____

8. **exile** (ĕg'zīl') *noun*   **a.** The condition of being forced to leave one's country or native land.   **b.** An outcast.   *verb*   To send into banishment.

    Example   The *exile* wandered from country to country seeking a welcome.

8. _____

9. **extinguish** (ĭk-stĭng'gwĭsh) *verb*   To put out, such as a fire or a light; put an end to. (From the Latin *ex-*, meaning "out," and *stinguere*, meaning "to quench")

    Related Word   **extinguisher** *noun*
    Example   The rangers fought to *extinguish* the forest fire.

9. _____

10. **purge** (pûrj) *verb*   To get rid of a part or an element that is not pure or desirable.   *noun*   The act or process of getting rid of an impure element. (From the Latin word *purgare*, meaning "to cleanse")

    Example   City officials promised to *purge* the drinking water of any harmful substances.

10. _____

EXERCISE 1 COMPLETING DEFINITIONS

On the answer line, write the word from the vocabulary list that best completes each definition.

1. To get rid of an undesirable part or element is to _____ it.

2. If you remove a bruise from an apple by cutting it out, you _____ it.

3. If you rid your mind of fears, you _____ them.

4. If you force people to move from a dwelling, you _____ them.

5. If a crowd is forced to scatter, it is _____.

6. A person who has been banished from his or her country is in _____.

7. If you put out a fire, you _____ it.

8. If you throw your newspaper away, you _____ it.

9. To declare someone ineligible is to _____ him or her.

10. If you remove someone from his or her usual area, you _____ that person.

1. _____

2. _____

3. _____

4. _____

5. _____

6. _____

7. _____

8. _____

9. _____

10. _____

EXERCISE 2 USING WORDS CORRECTLY

Each of the following statements contains an italicized vocabulary word. Decide whether the sentence is true or false, and write *True* or *False* on the answer line.

1. Failing two courses *dispelled* Bob's doubts about his ability.

2. Firefighters often *extinguish* fires with water.

3. Turning professional will *disqualify* an athlete from some events in the Olympic Games.

4. The automobile has almost completely *displaced* the horse as a means of transportation.

5. You would *purge* the water in a swimming pool by adding polluted water to it.

6. When you write a composition, you should *excise* paragraphs that are not on the subject.

7. A person who has been *exiled* can return to his or her country at will.

8. A landlord *evicts* a good tenant by renewing his or her lease.

9. Antique collectors carefully *discard* and preserve their antiques.

10. The sight of a large bear can easily *disperse* a group of campers.

1. _____

2. _____

3. _____

4. _____

5. _____

6. _____

7. _____

8. _____

9. _____

10. _____

Decide which vocabulary word or related form best completes the sentence, and write the letter of your choice on the answer line.

1. The speaker _____ any doubts that we may have had about the value of moderate exercise.
   a. purged   b. displaced   c. evicted   d. dispelled

   1. _____

2. Some charity organizations collect clothes that people might otherwise _____ .
   a. disperse   b. discard   c. displace   d. excise

   2. _____

3. "Breaking training will _____ you from the track meet this weekend," warned the coach.
   a. evict   b. disqualify   c. displace   d. dispel

   3. _____

4. George knew how to _____ the boiler of sediment.
   a. evict   b. displace   c. extinguish   d. purge

   4. _____

5. At midnight, the campers _____ their flashlights and watched the stars.
   a. displaced   b. excised   c. extinguished   d. dispelled

   5. _____

6. The charitable organization tried to find homes for _____ people.
   a. displaced   b. discarded   c. extinguished   d. excised

   6. _____

7. Because some people would not move out, city officials had to _____ them from the unsafe building.
   a. purge   b. evict   c. disqualify   d. dispel

   7. _____

8. The doctor can either burn or _____ that knobby growth on Sylvia's hand.
   a. exile   b. discard   c. excise   d. disqualify

   8. _____

9. In the story "The Man Without a Country," a young army officer is sent into _____ .
   a. exile   b. eviction   c. displacement   d. dispersion

   9. _____

10. After raking the leaves, Robert jumped into the pile and _____ them again.
    a. dispelled   b. dispersed   c. excised   d. evicted

    10. _____

Decide which form of the vocabulary word in parentheses best completes the sentence. The form given may be correct. Write you answer on the answer line.

1. After his defeat at Waterloo, Napoleon was _____ to the island of St. Helena. (exile)

   1. _____

2. The _____ of Susan's essay in the contest created an uproar. (disqualify)

   2. _____

3. _____ the grease fire was a difficult task. (extinguish)

   3. _____

4. When you put ice cubes into a glass of water, the liquid rises because of the process of _____ . (displace)

   4. _____

5. Yasuki had several warts _____ . (excise)

   5. _____

6. Many communities have laws that tightly regulate the _____ of tenants by landlords. *(evict)*

6. _____

7. "Do you want to keep this sweater," asked Cindy, "or is it a _____?" *(discard)*

7. _____

8. After the _____ of the crowd, the theater was surprisingly clean. *(disperse)*

8. _____

9. Veterans in the political party were expecting a _____ of members who had not supported the candidate. *(purge)*

9. _____

10. When Justin is feeling low, writing in his journal sometimes helps to _____ his gloom. *(dispel)*

10. _____

READING COMPREHENSION

Each numbered sentence in the following passage contains an italicized vocabulary word or related form. After you read the passage, you will complete an exercise.

THE SAN FRANCISCO EARTHQUAKE AND FIRE

(1) At 5:13 on the morning of April 18, 1906, a violent *displacement* within the San Andreas fault occurred. The fault can be described as a lengthy fracture in the crust of the earth that runs for almost eight hundred miles in California. As a result of the sudden shift in the earth's surface, the city of San Francisco suffered a bruising earthquake. (2) This disaster took the lives of 452 people, destroyed 28,000 buildings, and *evicted* countless families from their homes.

The tremor, which lasted forty-seven seconds, shook the city violently. (3) People *discarded* all caution as they rushed out of their homes and looked for ways to escape the quaking buildings. (4) The effect of the quake *dispersed* the crowds of people into the streets. (5) Women in nightgowns and men in long underwear must have looked like *exiles* from a strange land.

Immediately following the quake, fires were started by overturned stoves, broken electric wires, gas from exploding pipes, and damaged chimneys. (6) Fire *purged* the city of both ramshackle buildings and stately homes. The fires spread quickly because 90 percent of the city's structures were made of wood. (7) Although fire had destroyed San Francisco six times before 1906, building codes had still not *disqualified* wood as a construction material. In areas with frequent earthquakes, builders were afraid to use bricks because they collapse too easily.

The only way that firefighters found to rid the city of burning buildings was to use dynamite to destroy entire blocks. (8) It took three days to *extinguish* the fire. San Francisco quickly rebuilt those huge parts of the city that had been destroyed. (9) In spite of this rapid recovery, the 1906 earthquake and fire are a part of the city's history that will never be *excised*. (10) It was difficult for people to *dispel* the frightening idea that a disaster like this might happen again. Indeed, a sizable earthquake hit San Francisco in October 1989. However, this time the city was better prepared. The special construction that the city's buildings now use helped to limit the damage the earthquake caused.

READING COMPREHENSION EXERCISE

Each of the following statements corresponds to a numbered sentence in the passage. Each statement contains a blank and is followed by four answer choices. Decide which choice fits best in the blank. The word or phrase that you choose must express roughly the same meaning as the italicized word in the passage. Write the letter of your choice on the answer line.

1. Early on an April morning in 1906, there was a tremendous _____ within the San Andreas fault.
   a. natural disaster
   b. change of position
   c. ear-shattering noise
   d. flood of water

   1. _____

2. As a result of the disaster, many people were _____ their homes.
   a. desperate about
   b. trapped in
   c. forced out of
   d. anxious about

   2. _____

3. As they escaped from the buildings, people _____ all caution.
   a. rejected
   b. tried to use
   c. ran to find
   d. exercised

   3. _____

4. The effect of the quake _____ crowds of people into the streets.
   a. panicked
   b. pushed
   c. scattered
   d. detoured

   4. _____

5. Dressed in their nightclothes, people must have looked like _____ from another country.
   a. outcasts
   b. visitors
   c. tourists
   d. officials

   5. _____

6. Fire _____ the city of homes as well as shacks.
   a. developed
   b. rid
   c. released
   d. added

   6. _____

7. San Francisco had not yet _____ wood as a construction material.
   a. tried
   b. banned
   c. guaranteed
   d. allowed

   7. _____

8. San Francisco's fire took three days to _____.
   a. put out
   b. spread
   c. investigate
   d. escape from

   8. _____

9. The 1906 earthquake and fire are impossible to _____ the city's history.
   a. understand in
   b. add to
   c. transform in
   d. remove from

   9. _____

10. The idea that a similar disaster would occur was hard to _____.
    a. recognize
    b. drive away
    c. understand
    d. remember

    10. _____

WRITING ASSIGNMENT

Imagine that you are a newspaper reporter. It is late at night and all is quiet. Suddenly a fire alarm goes off. You find out that a fire has started from a faulty electrical wire in an apartment building. Write a news story, using at least five of the words from this lesson, to recount the events of that night. Underline each word.

The roots *-mov-* and *-mot-* are two forms of the same Latin root, meaning "move." They come from the Latin word *movere*, meaning "to move." Many English words are derived from these roots. For example, a *locomotive* is a train that moves from place to place. A *motor* has parts that move. When you are in *motion*, you are in the process of moving. A *movie* projector moves film along at a rapid rate. In this lesson, you will learn other words that have something to do with movement.

WORD LIST
commotion
demotion
emotional
immobilize
mobility
momentary
momentum
motive
promotion
remote

DEFINITIONS

After you have studied the definitions and example for each word, write the vocabulary word on the line to the right.

1. **commotion** (kə-mō′shən) *noun*   A violent or turbulent motion; a disturbance that creates disorder. (From the Latin *com-*, meaning "together," and *movere*, meaning "to move")

   Example   Laura slammed her locker angrily, creating a *commotion* in the otherwise quiet hall.

   1. _____

2. **demotion** (dĭ-mō′shən) *noun*   A lowering in rank or position. (From the Latin *de-*, meaning "down," and *movere*)

   Related Word   **demote** *verb*
   Example   The job *demotion* meant less pay for the employee.

   2. _____
   See *promotion*.

3. **emotional** (ĭ-mō′shə-nəl) *adjective*   Showing strong feelings; easily stirred by one's feelings; agitated. (From the Latin *ex-*, meaning "out," and *movere*)

   Related Word   **emotion** *noun*
   Example   Larry became very *emotional* after watching the sad movie on television.

   3. _____

4. **immobilize** (ĭ-mō′bə-līz′) *verb*   To make motionless or incapable of moving. (From the Latin *in-*, meaning "not," and *mobilis*, meaning "movable")

   Related Words   **immobile** *adjective*; **immobilization** *noun*
   Example   The traffic in the park was *immobilized* when three bears sat down in the middle of the road.

   4. _____
   See *mobility*.

5. **mobility** (mō-bĭl′ĭ-tē) *noun*   Ability to move or be moved from place to place. (From the Latin word *movere*)

   Related Word   **mobile** *adjective*
   Example   One of the advantages of a four-wheel-drive vehicle is its *mobility* over rough terrain.

5. _____
MEMORY CUE: *Mobility* refers to the ability to move easily. *Immobilize* has to do with the inability to move freely.

6. **momentary** (mō′mən-tĕr′ē) *adjective*   Lasting for only an instant or a moment. (From the Latin word *movere*)

   Related Word   **momentarily** *adverb*
   Example   Irene had a *momentary* fear that she had lost her wallet, but she found it in her purse.

6. _____

7. **momentum** (mō-mĕn′təm) *noun*   Force or speed of motion. (From the Latin word *movere*)

   Example   The snowball gained *momentum* as it rolled down the slope.

7. _____

8. **motive** (mō′tĭv) *noun*   A reason or an emotion that makes one act in a certain way. (From the Latin word *motivus*, meaning "causing motion")

   Related Words   **motivate** *verb;* **motivation** *noun*
   Example   In many mystery novels, the criminal's *motive* is greed.

8. _____

9. **promotion** (prə-mō′shən) *noun*   **a.** An advancement to a higher grade, rank, or position.   **b.** Publicity for a product or a business venture. (From the Latin *pro-*, meaning "forward," and *movere*)

   Related Words   **promote** *verb;* **promoter** *noun*
   Example   Jane earned her job *promotion* by working extra hours at the office.

9. _____
MEMORY CUE: *Promotion* is the opposite of *demotion*.

10. **remote** (rĭ-mōt′) *adjective*   **a.** Located far away; distant in time, space, connection, or relation.   **b.** Slight. (From the Latin *re-*, meaning "back," and *movere*)

    Related Words   **remotely** *adverb;* **remoteness** *noun*
    Example   It took the campers three days to hike to the *remote* lake.

10. _____
MEMORY CUE: A *remote* control allows you to change channels on your TV from a distance.

EXERCISE 1 COMPLETING DEFINITIONS

On the answer line, write the word from the vocabulary list that best completes each definition.

1. If someone shows strong feelings, he or she might be called _____.

2. Something that lasts only for a brief period of time is _____.

3. A disturbance that creates disorder is called a _____.

4. If you are able to move about freely, you have _____.

5. An advancement to a higher position is called a _____.

6. The motion or force of a moving object is called its _____.

7. Something that is distant or far away is _____.

8. When a person is lowered in position or rank, he or she receives a _____.

9. A reason or emotion that causes a person to act in a certain way is called a _____.

10. When you prevent something from moving, you _____ it.

1. _____

2. _____

3. _____

4. _____

5. _____

6. _____

7. _____

8. _____

9. _____

10. _____

EXERCISE 2 USING WORDS CORRECTLY

Each of the following statements contains an italicized vocabulary word. Decide whether the sentence is true or false, and write *True* or *False* on the answer line.

1. Touring five European countries in one week requires *mobility*.

2. *Momentary* grief does not last.

3. A *demotion* is usually accompanied by an increase in salary.

4. Establishing a realistic *motive* for a crime is important to the writers of detective stories.

5. The possibility of people living on Mars in the next twenty years is very *remote*.

6. The *momentum* of a large wave can easily knock a person over.

7. A horse is *immobilized* after it leaves the starting gate in a race.

8. People who receive *promotions* usually feel that no one appreciates their work.

9. Arguing with a friend can be an *emotional* experience.

10. A lot of *commotion* helps people to fall asleep easily.

1. _____

2. _____

3. _____

4. _____

5. _____

6. _____

7. _____

8. _____

9. _____

10. _____

EXERCISE 3 CHOOSING THE BEST DEFINITION

For each italicized vocabulary word in the following sentences, write the
letter of the best definition on the answer line.

1. There is a *remote* possibility that Mt. Vesuvius will erupt within the next
   twenty-four hours.
   a. likely   **b.** unbelievable   **c.** scientific   **d.** slight

   1. _____

2. "Which would you prefer, Charles," the boss asked, "a transfer or a(n)
   promotion?"
   a. vacation   **b.** demotion   **c.** advancement   **d.** commitment

   2. _____

3. Inspector Drayfish tried to solve the mystery by looking for a(n) *motive*.
   a. reason   **b.** fingerprint   **c.** impulse   **d.** lack of reason

   3. _____

4. The football player's *momentum* carried him over the goal line for a
   touchdown.
   a. teammates   **b.** energy   **c.** cleats   **d.** force

   4. _____

5. Joe was irritated with the *momentary* interruption.
   a. long   **b.** brief   **c.** important   **d.** annoying

   5. _____

6. Martha enjoyed the *mobility* provided by driving a car.
   a. power   **c.** restrictiveness
   b. freedom of movement   **d.** feeling of adventure

   6. _____

7. The captain signaled for help for his *immobilized* yacht.
   a. motionless   **b.** fragile   **c.** movable   **d.** powerful

   7. _____

8. Frank reacted to the play in an *emotional* way.
   a. logical and unfeeling   **c.** personal
   b. hysterical   **d.** strongly felt

   8. _____

9. As a result of his *demotion*, Walter found he had more time.
   a. long vacation   **b.** resignation   **c.** drop in rank   **d.** promotion

   9. _____

10. Mr. Blake found his chickens in a state of wild *commotion*.
    a. hunger   **b.** disorder   **c.** impatience   **d.** happiness

    10. _____

EXERCISE 4 USING DIFFERENT FORMS OF WORDS

Decide which form of the vocabulary word in parentheses best completes
the sentence. The form given may be correct. Write you answer on the
answer line.

1. It is important to find a good facility for a _____ home. *(mobility)*

   1. _____

2. Mr. Thompson threatened to _____ the employee. *(demotion)*

   2. _____

3. The mountains were difficult to reach because of their _____. *(remote)*

   3. _____

4. When the raccoon broke into the kitchen, there was a great deal of _____.
   (commotion)

   4. _____

5. The manager promised to _____ the machine operator as soon as there
   was an opening. *(promotion)*

   5. _____

6. Surrounded on all sides, the troops were _____. *(immobilize)*

   6. _____

7. The roller coaster car gained _____ as it sped down the track. (*momentum*)

7. _____

8. _____ is an important ingredient in learning. (*motive*)

8. _____

9. Alexis was _____ dazed when she bumped her head. (*momentary*)

9. _____

10. Debbie showed a great deal of _____ after losing the class election. (*emotional*)

10. _____

READING COMPREHENSION

Each numbered sentence in the following passage contains an italicized vocabulary word or related form. After you read the passage, you will complete an exercise.

AUTOMOBILES: COSTS AND BENEFITS TO SOCIETY

At one time, people dependent upon the horse as the best means of transportation had to live close to the places they worked. Visits to far-off relatives were long and costly events. A twenty-mile trip could take all day.

(1) A *momentary* thought about modern life shows how the automobile has changed all of this. (2) *Mobility* is now common in modern society. A trip of twenty miles usually takes less than an hour. In fact, many people travel this distance daily to their places of work. (3) The *commotion* of automobile traffic has become common in the streets of large cities. (4) Efficient, high-speed highways cross our states, linking *remote* areas to each other and to major cities.

The automobile has greatly benefited society, yet it also has had certain negative effects. The gasoline used in most automobiles can harm the environment. Much of the oil used in gasoline has to be carried long distances. There have been some large spills and leaks from tankers carrying

oil. These disasters have harmed nearby wildlife. News programs have carried sad stories showing thousands of birds and seals covered with oil. (5) Not surprisingly, viewers have had *emotional* reactions to the tragedy. (6) At times, *immobilized* tankers have been difficult to repair and have continued to leak oil for several days. (7) Captains and other crew members of the tankers have been *demoted* or have lost their jobs. The companies that sponsor them have been involved in major law suits.

Gasoline can have other negative effects that are more difficult to notice. When gasoline is used in engines, cars give off carbon monoxide, a gas that can injure health. (8) In crowded cities, where cars are forced to travel slowly and cannot achieve rapid *momentum*, carbon monoxide increases. Under these circumstances, it may affect people's health and well being. Carbon dioxide, another gas, can harm the environment by contributing to the pollution in the air. When

this gas increases to a certain level, it can become trapped in our atmosphere, gradually warming our environment. This is often called the "greenhouse effect."

(9) All these things provide strong *motivations* to replace gasoline. Ethanol, a fuel made from food products such as corn, can be used in place of gasoline. Since many farmers in North America are producing more food products than they can sell, ethanol is easy to supply. In addition, food products are less likely than oil to cause dangerous accidents when they are transported.

(10) Some companies are *promoting* cars that burn ethanol. Ethanol fuel can perform to high standards. It has been used in prize-winning race cars and in airplanes that have flown faster than the speed of sound. With the development of fuels such as ethanol, our society can keep its fast pace while reducing the environmental harm that may be caused by such fuels as gasoline.

Each of the following statements corresponds to a numbered sentence in the passage. Each statement contains a blank and is followed by four answer choices. Decide which choice fits best in the blank. The word or phrase that you choose must express roughly the same meaning as the italicized word in the passage. Write the letter of your choice on the answer line.

1. A _____ thought about modern life shows how the automobile has changed all of this.
   a. short   b. moving   c. long   d. first

2. _____ is now common in modern society.
   a. Quickness   b. Movement   c. Rudeness   d. Helpfulness

3. The _____ of automobile traffic has become common in the streets of large cities.
   a. boredom   b. noise   c. disorder   d. sight

4. Efficient, high-speed highways cross our states, linking _____ areas to each other and to major cities.
   a. small   b. distant   c. friendly   d. huge

5. Not surprisingly, viewers have had _____ reactions to the tragedy.
   a. small   b. agitated   c. moving   d. many

6. At times, _____ tankers have been difficult to repair and have continued to leak oil for several days.
   a. dangerous   b. motionless   c. numerous   d. sinking

7. Captains and other crew members of the tankers have been _____ or have lost their jobs.
   a. lowered in respect   c. lowered in health
   b. lowered in pay   d. lowered in rank

8. In crowded cities, where cars are forced to travel slowly and cannot achieve rapid _____, carbon monoxide increases.
   a. speed   b. acceleration   c. stopping   d. turns

9. All these things provide strong _____ to replace gasoline.
   a. feelings   b. money   c. reasons   d. advances

10. Some companies are _____ cars that burn ethanol.
    a. producing   b. trying   c. advertising   d. developing

1. _____

2. _____

3. _____

4. _____

5. _____

6. _____

7. _____

8. _____

9. _____

10. _____

Imagine that you are going away for the summer. A friend is treating you to a farewell movie. When you arrive at the friend's house, you are amazed to find a large group of people waiting for you. "Surprise! Happy vacation!" they yell. Write a paragraph using five words from this lesson that tells about this experience. Underline each word. Try to include humor in your narrative.

READING SKILLS

THE PREFIX *SUB-*

Like other prefixes, the prefix *sub-* changes the meaning of the roots to which it is added. This prefix has two possible meanings.

Prefix Meaning	Word	Definition
1. below or under	substandard	below standard
	subconscious	below consciousness = not fully conscious
2. secondary	subplot	secondary plot
	subcommittee	secondary committee

EXERCISE USING THE PREFIX *SUB-*

Step 1: Write your definition of the italicized word in each of the following sentences. *Step 2:* Write the dictionary definition of the word. Choose the definition that best fits the way the word is used in the sentence. *Step 3:* Write a sentence of you own in which you use the word correctly.

1. Pam had never ridden a *subway* train until she moved to Boston.

   Your Definition _____

   Dictionary Definition _____

   Sentence _____

2. The *subtotal* for the groceries was fifty-six dollars.

   Your Definition _____

   Dictionary Definition _____

   Sentence _____

3. The farmer hired an expert to test the *subsoil* of his wheat fields.

   Your Definition _____

   Dictionary Definition _____

   Sentence _____

4. The Welmers purchased a home in a *subdivision* outside Tulsa.

   Your Definition _____

   Dictionary Definition _____

   Sentence _____

5. The nation of India is also a *subcontinent* of Asia.

   Your Definition _____

   Dictionary Definition _____

   Sentence _____

6. The increase in ocean water temperature was caused by the eruption of a *submarine* volcano.

   Your Definition _____

   Dictionary Definition _____

   Sentence _____

7. We went to see a movie at a theater in the *suburbs*. (Clue: -*urb*- is a Latin root meaning "city.")

   Your Definition _____

   Dictionary Definition _____

   Sentence _____

8. Ten city blocks close to the river were *submerged* by the flood. (Clue: -*merg*- is a Latin root meaning "to plunge.")

   Your Definition _____

   Dictionary Definition _____

   Sentence _____

9. The number in the chemical formula for water, H_2O, is a *subscript*. (Clue: -*script*- is a Latin root meaning "written.")

   Your Definition _____

   Dictionary Definition _____

   Sentence _____

10. Town residents were not allowed to return to their homes until the flood waters *subsided*. (Clue: -*sid*- is a Latin root meaning "to settle.")

    Your Definition _____

    Dictionary Definition _____

    Sentence _____

11. The fire marshall determined that *substandard* electrical work had caused the fire.

    Your Definition _____

    Dictionary Definition _____

    Sentence _____

LESSON 25 ETIQUETTE AND BEHAVIOR

Many people think that etiquette consists of rigid rules for introducing people or for setting a table correctly. However, etiquette simply means good manners—guidelines that help us in our relationships with others. Good manners are not restricted to certain social occasions; instead, they require courteous and considerate behavior in everyday life. This lesson covers words used to describe and explain good manners.

WORD LIST

dignity
formal
hospitable
morality
nicety
propriety
puritanical
refinement
suave
tact

DEFINITIONS

After you have studied the definitions and example for each word, write the vocabulary word on the line to the right.

1. **dignity** (dĭg′nĭ-tē) *noun*   **a.** Pride and self-respect.   **b.** The quality or condition of being worthy.   **c.** The quality or condition of being respected or honored by others. (From the Latin word *dignus*, meaning "worthy")

   Related Words   **dignified** *adjective;* **dignify** *verb*
   Example   Skipping in a graduation procession is inappropriate; students should walk with *dignity*.

   1. _____

2. **formal** (fôr′məl) *adjective*   **a.** Following accepted requirements or customs.   **b.** Calling for elegant clothes and fine manners: *a formal dance.* (From the Latin word *forma*, meaning "shape" or "form")

   Related Words   **formality** *noun;* **formally** *adverb*
   Example   The master of ceremonies gave the speaker a *formal* introduction.

   2. _____
   MEMORY CUE: To be *formal* means to follow certain *forms*.

3. **hospitable** (hŏs′pĭ-tə-bəl) *adjective*   **a.** Treating guests or strangers warmly and generously.   **b.** Favorably open to or accepting of: *hospitable to new ideas.* (From the Latin word *hospes*, meaning both "host" and "guest")

   Related Words   **hospitably** *adverb;* **hospitality** *noun*
   Example   Clarisse found it difficult to be *hospitable* toward her uninvited weekend guests.

   3. _____

4. **morality** (mə-răl′ĭ-tē) *noun*   **a.** A set of rules about what is right and wrong in human conduct.   **b.** The ability to distinguish between right and wrong. (From the Latin word *mores*, meaning "customs")

    Related Words   **moral** *noun;* **moral** *adjective;* **moralize** *verb*
    Example   Citizens expect public officials to act according to a high standard of *morality.*

4. _____

5. **nicety** (nī′sĭ-tē) *noun*   **a.** A fine point or small detail.   **b.** Carefulness and delicacy in handling.   **c.** An elegant feature: *the nicety of dining in a fine restaurant.*

    Example   Although I know how to prepare simple foods, I would enjoy learning the *niceties* of gourmet cooking.

5. _____

6. **propriety** (prə-prī′ĭ-tē) *noun*   The quality of being suitable or proper; suitability of behavior to the circumstances.

    Example   The small child showed that he did not understand the *propriety* expected at Symphony Hall.

6. _____

7. **puritanical** (pyŏor′ĭ-tăn′ĭ-kəl) *adjective*   Strict; rigid in matters of religion or behavior. (From the Latin word *purus*, meaning "pure")

    Related Words   **puritan** *noun;* **puritanically** *adverb*
    Example   Her grandmother's *puritanical* beliefs prevented Jill from wearing shorts or blue jeans.

7. _____

8. **refinement** (rĭ-fīn′mənt) *noun*   **a.** Good taste and polish in manner or in means of expression.   **b.** The removal of impurities from a substance, such as oil.

    Related Word   **refine** *verb*
    Example   Early in the twentieth century, wealthy young women sometimes attended finishing schools, which emphasized *refinement* in behavior.

8. _____

9. **suave** (swäv) *adjective*   Smoothly agreeable or polite; sophisticated. (From the Latin word *suavis*, meaning "pleasant")

    Related Words   **suavely** *adverb;* **suaveness** *noun*
    Example   Television talk-show hosts must be able to talk with their guests in a *suave* fashion.

9. _____

10. **tact** (tăkt) *noun*   A sense of knowing what to say and do to avoid offending others or to handle a difficult situation well. (From the Latin word *tactus*, meaning "touch")

    Related Words   **tactful** *adjective;* **tactfully** *adverb*
    Example   The two women showed great *tact* when both appeared at the party wearing identical dresses.

10. _____

EXERCISE I COMPLETING DEFINITIONS

On the answer line, write the word from the vocabulary list that best completes each definition.

1. A person who has pride and self-respect has _____.

2. To have good taste and polish is to have _____.

3. People who are extremely strict in their manner of living may be considered _____.

4. Someone who is agreeable, polite, and sophisticated is said to be _____.

5. To behave appropriately in a situation is to show _____.

6. To be kind and generous to guests is to be _____.

7. To follow accepted customs is to be _____.

8. A code of _____ consists of rules of right and wrong.

9. People who say and do the right thing at the right time show _____.

10. A fine point or small detail is a _____.

1. _____
2. _____
3. _____
4. _____
5. _____
6. _____
7. _____
8. _____
9. _____
10. _____

EXERCISE 2 USING WORDS CORRECTLY

Decide whether the italicized vocabulary word has been used correctly in the sentence. On the answer line, write *Correct* for correct use and *Incorrect* for incorrect use.

1. Sarah believes that the *refinement* of one's manners is a continuing process.

2. Dave wore a blue tuxedo and blue *suave* shoes to the prom.

3. Only Jorey had the *propriety* to dare to cross the swinging bridge.

4. Ian treats all people with *dignity*.

5. Sheila was being *hospitable* when she abruptly hung up the telephone.

6. Glynnis took the posters and *tact* them onto the bulletin board.

7. Charlie installed a *puritanical* water filter in his cottage.

8. The Dexters were uncomfortable at the *formal* dinner.

9. Robert completely missed the *niceties* of Leonard's argument.

10. Cassie questioned the *morality* of Oliver's attitudes.

1. _____
2. _____
3. _____
4. _____
5. _____
6. _____
7. _____
8. _____
9. _____
10. _____

EXERCISE 3 CHOOSING THE BEST DEFINITION

For each italicized vocabulary word in the following sentences, write the letter of the best definition on the answer line.

1. Elise questioned the *propriety* of wearing a poncho to a wedding.
   a. humor **b.** attractiveness **c.** suitability **d.** wisdom

1. _____

2. The exchange student said that she had never met a more *hospitable* family than ours.
   a. welcoming   **b.** hopeful   **c.** unusual   **d.** sizable

   2. _____

3. In the Middle Ages, plays were a common method of teaching *morality*.
   a. good manners   **c.** history
   b. common sense   **d.** rules of conduct

   3. _____

4. LaMar would make a good guidance counselor because he has understanding and *tact*.
   a. skill in guiding others
   b. knowledge of right and wrong
   c. knowledge of careers
   d. skill in knowing what to say and do in all situations

   4. _____

5. "Paul, you are *puritanical* in your interpretation of literature," said Louise.
   a. rigid   **b.** confusing   **c.** entertaining   **d.** helpful

   5. _____

6. Mr. Zwahlen enjoyed the *nicety* of afternoon tea.
   a. pleasure   **c.** unusual aspect
   b. elegant feature   **d.** custom

   6. _____

7. We chose John to be the speaker because he is both *suave* and entertaining.
   a. intelligent   **b.** silly   **c.** sophisticated   **d.** honest

   7. _____

8. Everyone respected Phillip for the *refinement* of his social skills.
   a. lack   **b.** polish   **c.** summary   **d.** location

   8. _____

9. The company has a *formal* policy that all reports must be signed by the president.
   a. written   **c.** following accepted requirements
   b. widely publicized   **d.** old

   9. _____

10. Mr. Dill believes in the *dignity* of manual labor.
    a. requirement   **c.** honorable nature
    b. difficulty   **d.** challenge and excitement

    10. _____

EXERCISE 4 USING DIFFERENT FORMS OF WORDS

Decide which form of the vocabulary word in parentheses best completes the sentence. The form given may be correct. Write your answer on the answer line.

1. Aesop's fables end with _____ that we can apply to our own lives. *(morality)*

   1. _____

2. Watch how Mrs. Kozlowski _____ gets her point across. *(tact)*

   2. _____

3. Between friends, signing a contract is a mere _____. *(formal)*

   3. _____

4. While living in Austria, Erik is _____ his skills in speaking German. *(refinement)*

   4. _____

5. Jeff knows how to win in a _____ manner. *(dignity)*

   5. _____

6. The Trojan War started when Paris abused the _____ extended to him by Menelaus. *(hospitable)*

   6. _____

7. "Ladies and gentlemen, let us not waste time worrying about the _____ of raising taxes." *(propriety)*

   7. _____

8. Jason behaves _____ when he meets new people. *(suave)*   8. _____

9. In spite of appearances, Harriet's thinking is not at all _____. *(puritanical)*   9. _____

10. Endora enjoys the _____ of a beautifully set table and well-prepared food. *(nicety)*   10. _____

READING COMPREHENSION

Each numbered sentence in the following passage contains an italicized vocabulary word. After you read the passage, you will complete an exercise.

EMILY POST: AUTHORITY ON ETIQUETTE

Emily Post, well known for her newspaper columns, radio broadcasts, and books, made a career out of good manners. **(1)** Her first book on etiquette, published in 1922, established her as an authority on social *refinement.* **(2)** Although she frequently revised her book to allow for changing social conditions, the *niceties* of conduct that she described did not really change much over the years.

Mrs. Post emphasized that good manners are based on common sense and regard for the feelings of others. **(3)** In her books she covered the *proprieties* of all types of situations, from using the telephone to driving a car. Her advice became so popular that she was soon doing weekly radio shows and daily newspaper columns. **(4)** People asked questions about giving *formal* dinner parties or sending thank-you notes. **(5)** Others requested suggestions on how to be *hospitable* to guests. **(6)** Young people sought her advice on how to appear *suave* on important dates.

(7) In her books Emily Post also wrote about questions of *morality.* **(8)** She was not *puritanical,* however, for she realized that there has to be flexibility in peoples' attitudes. **(9)** She simply encouraged people to respect the *dignity* of others. **(10)** She believed that if everyone could learn *tact,* people would get along better, and life in general would be more enjoyable.

READING COMPREHENSION EXERCISE

Each of the following statements corresponds to a numbered sentence in the passage. Each statement contains a blank and is followed by four answer choices. Decide which choice fits best in the blank. The word or phrase that you choose must express roughly the same meaning as the italicized word in the passage. Write the letter of your choice on the answer line.

1. Emily Post was an authority on social _____.   1. _____
   a. mistakes   **b.** polish   **c.** conversation   **d.** plans

2. The _____ of behavior that Mrs. Post wrote about did not change very much over the years.   2. _____
   a. freedom   **b.** simple errors   **c.** limitation   **d.** fine points

3. Emily Post described _____ for all types of situations.   3. _____
   a. appropriate behavior   **c.** critical conditions
   b. oversights   **d.** meetings

4. People asked Emily Post how to give _____ dinner parties.
   a. frequent   b. exciting   c. elegant   d. unusual

4. _____

5. Other people asked for advice about how to be _____ to guests.
   a. generous   b. abrupt   c. cool   d. adventurous

5. _____

6. Young people asked how to appear _____ on dates.
   a. gentle   b. intelligent   c. correct   d. sophisticated

6. _____

7. Emily Post also wrote about questions of _____.
   a. respect   b. telephoning   c. right conduct   d. cooking

7. _____

8. Emily Post was not _____.
   a. adequately prepared   c. scholarly
   b. helpful   d. extremely strict

8. _____

9. She believed that people should respect the _____ of others.
   a. kindness   b. worth   c. humor   d. creativity

9. _____

10. Emily Post believed that people would get along well if they _____.
    a. were sensitive in knowing what to say and do
    b. developed a sense of humor
    c. followed rigid rules
    d. said whatever came into their minds

10. _____

PRACTICE WITH ANALOGIES

See pages 26, 52, 78, and 98 for some strategies to use with analogies.

Directions   On the answer line, write the vocabulary word or a form of it that completes each analogy.

1. Dispel is to falsehood as _____ is to object. (Lesson 23)

1. _____

2. Expel is to student as _____ is to tenant. (Lesson 23)

2. _____

3. Eradicate is to pest as _____ is to fire. (Lesson 23)

3. _____

4. Tact is to diplomat as _____ is to host. (Lesson 25)

4. _____

VOCABULARY ENRICHMENT

The word *puritanical* comes from *Puritan*, a term describing a famous religious group whose members left England in the sixteenth and seventeenth centuries to seek religious freedom in America. The Puritans viewed their religion as purified, since they had simplified many ceremonies and customs of the Church of England. They regarded excessive luxury and pleasure as sinful; members of the community did not read worldly books or see plays. Instead, they worked hard and closely regulated their lives. Thus, the word *puritanical* has come to mean "strictness in religious duties or moral conduct."

Activity   Many words used today are derived from the names of nations or groups. In a high school or college dictionary, look up the words listed below. Write the definition of the word and description of the group or nationality whose name is associated with the word.

1. barbaric   2. gothic   3. spartan   4. tartar

"I *think* that water lilies are the most beautiful flowers."
"I *believe* that sunlight is necessary for health."
"I *feel* strongly about the conservation of our natural resources."

These statements are among the most common types that people can make: thoughts, beliefs, and opinions. By using such statements, you can express a range of judgments and ideas. In this lesson, you will learn words that refer to some of the ways in which people consider, develop, and express their thoughts and beliefs.

<table>
<tr><td>WORD LIST</td></tr>
<tr><td>analyze
comprehend
contemplate
conviction
engross
intellect
intuition
logical
lucid
profound</td></tr>
</table>

DEFINITIONS

After you have studied the definitions and example for each word, write the vocabulary word on the line to the right.

1. **analyze** (ăn'ə-līz') *verb*   To break down into parts in order to understand. (From the Greek word *analyein,* meaning "to undo")

   Related Words   **analysis** *noun;* **analyst** *noun;* **analytical** *adjective*
   Example   The reviewer *analyzed* the movie to identify the qualities that made it so entertaining.

1. _____

2. **comprehend** (kŏm'prĭ-hĕnd') *verb*   To understand or know in depth; grasp with the mind. (From the Latin *com-,* meaning "together," and *prehender,* meaning "to grasp")

   Related Words   **comprehensible** *adjective;* **comprehension** *noun*
   Example   Eli *comprehends* all aspects of computer programming.

2. _____

3. **contemplate** (kŏn'təm-plāt') *verb*   **a.** To look at and think about something in a detached way.   **b.** To think about doing something; consider: *contemplate a career in physics.*

   Related Words   **contemplation** *noun;* **contemplative** *adjective*
   Example   Mark *contemplated* the antics of the sandpipers as he walked along the beach.

3. _____
   MEMORY CUE: When you *contemplate,* you use what's between your *temples.*

4. **conviction** (kən-vĭk'shən) *noun*   **a.** A very strong belief or opinion. **b.** The act or process of finding or proving guilty; the state of being found guilty. (From the Latin word *convincere,* meaning "to overcome")

   Related Word   **convict** *verb*
   Example   Nothing could shake Jeremy's *conviction* that the environment should be protected.

4. _____

5. **engross** (ĕn-grōs') *verb*   To occupy the mind completely; absorb. (From the Latin word *grossus*, meaning "thick")

   Example   The conversation about space exploration *engrossed* Patricia.

5. _____

6. **intellect** (ĭn'tl-ĕkt') *noun*   The ability to think, reason, and understand. (From the Latin *inter-*, meaning "between," and *legere*, meaning "to choose")

   Related Words **intellectual** *noun;* **intellectual** *adjective*
   Example   Simon and Gloria scored well on the aptitude tests because of their superior *intellects.*

6. _____

7. **intuition** (ĭn'tōō-ĭsh'ən) *noun*   A sense or feeling; knowledge or understanding that one gains immediately, without going through a step-by-step process of reasoning. (From the Latin word *inteuri*, meaning "to look at")

   Related Words **intuitive** *adjective;* **intuitively** *adverb*
   Example   Fred's *intuition* told him not to enter the cave.

7. _____

8. **logical** (lŏj'ĭ-kəl) *adjective*   **a.** Clearly thought out or reasoned: *a logical conclusion.*   **b.** Based reasonably on earlier statements or events. (From the Greek word *logos*, meaning "reason")

   Related Words **logic** *noun;* **logically** *adverb*
   Example   Maria does well in geometry because she is *logical.*

8. _____

9. **lucid** (lōō'sĭd) *adjective*   Easily understood; clear. (From the Latin word *lucere*, meaning "to shine")

   Related Words **lucidity** *noun;* **lucidly** *adverb*
   Example   The prosecutor gave a *lucid* summary of the evidence against the defendant.

9. _____
   MEMORY CUE: When something is presented *lucidly,* you "see the light."

10. **profound** (prə-found') *adjective*   **a.** Deep; thorough; going beneath the surface.   **b.** Having intellectual depth. (From the Latin *pro-*, meaning "before," and *fundus*, meaning "bottom")

    Related Words **profoundly** *adverb;* **profundity** *noun*
    Example   In her composition about the strengths of democracy, Geraldine made several *profound* points.

10. _____

EXERCISE 1 WRITING CORRECT WORDS

On the answer line, write the word from the vocabulary list that fits
each definition.

1. To look at and think about something in a detached way; think about
   doing something

2. To occupy the mind completely; absorb

3. Immediate knowledge or understanding

4. A fixed, strong belief

5. Easily understood; clear

6. To understand or know; grasp with the mind

7. The ability to think and reason

8. Clearly thought out or reasoned

9. Thorough; having intellectual depth

10. To break down into parts in order to understand

1. _____

2. _____

3. _____

4. _____

5. _____

6. _____

7. _____

8. _____

9. _____

10. _____

EXERCISE 2 USING WORDS CORRECTLY

Each of the following questions contains an italicized vocabulary word.
Decide the answer to the question, and write *Yes* or *No* on the answer line.

1. If you were *engrossed* in a story, would you have trouble concentrating
   on it?

2. If you have a *conviction* about something, do you have a strong belief
   about it?

3. Might a coach *analyze* a swimmer's strokes to help her improve?

4. Would weightlifting be the best way to improve your *intellect*?

5. If you *contemplate* a flower, do you look at it for a length of time?

6. Are people being *logical* when they rely only on their feelings in making
   a decision?

7. Are you likely to understand an explanation that is *lucid*?

8. If you rely on *intuition* to solve a problem, do you break that problem into
   steps and think about each step in depth?

9. If you *comprehend* a newspaper article, are you confused by what it is
   saying?

10. If a speaker says something *profound*, has he or she presented
    shallow ideas?

1. _____

2. _____

3. _____

4. _____

5. _____

6. _____

7. _____

8. _____

9. _____

10. _____

Decide which vocabulary word or related form best completes the sentence, and write the letter of your choice on the answer line.

1. The scientist _____ the substance and discovered that it contained a small amount of lead.
   a. comprehended
   b. analyzed
   c. engrossed
   d. convicted

   1. _____

2. By following the _____ directions, Rosita quickly put the toy together.
   a. lucid   b. engrossed   c. contemplative   d. profound

   2. _____

3. After much _____, Carol decided to work a year before going to college.
   a. conviction
   b. contemplation
   c. comprehension
   d. intellect

   3. _____

4. Mr. Swanson urged Kevin to be _____ and think about the pros and cons of each job offer.
   a. engrossed
   b. comprehensible
   c. logical
   d. intuitive

   4. _____

5. Jamie's knowledge of Spanish helped him to _____ French.
   a. comprehend
   b. be lucid in
   c. contemplate
   d. be engrossed in

   5. _____

6. In England, some Puritans were persecuted for their religious _____.
   a. intuitions   b. intellects   c. logic   d. convictions

   6. _____

7. In the legend of Pyramus and Thisbe, Pyramus' love for Thisbe is so _____ that he kills himself when he thinks that she has died.
   a. logical   b. lucid   c. profound   d. comprehensible

   7. _____

8. According to the reviewer, the exciting new novel will _____ most readers.
   a. contemplate   b. engross   c. analyze   d. comprehend

   8. _____

9. The professor was known for her great _____; she understood ideas that confused most people.
   a. conviction   b. intellect   c. engross   d. lucid

   9. _____

10. Although I could not explain why I felt this way, my _____ gave me the feeling that something was wrong.
    a. logic   b. analysis   c. lucidity   d. intuition

    10. _____

Decide which form of the vocabulary word in parentheses best completes the sentence. The form given may be correct. Write your answer on the answer line.

1. The study committee completed its _____ of the proposed dam. (analyze)

   1. _____

2. Brian found the adventure story very _____. (engross)

   2. _____

3. Geometry helps people to expand their _____ powers. (intellect)

   3. _____

4. Gwen was _____ affected by her experiences as a hospital volunteer. (profound)

   4. _____

5. Directness and simplicity help to make one's writing _____. *(comprehend)*

6. Greg knew _____ that someone was following him as he walked down the street. *(intuition)*

7. Christopher Columbus held the _____ that the world was round. *(conviction)*

8. Some people choose _____ as the surest road to wisdom. *(contemplate)*

9. The lawyer's argument was a model of _____. *(lucid)*

10. Maria argued _____ in favor of a larger allowance. *(logical)*

5. _____

6. _____

7. _____

8. _____

9. _____

10. _____

READING COMPREHENSION

Each numbered sentence in the following passage contains an italicized vocabulary word or related form. After you read the passage, you will complete an exercise.

THE DISCOVERY OF PENICILLIN BY ACCIDENT AND LOGIC

(1) Most of the time, scientists make discoveries through *logical* thinking. (2) But on occasion, *intuition* can play an important role in science. One such story is the discovery of penicillin by Alexander Fleming. (3) In this case, a small, careless act had *profound* effects on medical science. In 1928, researcher Alexander Fleming went on a vacation, leaving a culture of bacteria on an open plate. When he returned, he noticed that an unusual blue mold had grown on the dish, killing the bacteria right around it. Later, Fleming realized that he had accidentally made one of the most important discoveries of the twentieth century: penicillin, a mold that could cure human disease by destroying many types of bacteria.

(4) Was Fleming so *engrossed* in his research that he accidentally left the bacteria dish open for weeks, or did he leave it there purposely? We will never know the answer to that question.

(5) However, we do know that Fleming held the *conviction* that good research was partially accidental.

Fleming felt that some carelessness could lead to discovery. (6) Even if he could not give a *lucid* explanation for what he was doing, he felt it was important to allow things to "happen" in his laboratory. He did not like to keep a neat laboratory. He also liked to have fun. In his lab, he made "germ paintings" of bacteria. When he started them they were invisible, but later they grew into different colors.

However, the full significance of penicillin was not appreciated for at least ten years. (7) Fleming, *contemplating* its uses, suggested it might help to treat disease. However, he did not attempt to purify it for medicinal use.

In the late 1930s, however, Howard Florey became interested in it. (8) Using a more *intellectual* approach, Florey tested it in the laboratory and showed

that it was a highly effective medicine. By 1940, penicillin was being used to cure infections.

(9) Researchers have been able to *analyze* why penicillin and other antibiotics cure many infections. (10) To *comprehend* this problem, we must consider that penicillin works in a special way. It kills the bacteria that cause infection, but it does not harm the human body. How can this happen? The answer is that bacteria are very different from the human body. Because of this, penicillin can kill the harmful bacteria without harming human beings.

Fleming's accident and Florey's logic combined to make one of the most important discoveries of the twentieth century. The use of penicillin has saved thousands of lives. For their efforts, Fleming and Florey were awarded the Nobel Prize for Medicine in 1945.

Thoughts and Beliefs

Each of the following statements corresponds to a numbered sentence in the passage. Each statement contains a blank and is followed by four answer choices. Decide which choice fits best in the blank. The word or phrase that you choose must express roughly the same meaning as the italicized word in the passage. Write the letter of your choice on the answer line.

1. Most of the time, scientists make discoveries through _____ thinking.
   a. reasoned   **b.** helpful   **c.** intelligent   **d.** creative

   1. _____

2. But on occasion, _____ *can* play an important role in science.
   a. importance   **b.** feeling   **c.** belief   **c.** depth

   2. _____

3. In this case, a small, careless act had _____ effects on medical science.
   a. hopeful   **b.** helpful   **c.** deep   **d.** accidental

   3. _____

4. Was Fleming so _____ in his research that he accidentally left the bacteria dish open for weeks, or did he leave it there purposely?
   a. convinced   **b.** affected   **c.** thoughtful   **d.** involved

   4. _____

5. However, we do know that Fleming held the _____ that good research was partially accidental.
   a. conclusion   **b.** feeling   **c.** belief   **d.** understanding

   5. _____

6. Even if he could not give a _____ explanation for what he was doing, he felt it was important to allow things to "happen" in his laboratory.
   a. clear   **b.** deep   **c.** helpful   **d.** convincing

   6. _____

7. Fleming, _____ its uses, suggested it might help to treat disease.
   a. reporting on   **c.** reading about
   b. writing about   **d.** thinking about

   7. _____

8. Using a more _____ approach, Florey tested it in the laboratory and showed that it was a highly effective medicine.
   a. slow   **b.** thinking   **c.** clear   **d.** intelligent

   8. _____

9. Researchers have been able to _____ why penicillin and other antibiotics cure many infections.
   a. predict   **c.** guess
   b. figure out   **d.** make theories about

   9. _____

10. To _____ this problem, we must consider that penicillin works in a special way.
    a. understanding   **c.** solve
    b. help   **d.** create

    10. _____

WRITING ASSIGNMENT

Write a dialogue (conversation) between two people who disagree over some issue. The topic could be related to your school, your community, or even the nation. In your account, include explanatory details that identify the two people who are discussing the issue. Use at least five of the vocabulary words from this lesson, and underline each word that you use.

Anything worth preserving is worth protecting. Throughout history you will find examples of men and women defending their honor, their beliefs, their countries, their families, and their property. People succeed in defending these things because they are stronger and more courageous than those who are challenging them. In this lesson you will study words concerning defense and strength.

buttress
defensible
durable
fortify
invigorate
outpost
potent
quell
resistant
valor

DEFINITIONS

After you have studied the definitions and example for each word, write the vocabulary word on the line to the right.

1. **buttress** (bŭt′rĭs) *noun*   Something that supports or reinforces.
   verb   To support or reinforce. (From the Old French word *bouter*, meaning "to strike against")

   Example   Connie used accident statistics to *buttress* her argument for wearing seat belts.

1. _____
   See *fortify.*

2. **defensible** (dĭ-fĕn′sə-bəl) *adjective*   **a.** Capable of being proven reasonable; excusable.   **b.** Capable of being protected.

   Related Words defense *noun;* **defensibly** *adverb*
   Example   Our team won the debate because our position was more *defensible* than that of our opponents.

2. _____

3. **durable** (dŏŏr′ə-bəl) *adjective*   Capable of withstanding wear and tear; sturdy; long-lasting. (From the Latin word *durus*, meaning "hard")

   Related Words durability *noun;* **durably** *adverb*
   Example   Mr. and Mrs. Rodriguez have a *durable* marriage that has lasted sixty years.

3. _____

4. **fortify** (fôr′tə-fī′) *verb*   To strengthen and make secure. (From the Latin word *fortis*, meaning "strong")

   Related Word   fortification *noun*
   Example   When the Mississippi River rose, the residents of New Orleans *fortified* the banks of the river with sandbags.

4. _____
   USAGE NOTE: To *fortify* suggests adding strength; to *buttress* suggests adding support.

5. **invigorate** (ĭn-vĭg′ə-rāt′) *verb*   To give life and energy to; stimulate; animate. (From the Latin word *vigere*, meaning "to be lively")

   Example   The brisk autumn weather *invigorates* me each year.

5. _____

6. **outpost** (out′pōst′) *noun*   **a.** A group of soldiers located some distance from the main body of troops.   **b.** Any distant, isolated settlement.

   Example   The *outpost* maintained a constant watch to prevent a surprise attack.

6. _____

7. **potent** (pōt′nt) *adjective*   **a.** Strong; powerful.   **b.** Having a strong influence. (From the Latin word *potens*, meaning "having power")

   Related Word   **potency** *noun*
   Example   Penicillin is a *potent* drug used for combating infection.

7. _____

8. **quell** (kwĕl) *verb*   **a.** To quiet; pacify.   **b.** To put down forcibly; overpower. (From the Old English word *cwellan*, meaning "to kill")

   Example   The telephone call from her boss *quelled* Irene's fear of losing her job.

8. _____

9. **resistant** (rĭ-zĭs′tənt) *adjective*   Tending to oppose or hold off. (From the Latin *re-*, meaning "against," and *sistere*, meaning "to place")

   Related Words   **resist** *verb;* **resistance** *noun*
   Example   At first Michael was *resistant* to the idea of going away to school.

9. _____

10. **valor** (văl′ər) *noun*   Courage and boldness, such as one might show in battle. (From the Latin word *valere*, meaning "to be strong")

   Related Word   **valiant** *adjective*
   Example   Sergeant York was widely acclaimed for his *valor* on the front lines during World War I.

10. _____

EXERCISE I WRITING CORRECT WORDS

On the answer line, write the word from the vocabulary list that fits
each definition.

1. Able to be proven reasonable or to be protected

2. To give life and energy to; stimulate

3. Tending to oppose or hold off

4. A support or reinforcement

5. Courage and boldness

6. Able to withstand wear and tear; long-lasting

7. To strengthen and make secure

8. Troops stationed at a distance from the main forces

9. To quiet; put down forcibly

10. Strong; powerful

1. _____
2. _____
3. _____
4. _____
5. _____
6. _____
7. _____
8. _____
9. _____
10. _____

EXERCISE 2 USING WORDS CORRECTLY

Decide whether the italicized vocabulary word has been used correctly in the
sentence. On the answer line, write *Correct* for correct use and *Incorrect* for
incorrect use.

1. Mother's yoga exercises *invigorate* her so much that she no longer
gets tired.

2. Additional troops were called in to *fortify* the blockade.

3. Aaron is often *resistant* to new ideas and welcomes them with an
open mind.

4. With skill and *valor*, Joan of Arc fought the English at Orleans.

5. Napoleon's army was so *potent* that his military campaign started to fail.

6. The small army found a *defensible* position and thus was defeated by
the enemy.

7. Joshua is said to have used his trumpet as a *buttress* to knock down the
walls of Jericho.

8. The jacket is made of *durable* material; I have worn it every day for
five winters.

9. William found duty with the *outpost* to be tedious and lonely because he
wanted to be in a city.

10. After being awakened by a bad dream, the child cried until his father
comforted him and *quelled* his fears.

1. _____
2. _____
3. _____
4. _____
5. _____
6. _____
7. _____
8. _____
9. _____
10. _____

EXERCISE 3 CHOOSING THE BEST WORD

Decide which vocabulary word or related form best completes the sentence, and write the letter of your choice on the answer line.

1. The carpet is so _____ that it will last for years.
   a. fortified   **b.** durable   **c.** resistant   **d.** potent

   1. _____

2. Have you noticed that Vera is _____ to colds and stays healthy all winter?
   a. fortified   **b.** durable   **c.** resistant   **d.** potent

   2. _____

3. A prop or support called a(n) _____ can be seen on many medieval cathedrals.
   a. potent   **b.** buttress   **c.** outpost   **d.** quell

   3. _____

4. To make bread more nutritious, many bakers _____ it with vitamins.
   a. resist   **b.** quell   **c.** invigorate   **d.** fortify

   4. _____

5. Andrew and Elizabeth find a cold swim in the ocean _____ on a hot day.
   a. resistant   **b.** invigorating   **c.** defensible   **d.** durable

   5. _____

6. Every spring the college students have a water fight, and every year the president of the college has to _____ it.
   a. quell   **b.** resist   **c.** buttress   **d.** fortify

   6. _____

7. Every point of Alicia's argument is _____ and cannot be contradicted.
   a. resistant   **b.** quelled   **c.** durable   **d.** defensible

   7. _____

8. North of the Arctic Circle, the government maintains its _____ for tracking satellites.
   a. buttress   **b.** valor   **c.** resistance   **d.** outpost

   8. _____

9. John F. Kennedy's book *Profiles in Courage* tells of the _____ of political leaders in the United States from John Quincy Adams to William Howard Taft.
   a. invigoration   **b.** valor   **c.** fortifications   **d.** outposts

   9. _____

10. The venom of some scorpions is so _____ that it can cause paralysis.
    a. defensible   **b.** potent   **c.** invigorating   **d.** durable

    10. _____

EXERCISE 4 USING DIFFERENT FORMS OF WORDS

Decide which form of the vocabulary word in parentheses best completes the sentence. The form given may be correct. Write your answer on the answer line.

1. Phillip thought that his _____ of his actions would be easily understood and accepted. *(defensible)*

   1. _____

2. The walls of the cathedral of Notre Dame have many supporting devices known as "flying," or arched, _____. *(buttress)*

   2. _____

3. The _____ built by France along its eastern border before World War II was called the Maginot Line. *(fortify)*

   3. _____

4. "Eat Vital-O Cereal," read the advertisement, "for an _____ breakfast!" *(invigorate)*

   4. _____

5. Someday a space station may be our _____ on the frontiers of space. (*outpost*)

5. _____

6. Vitamins may lose some of their _____ after the expiration date has passed. (*potent*)

6. _____

7. The American Revolution began as a colonial uprising that the British were unable to _____. (*quell*)

7. _____

8. Copernicus's theory that the planets revolve around the sun met with much _____. (*resistant*)

8. _____

9. Maple has great _____ because it is a hard wood. (*durable*)

9. _____

10. In Homer's epic poem the *Iliad*, Achilles, a _____ Greek warrior, slays the Trojan Hector. (*valor*)

10. _____

READING COMPREHENSION

Each numbered sentence in the following passage contains an italicized vocabulary word or related form. After you read the passage, you will complete an exercise.

OLD VINCENNES

Vincennes, Indiana, is one of the oldest settlements in the United States outside the thirteen colonies. (1) Settled soon after 1700 as a French *outpost* in the wilderness, it was named after one of the early military commanders, Sieur de Vincennes. (2) The French selected the site because of its *defensible* location. (3) They *fortified* the village against invaders. (4) It was to be a *buttress* for the French claims in the Northwest Territory. (5) This *durably* built fort was, however, ceded to the British at the end of the French and Indian War and renamed Fort Sackville.

The colonists occupied Fort Sackville during the Revolutionary War. (6) The British, looking upon the fort as a *potent* defense post for controlling the Northwest Territory, seized it again in 1778.

(7) The *valor* and cunning of one man, George Rogers Clark, was responsible for the colonies' recapturing Vincennes. His army of two hundred men arrived as the Wabash River flooded the plains around the town. (8) The cold water *invigorated* Clark's soldiers as they attacked. (9) Since the attack was made during a flood, it caught the British off guard and hampered their *resistant* maneuvers. (10) Soon the colonists *quelled* all resistance, and the British surrendered the fort to the colonists. This victory helped to secure the Northwest Territory for the American colonies.

READING COMPREHENSION EXERCISE

Each of the following statements corresponds to a numbered sentence in the passage. Each statement contains a blank and is followed by four answer choices. Decide which choice fits best in the blank. The word or phrase that you choose must express roughly the same meaning as the italicized word in the passage. Write the letter of your choice on the answer line.

1. The French constructed Vincennes as a(n) _____ in the wilderness.
   a. isolated settlement
   b. city
   c. trading post
   d. shelter for emigrants

1. _____

2. The French chose the site because of its _____ location.
   a. wilderness
   b. capable of being protected
   c. central
   d. capable of being hidden
   2. _____

3. Anticipating a possible invasion, the French _____ the village.
   a. abandoned   b. strengthened   c. moved   d. developed
   3. _____

4. The French hoped that Vincennes would serve as a _____ for their claims in the Northwest Territory.
   a. trading post
   b. meeting place
   c. reinforcement
   d. border city
   4. _____

5. The _____ built fortress at Vincennes was renamed Fort Sackville.
   a. comprehensively
   b. newly
   c. systematically
   d. sturdily
   5. _____

6. The British looked upon Vincennes as a(n) _____ defense post for the control of the Northwest Territory.
   a. powerful   b. unnecessary   c. inadequate   d. outdated
   6. _____

7. George Rogers Clark showed great _____ in leading his men to retake Vincennes.
   a. stupidity   b. courage   c. durability   d. knowledge
   7. _____

8. The cold water of the Wabash River _____ the soldiers.
   a. stimulated   b. froze   c. irritated   d. defeated
   8. _____

9. The attack hampered the _____ maneuvers of the British.
   a. military   b. weak   c. opposing   d. capable
   9. _____

10. All resistance was soon _____ by the invading colonists.
    a. ignored   b. encouraged   c. put down   d. scattered
    10. _____

WRITING ASSIGNMENT

Imagine you are called upon to write a brief essay for foreign students about a courageous defender of this country. Choose a person who exemplifies such courage. In your essay explain what this person did and why it is important. Use at least five of the words from the lesson to describe his or her exploits, and underline each word that you use.

VOCABULARY ENRICHMENT

The word *buttress*, which is of Germanic origin, was initially an architectural term. In northern Europe during the Middle Ages, architects designed Gothic-style churches with high roofs and steeples that reached toward the heavens. The weight of these tall roofs and steeples pressed downward, exerting great pressure on the walls. To prevent the walls from collapsing, the architects designed a series of buttresses, or props, to provide additional support.

   Today, in addition to being used in its architectural sense, the term *buttress* refers to anything that serves as a means of support.

Activity   Other words besides *buttress* are derived from architectural terms. Find each of the following words in a dictionary. Write the architectural definition and the general definition of the word. Then write an explanation of the connection between the two definitions for each word.

1. cornerstone   2. eavesdrop   3. keystone   4. labyrinth

The **Test** for Lessons 25, 26, and 27 is on page T30.

READING SKILLS

THE SUFFIXES -*ANCE*, -*ENCE*, AND -*ANCY*

You can add to your vocabulary if you know the meanings of common suffixes. A **suffix** is a letter or group of letters added to the end of a root. To determine the meaning of a word with a suffix, add the definition of the suffix to the definition of the root to which it is attached.

Suffixes change the part of speech of a root. For example, the suffixes -*ance*, -*ence*, and -*ancy* change verbs and adjectives into nouns. These suffixes have three common meanings.

Suffix Meaning	Word	Definition
1. capacity for	tolerance (*tolerate* + -*ance*)	the capacity for tolerating others
2. act of	persistence (*persist* + -*ence*)	the act of persisting
3. state, quality, or condition of	hesitancy (*hesitate* + -*ancy*)	the state, quality or condition of hesitating

When these suffixes are added to a root, the spelling of the root sometimes changes. In the examples above, the letters *ate* are dropped when the suffixes are added to *tolerate* and *hesitate*. Here are three other examples.

perseverance = persevere + -ance (The final *e* is dropped.)
constancy = constant + -ancy (The letters *ant* are dropped.)
occurrence = occur + -ence (Another *r* is added.)

EXERCISE USING THE SUFFIXES -*ANCE*, -*ENCE*, AND -*ANCY*

Each sentence in this exercise contains an italicized verb or adjective. *Step 1:* Change the italicized word in each of the following sentences to a noun by adding the suffix -*ance*, -*ence*, or -*ancy*. Write the resulting word. *Step 2:* Write your definition of the noun. *Step 3:* Check your definition in the dictionary. Then write a sentence of your own in which you correctly use the noun.

1. Julie took an *abundant* supply of paper to her art class.

   Noun Form _____

   Your Definition _____

   Sentence _____

2. Mark's *reluctant* expression told us that he did not want to leave the party.

Noun Form _____

Your Definition _____

Sentence _____

3. The judge ruled that the statements of the witness were *relevant* to the case.

Noun Form _____

Your Definition _____

Sentence _____

4. Joan's *vibrant* personality makes her popular with her classmates.

Noun Form _____

Your Definition _____

Sentence _____

5. "You must *remit* your loan payment by the end of the month," the bank notice said.

Noun Form _____

Your Definition _____

Sentence _____

6. Because they are *buoyant,* the seat cushions in the boat can be used as life preservers.

Noun Form _____

Your Definition _____

Sentence _____

7. Marshall uses a cart to *convey* books to and from the library.

Noun Form _____

Your Definition _____

Sentence _____

8. Helga cheerfully admitted that she sometimes *indulges* her taste for raw onions.

Noun Form _____

Your Definition _____

Sentence _____

Whether an action is helpful or harmful is not always clear at first glance. For example, two people may witness a large dog growling and barking beside a young child. One individual may be convinced that the dog is going to hurt the child. Another person witnessing the scene may recognize that the dog is protecting the child.

In describing a situation like this, it is important to use words that clearly explain what is going on. When you do so, your reader or listener can reach a valid conclusion about whether the action is harmful or helpful. In this lesson you will learn words that will improve your ability to describe such situations.

belittle
envelop
exploit
facilitate
forsake
impair
inflict
inhumane
rehabilitate
rejuvenate

DEFINITIONS

After you have studied the definitions and example for each word, write the vocabulary word on the line to the right.

1. **belittle** (bǐ-lǐt'l) *verb*   To cause to seem small, unimportant, or inferior.

   Example   The Senator *belittled* the policies and voting record of his opponent.

   1. _____

2. **envelop** (ĕn-vĕl'əp) *verb*   To surround entirely; enclose or wrap. (From the Old French word *envoloper*, meaning "to wrap up in")

   Example   A thick fog *enveloped* the seaside community.

   2. _____
   MEMORY CUE: An envelope *envelops* a letter.

3. **exploit** (ĭk-sploit') *verb*   **a.** To take advantage of, often selfishly or unfairly.   **b.** To utilize; get full value or usefulness out of.
   verb (ĕk'sploit')   An act or deed, especially a brilliant or heroic accomplishment.

   Related Word   **exploitation** *noun*
   Example   The king *exploited* his subjects by forcing them to pay high taxes.

   3. _____

4. **facilitate** (fə-sǐl'ǐ-tāt) *verb*   To make easier; free from difficulty. (From the Latin word *facere*, meaning "to do")

   Example   Electing a group leader will *facilitate* the process of making decisions and accomplishing tasks.

   4. _____

5. **forsake** (fôr-sāk') *verb*   **a.** To abandon.   **b.** To give up or reject.

   Example   Justine's so-called friends have *forsaken* her when she needs them the most.

   5. _____

6. **impair** (ĭm-pâr′) *verb*   To diminish in strength, quantity, or quality; make worse; weaken or damage. (From the Latin word *pejorare*, meaning "to worsen")

   Related Word   **impairment** *noun*
   Example   David *impaired* his health by not getting enough rest.

   6. _____

7. **inflict** (ĭn-flĭkt′) *verb*   To impose or apply something unpleasant or painful, such as punishment. (From the Latin *in-*, meaning "on," and *fligere*, meaning "to strike")

   Example   Some people think that joggers *inflict* needless punishment on themselves.

   7. _____

8. **inhumane** (ĭn′hyōō-mān′) *adjective*   Lacking pity, kindness, or compassion; brutal.

   Related Word   **inhumanity** *noun*
   Example   The Society for the Prevention of Cruelty to Animals tries to stop the *inhumane* treatment of animals.

   8. _____

9. **rehabilitate** (rē′hə-bĭl′ĭ-tāt′) *verb*   **a.** To restore to a former state or condition.   **b.** To restore to useful life through education or training. (From the Latin *re-*, meaning "again," and *habilis*, meaning "able")

   Related Word   **rehabilitation** *noun*
   Example   Jack *rehabilitated* the house by giving it a fresh coat of paint.

   9. _____
   See *rejuvenate.*

10. **rejuvenate** (rĭ-jōō′və-nāt′) *verb*   To restore to youthful energy or appearance. (From the Latin *re-*, meaning "again," and *juvenis*, meaning "a youth")

    Related Word   **rejuvenation** *noun*
    Example   After a long winter, the hard-working students were *rejuvenated* by spring break.

    10. _____
    USAGE NOTE: To *rehabilitate* is to restore to a former state. To *rejuvenate* is to restore youthfulness to.

EXERCISE I COMPLETING DEFINITIONS

On the answer line, write the word from the vocabulary list that best completes each definition.

1. To restore to youthful energy or appearance is to _____.

2. To enclose or wrap is to _____.

3. To cause to seem inferior is to _____.

4. To lack compassion or pity is to be _____.

5. To restore to a previous state or condition is to _____.

6. To reject or abandon is to _____.

7. To take unfair advantage of is to _____.

8. To impose or apply something unpleasant is to _____.

9. To make something less strong or to damage it is to _____ it.

10. To make something easier is to _____ it.

1. _____

2. _____

3. _____

4. _____

5. _____

6. _____

7. _____

8. _____

9. _____

10. _____

EXERCISE 2 USING WORDS CORRECTLY

Each of the following statements contains an italicized vocabulary word. Decide whether the sentence is true or false, and write *True* or *False* on the answer line.

1. A subway breakdown at rush hour can *rejuvenate* hundreds of commuters.

2. If you *belittle* a person continually, he or she is likely to think well of you.

3. Carpenters are sometimes called in to *rehabilitate* old houses.

4. In the nineteenth century, workers were sometimes *exploited* by their employers.

5. Riding a bicycle over broken glass will never *impair* the performance of the bike's tires.

6. A bedtime story sometimes *facilitates* sleep for young children.

7. Heavyweight boxers do not *inflict* any pain or injury on one another.

8. Giving a thirsty person a drink of water is *inhumane* treatment.

9. A soldier who *forsakes* his or her duty is usually punished.

10. A winning runner might be *enveloped* by a crowd of fans as he or she crosses the finish line.

1. _____

2. _____

3. _____

4. _____

5. _____

6. _____

7. _____

8. _____

9. _____

10. _____

For each italicized vocabulary word in the following sentences, write the letter of the best definition on the answer line.

1. Reading in a poor light *impaired* Sonya's vision so much that she had to wear glasses at an early age.
   a. aided   **b.** strengthened   **c.** damaged   **d.** corrected

   1. _____

2. Using simple recipes *facilitates* the process of learning how to cook.
   a. helps   **b.** adds to   **c.** stops   **d.** discourages

   2. _____

3. The rescuers modestly tried to *belittle* their achievement, but the town rewarded them generously.
   a. make light of   **b.** advertise   **c.** brag about   **d.** ignore

   3. _____

4. The vocational school staff *rehabilitated* the young man who had not finished high school.
   a. irritated   **b.** reeducated   **c.** concerned   **d.** impressed

   4. _____

5. The reporter *exploited* people by revealing confidential information about their lives.
   a. praised in secret   **c.** took advantage of
   b. helped in a quiet way   **d.** alarmed and annoyed

   5. _____

6. Father felt *rejuvenated* after working out at the health club.
   a. delighted   **b.** ancient   **c.** miserable   **d.** youthful

   6. _____

7. A wasp can *inflict* a great deal of pain.
   a. cause   **b.** transfer   **c.** rush to   **d.** enjoy

   7. _____

8. Grandmother *enveloped* all three of us in a huge hug.
   a. stopped   **b.** welcomed   **c.** enclosed   **d.** frightened

   8. _____

9. The new zoo worker was fired because of his *inhumane* treatment of the animals.
   a. fair   **b.** brutal   **c.** entertaining   **d.** clumsy

   9. _____

10. In a well-known children's story, a country mouse decides to *forsake* the country.
    a. glorify   **b.** abandon   **c.** remain in   **d.** criticize

    10. _____

Decide which form of the vocabulary word in parentheses best completes the sentence. The form given may be correct. Write your answer on the answer line.

1. Roberta _____ the writing of her term paper by adequately researching her topic. (*facilitate*)

   1. _____

2. The program offered offenders a strong program of _____. (*rehabilitate*)

   2. _____

3. _____ the achievements of others can cause unhappiness. (*belittle*)

   3. _____

4. Some historians believe that feudalism was based on _____ of peasants. (*exploit*)

   4. _____

5. On a hot day, swimming usually has a _____ effect. (*rejuvenate*)

   5. _____

6. The dictator _____ a set of harsh rules on the people of the town. (*inflict*)

   6. _____

7. Court testimony revealed that the laboratory animals were treated in an _____ way. *(inhumane)*

7. _____

8. Exposure to constant noise can lead to the _____ of hearing ability. *(impair)*

8. _____

9. "Don't _____ me!" Samantha pleaded. "I refuse to ride this roller coaster alone!" *(forsake)*

9. _____

10. The mother lovingly _____ her baby in the blanket. *(envelop)*

10. _____

READING COMPREHENSION

Each numbered sentence in the following passage contains an italicized vocabulary word. After you read the passage, you will complete an exercise.

CHILD-LABOR LAWS: PROTECTING YOUNG WORKERS

Today laws govern the number of hours that young people may work as well as the conditions in which they work. This was not always so, however. (1) For example, until the twentieth century, the children of poor families in England were often *exploited* for inexpensive labor.

This exploitation took a number of forms. Children as young as nine years old were forced to work for fourteen to sixteen hours a day. (2) Poor working conditions seriously *impaired* the children's health. (3) Although many parents tried to *envelop* their children with protection and care, the families needed the money and could not fight the factory and mine owners.

(4) Many children must have felt *forsaken.*

English writers criticized the mistreatment of children. (5) Charles Dickens, the famous novelist, often described the *inhumane* waste of young lives. (6) The poet Elizabeth Barrett Browning, in her poem "The Cry of the Children," protested against a system that *inflicted* such suffering on youngsters. Other writers asserted that factory work cheated young people out of their childhoods. (7) Exhausted by their labor, the children could not be *rejuvenated* for even a minimum amount of schooling.

(8) Although these writers and others helped to call public attention to the abuse of child labor, their efforts did little to *facilitate* change. (9) In addition, some people *belittled* the problem. (10) They saw no need to *rehabilitate* a system that seemed to them to work well.

However, in time, public concern grew, and the British Parliament responded by passing a series of labor laws that protected young workers and freed them from long hours and terrible working conditions.

READING COMPREHENSION EXERCISE

Each of the following statements corresponds to a numbered sentence in the passage. Each statement contains a blank and is followed by four answer choices. Decide which choice fits best in the blank. The word or phrase that you choose must express roughly the same meaning as the italicized word in the passage. Write the letter of your choice on the answer line.

1. Manufacturers in England obtained cheap labor by _____ children.
   a. taking advantage of
   b. supporting
   c. taking care of
   d. restricting

1. _____

2. Unsatisfactory working conditions _____ the children's health.
   a. helped   **b.** didn't affect   **c.** damaged   **d.** improved

                                                           2. _____

3. Parents were unsuccessful in their attempts to _____ their children with care.
   a. burden   **b.** pamper   **c.** provide   **d.** restrict

                                                            3. _____

4. Children probably felt _____.
   a. abandoned   **b.** ridiculed   **c.** helped   **d.** promoted

                                                            4. _____

5. Charles Dickens wrote about the _____ treatment of young people.
   a. brutal   **b.** critical   **c.** unofficial   **d.** good

                                                            5. _____

6. Elizabeth Barrett Browning protested against a system that _____ so much suffering.
   a. approved   **b.** educated   **c.** stopped   **d.** imposed

                                                            6. _____

7. The young people could not be _____.
   a. encouraged greatly   **c.** helped financially
   b. made young again   **d.** rewarded significantly

                                                            7. _____

8. The writers were unable to _____ changes in the labor laws.
   a. stop   **c.** suggest
   b. bring about   **d.** force

                                                            8. _____

9. Some people even _____ the problems.
   a. magnified   **b.** ignored   **c.** minimized   **d.** agreed with

                                                            9. _____

10. They did not want to make any effort to _____ a system that they considered adequate.
   a. energize   **c.** develop logically
   b. disagree with   **d.** reform

                                                            10. _____

PRACTICE WITH ANALOGIES

Directions   On the answer line, write the letter of the phrase that best completes the analogy.

See pages 26, 52, 78, and 98 for some strategies to use with analogies.

1. Uncertain is to conviction as
   (A) furious is to anger   (C) shallow is to depth
   (B) juvenile is to youth   (D) handsome is to beauty

                                                            1. _____

2. Lucid is to clear as
   (A) ecstatic is to sad   (C) jealous is to lucky
   (B) hilarious is to funny   (D) bored is to curious

                                                            2. _____

3. Buttress is to support as
   (A) ornament is to decoration   (C) contract is to applause
   (B) keystone is to evidence   (D) schedule is to identity

                                                            3. _____

4. Valor is to hero as
   (A) wisdom is to sage   (C) resistance is to ally
   (B) idealism is to pragmatism   (D) dignity is to clown

                                                            4. _____

5. Rejuvenate is to youth as
   (A) reduce is to large   (C) revitalize is to tired
   (B) disclose is to private   (D) rehabilitate is to health

                                                            5. _____

When you agree with an idea or a cause, you may want to support it with your words or your actions. If you join an organization that protects endangered species of animals, for example, you are showing support for the organization's work. Your attitude may range from mild encouragement to strong approval. You may even volunteer your time to make others aware of the organization's proposals. The words in this lesson suggest different degrees of agreement with ideas as well as various degrees of support for projects.

DEFINITIONS

After you have studied the definitions and example for each word, write the vocabulary word on the line to the right.

1. **acknowledge** (ăk-nŏl′ĭj) *verb* **a.** To admit as true; confess. **b.** To recognize: *acknowledge a favor.*

   Related Word **acknowledgment** *noun*
   Example   After falling off the horse, John *acknowledged* that he didn't know how to ride.

   1. _____

2. **advocate** (ăd′və-kāt′) *verb* To write or speak in favor of; recommend or give support to. (ăd′və-kĭt′) *noun* A person who argues for a cause; a supporter. (From the Latin *ad-*, meaning "to," and *vocare*, meaning "call")

   Related Word **advocacy** *noun*
   Example   The conservationists *advocated* more effort to clean up the polluted rivers.

   2. _____
   MEMORY CUE: *Advocates* "call" others "to" their cause.

3. **comply** (kəm-plī′) *verb* To obey another's command, request, or wish. (From the Latin word *complere*, meaning "to complete")

   Related Word **compliance** *noun*
   Example   Monica will not *comply* with the unreasonable demands of her younger sister.

   3. _____
   USAGE NOTE: The word *comply* is used with the preposition *with*.

4. **concur** (kən-kûr′) *verb* To agree; have or express the same opinion as someone else. (From the Latin *com-*, meaning "together," and *currere*, meaning "to run")

   Related Words **concurrence** *noun*; **concurrent** *adjective*
   Example   The unanimous vote indicates that everyone *concurs* on the date of the dance.

   4. _____

5. **confirm** (kən-fûrm′) *verb* **a.** To prove to be true or to verify. **b.** To strengthen or make firmer. (From the Latin word *confirmare*, meaning "to strengthen")

   Related Word   **confirmation** *noun*
   Example   In a press release, the president of the university *confirmed* the news of her retirement.

   5. _____

6. **conform** (kən-fôrm′) *verb* To follow an established standard or pattern. (From the Latin *com-*, meaning "with," and *formare*, meaning "to shape")

   Related Words   **conformist** *noun*; **conformity** *noun*
   Example   Denise *conformed* easily to the rules for members of the choral group.

   6. _____
   USAGE NOTE: The word *conform* is used with the preposition *to*.

7. **justify** (jŭs′tə-fī′) *verb* To demonstrate or prove to be right, desirable, useful, or fair. (From the Latin words *justus*, meaning "just," and *facere*, meaning "to do")

   Related Words   **justifiable** *adjective;* **justification** *noun*
   Example   The tenant *justified* her complaints about the plumbing by pointing to the leaky faucet.

   7. _____

8. **sanction** (săngk′shən) *verb* To permit, approve, or encourage a course of action.   *noun* **a.** Permission or approval from an authority. **b.** A measure adopted by several nations against a nation considered to have violated international law. (From the Latin word *sanctus*, meaning "holy" or "sacred")

   Example   The relief agency *sanctioned* plans for sending food to the hurricane victims.

   8. _____

9. **sustain** (sə-stān′) *verb* **a.** To maintain or prolong; keep in existence. **b.** To endure or withstand. (From the Latin *sub-*, meaning "from below," and *tenere*, meaning "to hold")

   Related Word   **sustenance** *noun*
   Example   Through annual pledges the graduates *sustained* the scholarship fund.

   9. _____

10. **underlie** (ŭn′dər-lī′) *verb* **a.** To be the support or basis of. **b.** To be located under.

    Example   A desire for warmer weather *underlies* his parents' decision to move to Arizona.

    10. _____

EXERCISE I COMPLETING DEFINITIONS

On the answer line, write the word from the vocabulary list that best completes each definition.

1. To verify or prove that something is true is to _____ it.

2. To obey another's command or request is to _____ with that person's wishes.

3. To follow an established standard or pattern is to _____.

4. To maintain or keep in existence is to _____.

5. To be the support or basis of is to _____.

6. To speak or write in favor of or to recommend is to _____.

7. To have the same opinion as someone else is to _____.

8. To demonstrate or prove to be right or fair is to _____.

9. To admit as true or to recognize is to _____.

10. To permit, approve, or encourage is to _____.

1. _____

2. _____

3. _____

4. _____

5. _____

6. _____

7. _____

8. _____

9. _____

10. _____

EXERCISE 2 USING WORDS CORRECTLY

Each of the following questions contains an italicized vocabulary word. Decide the answer to the question, and write *Yes* or *No* on the answer line.

1. If the members of a committee are constantly arguing, do they *concur* with one another?

2. If you *conform* to unofficial dress standards at your school, do you generally wear the same type of clothing as other people do?

3. If you disagree with someone, would you try to *justify* his or her ideas?

4. Might the desire for a promotion *underlie* someone's hard work and dedication?

5. Is it a good idea to *confirm* hotel reservations before leaving on vacation?

6. Would a senator who opposed a certain bill *advocate* its passage?

7. Would a person who *complied* with a request have ignored that request?

8. Is it hard for fans to *sustain* enthusiasm when a team is playing poorly?

9. If you saw a stranger on the street, would you expect him to *acknowledge* you as an old friend?

10. Would a supervisor be likely to *sanction* extra vacation days for newly hired employees?

1. _____

2. _____

3. _____

4. _____

5. _____

6. _____

7. _____

8. _____

9. _____

10. _____

For each italicized vocabulary word in the following sentences, write the letter of the best definition on the answer line.

1. Actors and actresses *sustain* high levels of performance for many months during the run of a play.
   a. expect   b. concentrate   c. stay at   d. increase

   1. _____

2. The newspaper expected its reporters to *conform* to editorial policy.
   a. follow the standard   c. ignore
   b. speak highly of   d. think about

   2. _____

3. People who feel strongly about an issue often *advocate* their position publicly.
   a. deny   b. confuse   c. explore   d. recommend

   3. _____

4. Respect for the elderly *underlies* Rebecca's desire to volunteer at the Senior Citizens' Center.
   a. denies   c. serves as the basis of
   b. determines the extent of   d. illustrates

   4. _____

5. Sue *acknowledged* that she had not prepared well for the test.
   a. converted   b. admitted   c. denied   d. determined

   5. _____

6. Sometimes it is difficult to get everyone on a committee to *concur*.
   a. complain   b. assemble   c. start   d. agree

   6. _____

7. The attorneys hoped that the judge would *sanction* the introduction of new evidence.
   a. permit   b. prevent   c. punish   d. feature

   7. _____

8. Most parents feel *justified* in limiting their children's television viewing.
   a. guilty   b. wrong   c. right   d. old-fashioned

   8. _____

9. Each of us must *comply with* certain regulations.
   a. discover   b. remember   c. forget   d. obey

   9. _____

10. The owners of the team would neither *confirm* nor deny the rumor.
    a. invest   b. verify   c. hint   d. convert

    10. _____

Decide which form of the vocabulary word in parentheses best completes the sentence. The form given may be correct. Write your answer on the answer line.

1. _____ in art may lead to works that are too similar in style. *(conform)*

   1. _____

2. The runner could not _____ the grueling pace for the entire race. *(sustain)*

   2. _____

3. Mr. Delgado wished his boss would give him some _____ of his expected raise. *(confirm)*

   3. _____

4. The department head considers it _____ to request more money. *(justify)*

   4. _____

5. James readily _____ with all reasonable requests. *(comply)*

   5. _____

6. Ms. Huthar's _____ of minority group proposals won her praise from all parts of the city. (*advocate*)

6. _____

7. The class discussed the _____ theme of the poem. (*underlie*)

7. _____

8. Fifty-five governments voted to _____ the peace effort. (*sanction*)

8. _____

9. Matt claims to be a _____ bachelor. (*confirm*)

9. _____

10. Marion received the _____ she deserved for her volunteer service. (*acknowledge*)

10. _____

READING COMPREHENSION

Each numbered sentence in the following passage contains an italicized vocabulary word. After you read the passage, you will complete an exercise.

THE ORIGIN OF THE OLYMPIC GAMES

(1) Sports enthusiasts generally *concur* that the Olympic Games are one of the most exciting events in amateur athletics. (2) Historians *acknowledge* that the Olympics originated with the Greeks around 776 B.C. (3) The *underlying* reason for the first contests was the desire to honor Zeus. As time went on, however, the games became the setting for competition among the Greek city-states. (4) Contestants represented their city-states, and political leaders became great *advocates* of the games. Citizens were as proud of winning the contests as they were of winning battles.

Perfect coordination of mind and body was an ideal of the Greeks. (5) Therefore, the athletes had to *sustain* a rigorous training program for ten months prior to the games. (6) Before competition started, they pledged that they had *conformed* to training rules. (7) Failure to *comply* with these rules meant that they could not participate.

(8) Officials did not *sanction* the training of everyone for the Olympics, however. Women, slaves, and foreigners could not participate in the games. (9) Because of this prohibition, women felt *justified* in establishing their own games. These competitions were also held every four years, but they had fewer events.

The Olympic Games took place in Elis, where the plains of Olympia are located. Citizens of Elis regulated the events and the awarding of prizes. (10) Winners did not receive gold, silver, or bronze medals; instead, crowns made of olive branches *confirmed* the athletes' victories.

The glory and spirit of the ancient Olympics live again in our modern games, which were revived in 1896 through the efforts of Pierre, Baron de Coubertin. At their best, today's Olympic Games emphasize the ideals of healthy competition among nations and demonstrate the talents of athletes from around the world.

Each of the following statements corresponds to a numbered sentence in the passage. Each statement contains a blank and is followed by four answer choices. Decide which choice fits best in the blank. The word or phrase that you choose must express roughly the same meaning as the italicized word in the passage. Write the letter of your choice on the answer line.

1. People who like to watch sports usually _____ that the Olympic Games are exciting.
   a. demand   **b.** disagree   **c.** agree   **d.** suggest

   1. _____

2. Most historians _____ these competitions began in the eighth century B.C.
   a. learn that   **c.** recognize that
   b. deny that   **d.** question whether

   2. _____

3. The _____ reason for the first contests was to honor Zeus.
   a. basic   **b.** apparent   **c.** real   **d.** initial

   3. _____

4. The leaders of Greek city-states were great _____ the games.
   a. organizers of   **c.** critics of
   b. supporters of   **d.** participants in

   4. _____

5. Contestants were required to _____ strict training programs in preparation for the games.
   a. develop   **b.** avoid   **c.** endure   **d.** encourage

   5. _____

6. The athletes promised that they had _____ training rules.
   a. ignored   **b.** followed   **c.** thought about   **d.** created

   6. _____

7. If athletes did not _____ training regulations, they could not participate in the games.
   a. agree with   **b.** write   **c.** argue with   **d.** obey

   7. _____

8. Officials did not _____ the training of everyone for the Olympics.
   a. permit   **b.** fund   **c.** develop   **d.** eliminate

   8. _____

9. Greek women felt _____ in creating games of their own.
   a. right   **b.** wrong   **c.** unsure   **d.** courageous

   9. _____

10. The athletes' victories were _____ by crowns of olive branches.
   a. decorated   **b.** congratulated   **c.** established   **d.** denied

   10. _____

WRITING ASSIGNMENT

Imagine that you are a candidate running for a class office. In order to get elected, you want to win the support of as many people as possible. Using at least five vocabulary words from this lesson, write a short campaign speech, explaining specific policies and actions that you will emphasize if elected. Underline the vocabulary words that you use.

The ability to measure time has long been important to human beings. The Babylonians and Romans observed the movement of the sun in order to measure seconds, minutes, and hours. From these measurements they developed a calendar. People invented sundials and, later, clocks to measure the regularity of natural occurrences and to tell time. In this lesson you will study words that come from the Greek word *khronos (chronos)* and the Latin word *tempus*, which both mean "time."

DEFINITIONS

After you have studied the definitions and example for each word, write the vocabulary word on the line to the right.

1. **anachronism** (ə-năk′rə-nĭz′əm) *noun*   Something that is or seems to be out of its proper time in history. (From the Greek *ana-*, meaning "backward," and *khronizein*, meaning "to belong in time")

   Related Word   **anachronistic** *adjective*
   Example   The child's picture of ancient Incan life included several *anachronisms*, such as an automobile and a digital clock.

   1. _____

2. **chronic** (krŏn′ĭk) *adjective*   Lasting a long time or recurring often; habitual. (From the Greek word *khronos*, meaning "time")

   Related Word   **chronically** *adjective*
   Example   Older brothers and sisters are sometimes *chronic* teases.

   2. _____

3. **chronicle** (krŏn′ĭ-kəl) *noun*   A record of facts or events arranged in the order in which they happened.   *verb*   To record in the form of a chronicle. (From the Greek word *khronos*)

   Example   The detailed *chronicle* kept by Magellan helped historians to learn about early voyages of discovery.

   3. _____

4. **chronological** (krŏn′ə-lŏj′ĭ-kəl) *adjective*   Arranged in order of time of occurrence. (From the Greek word *khronos*)

   Related Word   **chronology** *noun*
   Example   The defense attorney asked the witness to give a *chronological* account of the events.

   4. _____

5. **extemporaneous** (ĭk-stĕm′pə-rā′nē-əs) *adjective*   **a.** Made, done, or spoken with little or no preparation.   **b.** Prepared ahead of time but delivered without notes. (From the Latin phrase *ex tempore*, meaning "on the spur of the moment")

Related Word	**extemporaneously** *adverb*
Example	Dr. Colgate's *extemporaneous* introductions of the speakers were more interesting than the speeches themselves.

6. **synchronize** (sĭng′krə-nīz′) *verb*   **a.** To cause to agree in time or rate. **b.** To occur at the same time; operate together. (From the Greek *syn-*, meaning "same," and *khronos*)

Related Word	**synchronization** *noun*
Example	The two groups of hikers *synchronized* their watches and agreed to meet at the camp in five hours.

7. **tempo** (tĕm′pō) *noun*   **a.** The rate of speed at which a musical composition is played.   **b.** The pace or rhythm of an activity. (From the Latin word *tempus*, meaning "time")

Example	The band played music at *tempos* much too fast for dancing.

8. **temporal** (tĕm′pər-əl) *adjective*   **a.** Of time; limited by time. **b.** Concerned with worldly rather than spiritual affairs. (From the Latin word *tempus*)

Example	The delicate wildflower has a *temporal* beauty.

MEMORY CUE: The opposite of *temporal* is *eternal*.

9. **temporary** (tĕm′pə-rĕr′ē) *adjective*   Lasting, used, or enjoyed for only a short time; not permanent.   *noun*   A person who serves for a limited time, such as an office worker. (From the Latin word *tempus*)

Related Word	**temporarily** *adverb*
Example	The candidate established *temporary* headquarters on Burlington Street.

MEMORY CUE: The opposite of *temporary* is *permanent*.

10. **temporize** (tĕm′pə-rīz′) *verb*   To delay in order to gain time or avoid a decision. (From the Latin word *tempus*)

Example	Raphael *temporized* with the builder, hoping to get a more realistic estimate.

5. _____

6. _____

7. _____

8. _____

9. _____

10. _____

EXERCISE 1 WRITING CORRECT WORDS

On the answer line, write the word from the vocabulary list that fits each definition.

1. To delay in order to gain time

2. Lasting for only a short time; not permanent

3. Lasting a long time or recurring

4. Of time; limited by time

5. To cause to agree in time or rate; occur at the same time

6. A record of facts or events in the order of their occurrence

7. The rate of speed of music; the pace of an activity

8. Something out of its proper time in history

9. Arranged in the order of occurrence

10. Done with little or no preparation

1. _____

2. _____

3. _____

4. _____

5. _____

6. _____

7. _____

8. _____

9. _____

10. _____

EXERCISE 2 USING WORDS CORRECTLY

Decide whether the italicized vocabulary word has been used correctly in the sentence. On the answer line, write *Correct* for correct use and *Incorrect* for incorrect use.

1. Reading from a typewritten script, the club president gave an *extemporaneous* speech to welcome the new members.

2. Martha tried hard not to lose her *temporal* with her younger brother.

3. The swimmers practiced long hours in order to *synchronize* their movements.

4. Jordan's *chronic* illness prevented him from participating in sports.

5. Julie always *temporizes* by making immediate decisions.

6. The *temporary* showers did little to relieve the drought.

7. Lucinda hoped that a new *anachronism* would make her job easier.

8. The teacher arranged the students' seats in *chronological* order.

9. The guitarist played at a slow *tempo* to fit the mood of the song.

10. Jennifer wrote a *chronicle* of her trip across the country.

1. _____

2. _____

3. _____

4. _____

5. _____

6. _____

7. _____

8. _____

9. _____

10. _____

EXERCISE 3 CHOOSING THE BEST DEFINITION

For each italicized vocabulary word or related form in the following sentences, write the letter of the best definition on the answer line.

1. The teacher asked us to list our vacation activities in *chronological* order.
    a. from the most recent to the earliest
    b. according to order of occurrence
    c. nonsensical
    d. shortened

1. _____

2. William Butler Yeats wrote many poems about the *temporal* dreams of youth.
   a. dark   **b.** active   **c.** limited by time **d.** positive

2. _____

3. The picture and sound of the movie were not *synchronized*.
   a. operating together   **c.** acceptable
   b. connected with wire   **d.** reviewed

3. _____

4. A suit of armor would be an *anachronism* in today's fashion world.
   a. something of great usefulness   **c.** stylish outfit
   b. something out of its proper time **d.** joke

4. _____

5. Judy's father worried that her *chronic* cough was a symptom of lung disease.
   a. loud   **b.** weak   **c.** occasional   **d.** lasting

5. _____

6. The *tempo* of life in tropical countries is usually much slower than that of life in New England.
   a. love   **b.** pace   **c.** volume   **d.** excitement

6. _____

7. Laura is excellent at speaking *extemporaneously*.
   a. to large groups   **c.** with little or no preparation
   b. dramatically   **d.** after several rehearsals

7. _____

8. Mr. Fiore wrote a *chronicle* of his family's contributions to science and medicine.
   a. poetic version **b.** diary   **c.** postcard   **d.** factual record

8. _____

9. The baby's interest in the new teddy bear was *temporary*.
   a. not permanent   **c.** endless
   b. amazing   **d.** not surprising

9. _____

10. When she talked with the mechanic, Annie *temporized*, since she knew that her mother would arrive at any moment.
    a. thought quickly   **c.** delayed
    b. stuttered   **d.** lost her temper

10. _____

EXERCISE 4 USING DIFFERENT FORMS OF WORDS

Decide which form of the vocabulary word in parentheses best completes the sentence. The form given may be correct. Write your answer on the answer line.

1. _____ of the office clocks eliminated arguments about the length of lunch hours. *(synchronize)*

1. _____

2. Because Tammy was _____ late for the bus, she now sets her alarm clock for an hour earlier. *(chronic)*

2. _____

3. The trio chose a song with a slow _____. *(tempo)*

3. _____

4. The Martins' telephone was _____ out of service. *(temporary)*

4. _____

5. Will knows his material well enough to speak _____ when telling the contest judges about his science project. *(extemporaneous)*

5. _____

6. One of the test questions required students to do a _____. *(chronological)*

6. _____

7. The _____ nature of spring weather is always a disappointment. *(temporal)*

7. _____

8. Quill pens are _____ in the space age. *(anachronism)*   8. _____

9. Caught on the mountain during a storm, the hikers made a _____ shelter   9. _____
   of the pine boughs along the trail. *(temporary)*

10. Over the past two years, Maria has _____ events that are related to the   10. _____
    women's movement. *(chronicle)*

READING COMPREHENSION

Each numbered sentence in the following passage contains an
italicized vocabulary word or related form. After you read the
passage, you will complete an exercise.

FOUR VIEWS OF TIME

Most people take time for
granted. We are aware of the
effect of crossing time zones
when we travel, however.
(1) Then, too, when we read or
watch a movie, we are able to
detect an occasional
anachronism—for example, a
teen-ager in a period film wearing braces. (2) Nevertheless, few
of us are conscious of how time
influences the *tempo* of our lives.
(3) Not until we try to *synchronize* our lives with the customs
of other countries do we begin to
understand how time affects us.

In this country we think of
time as a road that stretches into
the future. (4) The road has certain milestones that, ideally, we
reach in *chronological* order. We
perceive time as a resource—
something that we can spend,
save, or waste. We automatically
think of time as a quantity and
specify how much time is
required to do anything.

Given these ideas about time,
people from the United States
may have difficult adjustments to
make when exposed to the customs and time perceptions of different countries. For example,

American and European missionaries working with the Tiv in
Nigeria found it hard to understand their time sense. The Tiv
see time as a series of small capsules, each with a separate purpose. There is a time for working,
a time for cooking, one for visiting, and so forth. (5) When a person is in one of these *temporal*
capsules, shifting into another is
impossible. In addition, the Tiv
name each day after the product
sold in the local market on that
day. The missionaries simply
could not cope with changes in
the day of the week as they traveled around the country.

In Latin America, on the other
hand, people treat time much
more casually than North
Americans do. (6) A *chronic*
source of difficulty is the time at
which a meeting or event is
scheduled to take place.
(7) Trained by their culture to be
prompt, North American visitors
may have to wait *temporarily* in
offices, theaters, or stations.

Political and business negotia-
tions with people from the
Middle East also require adjustments to different views of time.

American negotiators like to
make appointments well in
advance, but people from the
Middle East tend not to consider
as real anything scheduled more
than a week ahead. Furthermore,
Saudi Arabians, Iranians, and
Egyptians use history as the basis
of making decisions.
(8) Middle Easterners give few
extemporaneous presentations,
for example. (9) Instead, they
chronicle the historical aspects of
a subject and then do a current
analysis. Meeting agendas are
also treated quite differently. In
the United States, if the discussion of a topic has been completed or if no progress can be
made, the meeting is cut short.
(10) Middle Easterners, on the
other hand, *temporize* at length
in order to fill the established
time period.

People's views of time play a
much greater role in their lives
than is immediately apparent.
How they see their past, present,
and future influences their language, customs, expectations,
and attitudes toward others.

READING COMPREHENSION EXERCISE

Each of the following statements corresponds to a numbered sentence in the passage. Each statement contains a blank and is followed by four answer choices. Decide which choice fits best in the blank. The word or phrase that you choose must express roughly the same meaning as the italicized word in the passage. Write the letter of your choice on the answer line.

1. In a book or film, we sometimes spot a(n) _____.
   a. naturally occurring event   c. mistake
   b. event out of its proper time in history   d. joke

2. Few of us are aware of how time influences the _____ of our lives.
   a. excitement   b. pace   c. beginning   d. music

3. As we _____ our lives and the customs of others, we begin to see how time affects us.
   a. separate   c. put on different schedules
   b. compare   d. put on the same schedule

4. Ideally, we reach each milestone of the road in _____ order.
   a. random   b. fixed   c. time   d. seasonal

5. When a person from Nigeria is in one of the _____ capsules, it is impossible to shift into another.
   a. time   b. space   c. revolving   d. previous

6. A _____ source of difficulty is the scheduled time for meetings and events.
   a. excessive   b. recurring   c. occasional   d. practical

7. Visitors from North America may have to wait _____ for appointments or transportation.
   a. for a short time   c. occasionally
   b. for a long time   d. permanently

8. Middle Easterners give few _____ presentations.
   a. interesting   b. lengthy   c. challenging   d. unprepared

9. They _____ the historical aspects of a subject first.
   a. eliminate   b. research   c. record   d. decide

10. Middle Easterners _____ in order to fill the prescribed time period.
    a. delay   b. meet   c. disagree   d. present

1. _____
2. _____
3. _____
4. _____
5. _____
6. _____
7. _____
8. _____
9. _____
10. _____

PRACTICE WITH ANALOGIES

Directions On the answer line, write the vocabulary word or a form of it that completes each analogy.

See pages 26, 52, 78, and 98 for some strategies to use with analogies.

1. Obey is to command as _____ is to order. *(Lesson 29)*

2. Misnomer is to name as _____ is to time. *(Lesson 30)*

3. Biography is to life as _____ is to event. *(Lesson 30)*

4. Pace is to race as _____ is to music. *(Lesson 30)*

5. Impromptu is to planning as _____ is to permanence. *(Lesson 30)*

1. _____
2. _____
3. _____
4. _____
5. _____

READING SKILLS

THE SUFFIX -ABLE

The adjective suffix -able and its two related forms, -ible and -ble, are among the most common and useful suffixes in the English language. The three possible meanings of this suffix and its related forms are as follows.

Suffix Meaning	Word	Definition
1. capable of	readable (read + -able)	capable of being read
2. worthy of or deserving	permissible (permission + -ible)	worthy of being permitted
3. inclined to	impressionable (impression + -able)	inclined to be easily impressed

Sometimes the addition of the suffix -able, -ible, or -ble causes a change in the spelling of the root. For example, when -ible is added to *permission*, the suffix -ion is dropped from the root.

These suffixes come from Latin and often appear in words with Latin roots as well as in words with English roots. For example, the word *audible* has the Latin root -audi, which comes from the Latin word that means "to hear."

EXERCISE USING THE SUFFIX -ABLE

Step 1: Write your definition of the italicized word in each of the following sentences. *Step 2:* Write the dictionary definition of the word. Choose the definition that best fits the way the word is used in the sentence. *Step 3:* Write a sentence of your own in which you use the word correctly.

1. The postal clerk asked if there was anything *breakable* in the package.

   Your Definition _____

   Dictionary Definition _____

   Sentence _____

2. I think Margarita gave a very *believable* performance in the play.

   Your Definition _____

   Dictionary Definition _____

   Sentence _____

3. Putting my savings in a high-interest account made an *appreciable* difference in my bank balance.

Your Definition _____

Dictionary Definition _____

Sentence _____

4. Car dealerships usually offer *comparable* prices.

Your Definition _____

Dictionary Definition _____

Sentence _____

5. The amount of work required in the course is quite *manageable*.

Your Definition _____

Dictionary Definition _____

Sentence _____

6. This meat is so tough that it is barely *edible*. (Clue: -*ed*- is a Latin root meaning "to eat.")

Your Definition _____

Dictionary Definition _____

Sentence _____

7. "How do you expect me to correct your spelling when your writing isn't *legible?*" Trudy asked Laverne. (Clue: -*leg*- is a Latin root meaning "to read.")

Your Definition _____

Dictionary Definition _____

Sentence _____

8. The Diebold twins' plan to build an airplane out of wooden crates wasn't *feasible*. (Clue: the Latin root of the italicized word means "to do.")

Your Definition _____

Dictionary Definition _____

Sentence _____

9. After sitting in traffic for three hours, we were all rather *irritable*.

Your Definition _____

Dictionary Definition _____

Sentence _____

LESSON I	LESSON I	LESSON 2	LESSON 2	LESSON 3	LESSON 3
abridge	gazetteer	academic	exhibit	calligraphy	monogram
browse	glossary	clarify	expound	cartography	monograph
citation	lexicography	confide	ingrained	epigram	seismograph
compendium	phonetics	disclose	sage	graphic	stenography
etymology	syllabication	enlighten	seminar	holography	typography

abridge (ə-brĭj′) *v.* To shorten a piece of writing.

© Great Source

browse (brouz) *v.* To read here and there in written material.

© Great Source

citation (sī-tā′shən) *n.* A quotation from a realiable source.

© Great Source

compendium (kəm-pĕn′dē-əm) *n.* A summary that is short but complete.

© Great Source

etymology (ĕt′ə-mŏl′ə-jē) *n.* The study of the origin and history of words.

© Great Source

gazetteer (găz′ĭ-tîr′) *n.* Section of dictionary with geographical data.

© Great Source

glossary (glô′sə-rē) *n.* A list of words and their definitions.

© Great Source

lexicography (lĕk′sĭ-kŏg′rə-fē) *n.* The process of compiling a dictionary.

© Great Source

phonetics (fə-nĕt′ĭks) *n.* The study of the sounds of language.

© Great Source

syllabication (sĭ-lăb′ĭ-kā′shən) *n.* The division of words into syllables.

© Great Source

academic (ăk′ə-dĕm′ĭk) *adj.* Scholarly; relating to school.

© Great Source

clarify (klăr′ə-fī′) *v.* To make clear or easy to understand.

© Great Source

confide (kən-fīd′) *v.* To share a secret (with) in private.

© Great Source

disclose (dĭ-sklōz′) *v.* To uncover or bring into view.

© Great Source

enlighten (ĕn-līt′n) *v.* To furnish with knowledge; to inform.

© Great Source

exhibit (ĭg-zĭb′ĭt) *v.* To show or display.

© Great Source

expound (ĭk-spound′) *v.* To make a detailed statement.

© Great Source

ingrained (ĭn-grānd′) *adj.* Impressed firmly on the mind.

© Great Source

sage (sāj) *n.* A person respected for wisdom and judgment.

© Great Source

seminar (sĕm′ə-när′) *n.* A conference or a discussion on a topic.

© Great Source

calligraphy (kə-lĭg′rə-fē) *n.* The art of fine handwriting.

© Great Source

cartography (kär-tŏg′rə-fē) *n.* The technique of making maps or charts.

© Great Source

epigram (ĕp′ĭ-grăm′) *n.* A short, clever saying or poem.

© Great Source

graphic (grăf′ĭk) *adj.* Described in a vivid manner.

© Great Source

holography (hō-lŏg′rə-fē) *n.* Laser-image photography.

© Great Source

monogram (mŏn′ə-grăm′) *n.* A design composed of one or more letters.

© Great Source

monograph (mŏn′ə-grăf′) *n.* A scholarly paper on a specialized subject.

© Great Source

seismograph (sīz′mə-grăf′) *n.* A device that monitors earthquakes.

© Great Source

stenography (stə-nŏg′rə-fē) *n.* The art of writing in shorthand.

© Great Source

typography (tī-pŏg′rə-fē) *n.* The appearance of printed material.

© Great Source

LESSON 4 allure	LESSON 5 audition	LESSON 6 image
LESSON 4 fervor	LESSON 5 melodious	LESSON 6 allusion
LESSON 4 avid	LESSON 5 orchestrate	LESSON 6 literary
LESSON 4 jubilant	LESSON 5 anthology	LESSON 6 pseudonym
LESSON 4 exhilarate	LESSON 5 ceramics	LESSON 6 dialogue
LESSON 4 motivate	LESSON 5 classical	LESSON 6 episode
LESSON 4 exult	LESSON 5 palette	LESSON 6 serialize
LESSON 4 zealous	LESSON 5 daub	LESSON 6 pantomime
LESSON 4 fanatic	LESSON 5 medley	LESSON 6 foreshadow
LESSON 4 zest	LESSON 5 texture	LESSON 6 volume

allure (ə-lŏŏr′) *n.* A strong attraction or fascination.
© Great Source

avid (ăv′ĭd) *adj.* Eager; very enthusiastic.
© Great Source

exhilarate (ĭg-zĭl′ə-rāt′) *v.* To make very happy; to invigorate.
© Great Source

exult (ĭg-zŭlt′) *v.* To rejoice greatly.
© Great Source

fanatic (fə-năt′ĭk) *n.* A person with an extreme belief in a cause.
© Great Source

fervor (fûr′vər) *n.* A state of intense emotion.
© Great Source

jubilant (jōō′bə-lənt) *adj.* Full of joy; rejoicing.
© Great Source

motivate (mō′tə-vāt′) *v.* To provide with an incentive.
© Great Source

zealous (zĕl′əs) *adj.* Fiercely dedicated, especially to a cause.
© Great Source

zest (zĕst) *n.* Spirited enjoyment; eagerness.
© Great Source

audition (ô-dĭsh′ən) *n.* A performance to demonstrate ability; a tryout.
© Great Source

ceramics (sə-răm′ĭks) *n.* Objects formed from clay and hardened by heat.
© Great Source

classical (klăs′ĭ-kəl) *adj.* Pertaining to arts of the 1700s or ancient times.
© Great Source

daub (dôb) *v.* To apply paint with crude strokes.
© Great Source

medley (mĕd′lē) *n.* Musical arrangement with a series of melodies.
© Great Source

melodious (mə-lō′dē-əs) *adj.* Pleasant to listen to.
© Great Source

orchestrate (ôr′kĭ-strāt′) *v.* To arrange music for an orchestra.
© Great Source

palette (păl′ĭt) *n.* A thin board on which an artist mixes paints.
© Great Source

pantomime (păn′tə-mīm′) *n.* Acting without speech.
© Great Source

texture (tĕks′chər) *n.* The feel of the surface of an object.
© Great Source

allusion (ə-lōō′zhən) *n.* An indirect reference to something.
© Great Source

anthology (ăn-thŏl′ə-jē) *n.* A collection of writings.
© Great Source

dialogue (dī′ə-lôg′) *n.* Conversation in a book, play, film, or TV show.
© Great Source

episode (ĕp′ĭ-sōd′) *n.* One part or event in a series.
© Great Source

foreshadow (fôr-shăd′ō) *v.* To hint at something before it happens.
© Great Source

image (ĭm′ĭj) *n.* A vivid word picture.
© Great Source

literary (lĭt′ə-rĕr′ē) *adj.* Having to do with literature and writing.
© Great Source

pseudonym (sōōd′n-ĭm′) *n.* A fictional name used by an author.
© Great Source

serialize (sîr′ē-ə-līz′) *v.* To present in a number of parts.
© Great Source

volume (vŏl′yōōm) *n.* A book.
© Great Source

LESSON 7 arboretum	LESSON 7 habitat	LESSON 8 antibiotic	LESSON 8 symbiosis	LESSON 9 audible	LESSON 9 impromptu
LESSON 7 aviary	LESSON 7 nurture	LESSON 8 biopsy	LESSON 8 viable	LESSON 9 coherent	LESSON 9 monologue
LESSON 7 botany	LESSON 7 talon	LESSON 8 biosphere	LESSON 8 vitality	LESSON 9 digress	LESSON 9 oratory
LESSON 7 chameleon	LESSON 7 terrarium	LESSON 8 devitalize	LESSON 8 vivacious	LESSON 9 eloquent	LESSON 9 proclaim
LESSON 7 cultivate	LESSON 7 zoology	LESSON 8 microbe	LESSON 8 vivid	LESSON 9 garble	LESSON 9 verbal

arboterum
(är′bə-rē′təm) n. A park where trees are displayed.

© Great Source

aviary
(ā′vē-ěr′ē) n. A structure for keeping birds in captivity.

© Great Source

botany
(bŏt′n-ē) n. The scientific study of plants.

© Great Source

chameleon
(kə-mēl′yən) n. A lizard whose skin changes color.

© Great Source

cultivate
(kŭl′tə-vāt′) v. To prepare land for growing crops; to raise plants or crops.

© Great Source

habitat
(hăb′ĭ-tăt′) n. The environment in which a plant or animal lives.

© Great Source

nurture
(nûr′chər) v. To nourish; to help grow.

© Great Source

talon
(tăl′ən) n. The claw of a hawk or other bird of prey.

© Great Source

terrarium
(tə-râr′ē-əm) n. A container for plants or animals.

© Great Source

zoology
(zō-ŏl′ə-jē) n. The scientific study of animals.

© Great Source

antibiotic
(ăn′tĭ-bī-ŏt′ĭk) n. A substance that kills harmful bacteria.

© Great Source

biopsy
(bī′ŏp′sē) n. The study of tissue taken from a living body.

© Great Source

biosphere
(bī′ə-sfîr′) n. The life-supporting part of the earth and atmosphere.

© Great Source

devitalize
(dē-vīt′l-īz′) v. To destroy the physical energy of.

© Great Source

microbe
(mī′krōb′) n. A tiny life form, visible only through a microscope.

© Great Source

symbiosis
(sĭm′bē-ō′sĭs) n. A close relationship between organisms.

© Great Source

viable
(vī′ə-bəl) adj. Capable of living and developing.

© Great Source

vitality
(vī-tăl′ĭ-tē) n. Physical or mental energy; vigor.

© Great Source

vivacious
(vĭ-vā′shəs) adj. Full of spirit; lively.

© Great Source

vivid
(vĭv′ĭd) adj. Bright, distinct, and intense.

© Great Source

audible
(ô′də-bəl) adj. Capable of being heard.

© Great Source

coherent
(kō-hîr′ənt) adj. Clearly thought out or expressed.

© Great Source

digress
(dī-grĕs′) v. To stray from the main subject.

© Great Source

eloquent
(ĕl′ə-kwənt) adj. Persuasive and graceful in speaking or writing.

© Great Source

garble
(gär′bəl) v. To mix up or scramble a piece of communication.

© Great Source

impromptu
(ĭm-prŏmp′tōō) adj. Performed without preparation.

© Great Source

monologue
(mŏn′ə-lôg′) n. A long speech made by one person.

© Great Source

oratory
(ôr′ə-tôr′ē) n. The art of speaking in public.

© Great Source

proclaim
(prō-klām′) v. To declare unmistakably.

© Great Source

verbal
(vûr′bəl) adj. Communicated through words.

© Great Source

LESSON 10 affable

LESSON 10 bliss

LESSON 10 compassion

LESSON 10 depress

LESSON 10 dismay

LESSON 10 ecstatic

LESSON 10 endear

LESSON 10 forlorn

LESSON 10 socialize

LESSON 10 somber

LESSON 11 acrophobia

LESSON 11 agoraphobia

LESSON 11 ailurophobia

LESSON 11 Anglophile

LESSON 11 audiophile

LESSON 11 bibliophile

LESSON 11 claustrophobia

LESSON 11 hydrophobia

LESSON 11 xenophobia

LESSON 11 zoophobia

LESSON 12 anticipate

LESSON 12 aspire

LESSON 12 covet

LESSON 12 enviable

LESSON 12 expectation

LESSON 12 inclination

LESSON 12 persevere

LESSON 12 reluctant

LESSON 12 voluntary

LESSON 12 wistful

affable
(ăf′ə-bəl) adj. Easy to speak to.

© Great Source

bliss
(blĭs) n. Extreme joy, leading to contentment.

© Great Source

compassion
(kəm-păsh′ən) n. The feeling of sharing the suffering of another.

© Great Source

depress
(dĭ-prĕs′) v. To lower in spirits or to sadden.

© Great Source

dismay
(dĭs-mā′) v. To fill with great dread or fear.

© Great Source

ecstatic
(ĕk-stăt′ĭk) adj. Overwhelmingly joyful.

© Great Source

endear
(ĕn-dîr′) v. To cause to be well-liked.

© Great Source

forlorn
(fər-lôrn′) adj. Appearing sad, lonely, or abandoned.

© Great Source

socialize
(sō′shə-līz′) v. To associate with others in a friendly way.

© Great Source

somber
(sŏm′bər) adj. Dark; gloomy.

© Great Source

acrophobia
(ăk′rə-fō′bē-ə) n. Intense fear of high places.

© Great Source

agoraphobia
(ăg′ər-ə-fō′bē-ə) n. Strong fear of open places.

© Great Source

ailurophobia
(ī-loor-ə-fō′bē-ə) n. A great fear or hatred of cats.

© Great Source

Anglophile
(ăng′glə-fīl′) n. One who admires English things.

© Great Source

audiophile
(ô′dē-ə-fīl′) n. One keenly interested in recorded sound.

© Great Source

bibliophile
(bĭb′lē-ə-fīl′) n. A devoted collector and preserver of books.

© Great Source

claustrophobia
(klô′strə-fō′bē-ə) n. Strong fear of small or enclosed places.

© Great Source

hydrophobia
(hī′drə-fō′bē-ə) n. Intense fear of water.

© Great Source

xenophobia
(zĕn′ə-fō′bē-ə) n. Fear or hatred of foreigners or strangers.

© Great Source

zoophobia
(zō′ə-fō′bē-ə) n. A strong fear of animals.

© Great Source

anticipate
(ăn-tĭs′ə-pāt′) v. To expect or look forward to.

© Great Source

aspire
(ə-spīr′) v. To have a great ambition.

© Great Source

covet
(kŭv′ĭt) v. To wish for longingly.

© Great Source

enviable
(ĕn′vē-ə-bəl) adj. Admirable enough to be wanted.

© Great Source

expectation
(ĕk′spĕk-tā′shən) n. Belief that a certain thing will occur.

© Great Source

inclination
(ĭn′klə-nā′shən) n. A preference for something.

© Great Source

persevere
(pûr′sə-vîr′) v. To continue in spite of obstacles.

© Great Source

reluctant
(rĭ-lŭk′tənt) adj. Unwilling to do something.

© Great Source

voluntary
(vŏl′ən-tĕr′ē) adj. Acting out of one's own free will.

© Great Source

wistful
(wĭst′fəl) adj. Full of a sad yearning or longing.

© Great Source

LESSON 13	LESSON 13	LESSON 14	LESSON 15	LESSON 15
annihilate	dismantle	compensate	idealize	drab
LESSON 13	LESSON 13	LESSON 14	LESSON 15	LESSON 15
contaminate	extinct	conserve	neutralize	chic
LESSON 13	LESSON 13	LESSON 14	LESSON 15	LESSON 15
corrode	negate	constructive	preservation	garb
LESSON 13	LESSON 13	LESSON 14	LESSON 14	LESSON 15
deplete	rancid	enhance	redeem	becoming
LESSON 13	LESSON 13	LESSON 14	LESSON 14	LESSON 15
deteriorate	squander	enrichment	restore	debonair
LESSON 15	LESSON 15	LESSON 15	LESSON 15	
disheveled	dowdy	rumpled	unsightly	veneer

annihilate (ə-nī′ə-lāt′) *v.* To destroy completely.

© Great Source

contaminate (kən-tăm′ə-nāt′) *v.* To make impure by contact or mixture.

© Great Source

corrode (kə-rōd′) *v.* To wear away or dissolve through chemical action.

© Great Source

deplete (dǐ-plēt′) *v.* To use up or reduce in quantity.

© Great Source

deteriorate (dǐ-tîr′ē-ə-rāt′) *v.* To become worse.

© Great Source

dismantle (dǐs-măn′tl) *v.* To take apart or tear down.

© Great Source

extinct (ǐk-stǐngkt′) *adj.* No longer existing or living.

© Great Source

negate (nǐ-gāt′) *v.* To make ineffective or worthless.

© Great Source

rancid (răn′sǐd) *adj.* Smelling or tasing like spoiled oils or fats.

© Great Source

squander (skwǒn′dər) *v.* To waste.

© Great Source

compensate (kŏm′pən-sāt′) *v.* To make up for or offset.

© Great Source

conserve (kən-sûrv′) *v.* To protect from loss or being used up.

© Great Source

constructive (kən-strŭk′tĭv) *adj.* Serving a useful purpose.

© Great Source

enhance (ĕn-hăns′) *v.* To add to or increase in value or beauty.

© Great Source

enrichment (ĕn-rĭch′mənt) *n.* Making an activity more meaningful.

© Great Source

idealize (ī-dē′ə-līz′) *v.* To regard as a model of excellence.

© Great Source

neutralize (noō′trə-līz′) *v.* To cancel or counteract the effect.

© Great Source

preservation (prĕz′ər-vā′shən) *n.* The act of guarding from injury.

© Great Source

redeem (rǐ-dēm′) *v.* To turn in for merchandise or money.

© Great Source

restore (rǐ-stôr′) *v.* To bring back into existence.

© Great Source

becoming (bǐ-kŭm′ĭng) *adj.* Attractive or suitable.

© Great Source

chic (shēk) *adj.* Stylish or fashionable.

© Great Source

debonair (dĕb′ə-nâr′) *adj.* Sophisticated in a lively, gracious manner.

© Great Source

disheveled (dǐ-shĕv′əld) *adj.* Untidy or messy.

© Great Source

dowdy (dou′dē) *adj.* Shabby and lacking in style.

© Great Source

drab (drăb) *adj.* Faded and dull in appearance.

© Great Source

garb (gärb) *n.* Clothing; clothing for a particular occasion.

© Great Source

rumpled (rŭm′pəld) *adj.* Wrinkled or creased.

© Great Source

unsightly (ŭn-sīt′lē) *adj.* Ugly or unpleasant to look at.

© Great Source

veneer (və-nîr′) *n.* An appearance that gives a favorable but false impression.

© Great Source

LESSON 16 amble	LESSON 16 mobilize	LESSON 17 affluent	LESSON 17 flume	LESSON 18 adjacent	LESSON 18 engulf
LESSON 16 convert	LESSON 16 modification	LESSON 17 deflect	LESSON 18 align	LESSON 18 indent	
LESSON 16 dawdle	LESSON 16 quiver	LESSON 17 flex	LESSON 17 influential	LESSON 18 brink	LESSON 18 solidify
LESSON 16 distort	LESSON 16 recede	LESSON 17 fluctuate	LESSON 17 influx	LESSON 18 contour	LESSON 18 symmetry
LESSON 16 itinerary	LESSON 16 traverse	LESSON 17 fluid	LESSON 17 reflex	LESSON 18 dimension	LESSON 18 tangible

amble (ăm′bəl) *v.* To walk slowly or leisurely.
© Great Source

convert (kən-vûrt′) *v.* To change in form, character, or function.
© Great Source

dawdle (dôd′l) *v.* To take more time than necessary.
© Great Source

distort (dĭ-stôrt′) *v.* To change the shape of something by twisting it.
© Great Source

itinerary (ī-tĭn′ə-rĕr′ē) *n.* A detailed plan for a proposed journey.
© Great Source

mobilize (mō′bə-līz′) *v.* To assemble for a particular purpose.
© Great Source

modification (mŏd′ə-fĭ-kā′shən) *n.* A change or adjustment.
© Great Source

quiver (kwĭv′ər) *v.* To shake with a slight but rapid motion.
© Great Source

recede (rĭ-sēd′) *v.* To move back or away from.
© Great Source

traverse (trə-vûrs′) *v.* To travel across, over, or through.
© Great Source

affluent (ăf′lo͞o-ənt) *adj.* Rich; wealthy.
© Great Source

deflect (dĭ-flĕkt′) *v.* To cause to turn aside.
© Great Source

flex (flĕks) *v.* To bend or contract.
© Great Source

fluctuate (flŭk′cho͞o-āt′) *v.* To change back and forth or vary greatly.
© Great Source

fluid (flo͞o′ĭd) *n.* A substance that flows easily.
© Great Source

flume (flo͞om) *n.* A gap through which a stream of water flows.
© Great Source

inflexible (ĭn-flĕk′sə-bəl) *adj.* Not able to change or be persuaded.
© Great Source

influential (ĭn′flo͞o-ĕn′shəl) *adj.* Having power or importance.
© Great Source

influx (ĭn′flŭks′) *n.* A steady stream of things or people flowing in.
© Great Source

reflex (rē′flĕks′) *n.* An instinctive or automatic physical response.
© Great Source

adjacent (ə-jā′sənt) *adj.* Next to or close to.
© Great Source

align (ə-līn′) *v.* To place in line.
© Great Source

brink (brĭngk) *n.* An edge or border.
© Great Source

contour (kŏn′to͝or′) *n.* The outline of a shape or figure.
© Great Source

dimension (dĭ-mĕn′shən) *n.* A measure of width, height, or length.
© Great Source

engulf (ĕn-gŭlf′) *v.* To surround or enclose.
© Great Source

indent (ĭn-dĕnt′) *v.* To make dents or impressions in.
© Great Source

solidify (sə-lĭd′ə-fī′) *v.* To make hard or compact.
© Great Source

symmetry (sĭm′ĭ-trē) *n.* A relationship of balance between objects.
© Great Source

tangible (tăn′jə-bəl) *adj.* Capable of being touched.
© Great Source

LESSON 19 aperture	LESSON 19 generator	LESSON 20 applicable	LESSON 20 obsolete	LESSON 21 inventory
LESSON 19 apparatus	LESSON 19 laser	LESSON 20 expedient	LESSON 21 barter	LESSON 21 merger
LESSON 19 centrifuge	LESSON 19 mechanism	LESSON 20 extraneous	LESSON 20 opportune	LESSON 21 commerce	LESSON 21 monopoly
LESSON 19 component	LESSON 19 prism	LESSON 20 functional	LESSON 20 pragmatic	LESSON 21 franchise	LESSON 21 transaction
LESSON 19 gauge	LESSON 19 treadmill	LESSON 20 futile	LESSON 20 relevant	LESSON 20 utilitarian	LESSON 21 inflation	LESSON 21 vender

aperture	(ăp′ər-chər) *n.* A hole, gap, slit, or other opening. © Great Source
apparatus	(ăp′ə-rā′təs) *n.* Tools that are put to a specific use. © Great Source
centrifuge	(sĕn′trə-fyōōj′) *n.* A machine used to separate substances. © Great Source
component	(kəm-pō′nənt) *n.* A part that with others makes up a whole. © Great Source
gauge	(gāj) *n.* A tool used for making measurements. © Great Source
generator	(jĕn′ə-rā′tər) *n.* A machine that changes mechanical energy. © Great Source
laser	(lā′zər) *n.* A device producing an intense beam of light. © Great Source
mechanism	(mĕk′ə-nĭz′əm) *n.* Arrangement of parts in a machine. © Great Source
prism	(prĭz′əm) *n.* Piece of transparent material that bends light. © Great Source
treadmill	(trĕd′mĭl′) *n.* A machine with a wheel or revolving belt. © Great Source
applicable	(ăp′lĭ-kə-bəl) *adj.* Appropriate; suitable. © Great Source
expedient	(ĭk-spē′dē-ənt) *adj.* In one's own interest. © Great Source
extraneous	(ĭk-strā′nē-əs) *adj.* Not essential or related. © Great Source
functional	(fŭngk′shə-nəl) *adj.* Able to operate or work. © Great Source
futile	(fyōōt′l) *adj.* Not successful; without result or effect. © Great Source
obsolete	(ŏb′sə-lēt′) *adj.* Not used anymore; old-fashioned. © Great Source
opportune	(ŏp′ər-tōōn′) *adj.* Well timed. © Great Source
pragmatic	(prăg-măt′ĭk) *adj.* Concerned with results. © Great Source
relevant	(rĕl′ə-vənt) *adj.* Related to the matter at hand. © Great Source
utilitarian	(yōō-tĭl′ĭ-târ′ē-ən) *adj.* Useful. © Great Source
backlog	(băk′lôg′) *n.* A quantity of unfinished work or unfilled orders. © Great Source
barter	(bär′tər) *v.* To trade goods or services without exchanging money. © Great Source
commerce	(kŏm′ərs) *n.* The buying and selling of merchandise. © Great Source
franchise	(frăn′chīz′) *n.* The right granted to sell a product or service. © Great Source
inflation	(ĭn-flā′shən) *n.* An expansion or increase. © Great Source
inventory	(ĭn′vən-tôr′ē) *n.* A quantity of articles in stock. © Great Source
merger	(mûr′jər) *n.* A process by which two or more groups join to make one. © Great Source
monopoly	(mə-nŏp′ə-lē) *n.* Complete control without competition. © Great Source
transaction	(trăn-săk′shən) *n.* A business activity. © Great Source
vender	(vĕn′dər) *n.* A person whose business is selling a product or service. © Great Source

LESSON 22 alliance	LESSON 22 collaborate	LESSON 22 colleague	LESSON 22 conspire	LESSON 22 federation
LESSON 22 harmony	LESSON 22 interact	LESSON 22 populous	LESSON 22 unanimous	LESSON 22 uniform
LESSON 23 discard	LESSON 23 dispel	LESSON 23 disperse	LESSON 23 displace	LESSON 23 disqualify
LESSON 23 evict	LESSON 23 excise	LESSON 23 exile	LESSON 23 extinguish	LESSON 23 purge
LESSON 24 commotion	LESSON 24 demotion	LESSON 24 emotional	LESSON 24 immobilize	LESSON 24 mobility
LESSON 24 momentary	LESSON 24 momentum	LESSON 24 motive	LESSON 24 promotion	LESSON 24 remote

alliance (ə-lī′əns) *n.* A formal agreement or union.

© Great Source

collaborate (kə-lăb′ə-rāt) *v.* To work together.

© Great Source

colleague (kŏl′ēg′) *n.* A member of one's profession.

© Great Source

conspire (kən-spīr′) *v.* To plan with others an illegal act.

© Great Source

federation (fĕd′ə-rā′shən) *n.* An association, usually permanent.

© Great Source

---

harmony (här′mə-nē) *n.* Agreement of opinion or feeling.

© Great Source

interact (ĭn′tər-ăkt′) *v.* To affect one another.

© Great Source

populous (pŏp′yə-ləs) *adj.* Having many people; thickly settled.

© Great Source

unanimous (yōō-năn′ə-məs) *adj.* Sharing the same opinion.

© Great Source

uniform (yōō′nə-fôrm′) *adj.* Having the same characteristics.

© Great Source

---

discard (dĭs-kärd′) *v.* To throw away; to reject.

© Great Source

dispel (dĭ-spĕl′) *v.* To drive away; to rid one's mind of an idea.

© Great Source

disperse (dĭ-spûrs′) *v.* To scatter; to send off in various directions.

© Great Source

displace (dĭs-plās′) *v.* To remove or put out of the usual place.

© Great Source

disqualify (dĭs-kwŏl′ə-fī′) *v.* To declare unable or unfit to participate.

© Great Source

---

evict (ĭ-vĭkt′) *v.* To force out; to eject.

© Great Source

excise (ĭk-sīz′) *v.* To remove or cut off.

© Great Source

exile (ĕg′zīl′) *n.* The condition of being forced to leave one's country.

© Great Source

extinguish (ĭk-stĭng′gwĭsh) *v.* To put out; to put an end to.

© Great Source

purge (pûrj) *v.* To rid of an element that is not pure.

© Great Source

---

commotion (kə-mō′shən) *n.* A violent motion or disturbance.

© Great Source

demotion (dĭ-mō′shən) *n.* A lowering in rank or grade.

© Great Source

emotional (ĭ-mō′shə-nəl) *adj.* Showing strong feelings.

© Great Source

immobilize (ĭ-mō′bə-līz′) *v.* To make motionless.

© Great Source

mobility (mō-bĭl′ĭ-tē) *n.* The ability to move.

© Great Source

---

momentary (mō′mən-tĕr′ē) *adj.* Lasting for only a short while.

© Great Source

momentum (mō-mĕn′təm) *n.* Force or speed of motion.

© Great Source

motive (mō′tĭv) *n.* A reason or emotion making one act in a certain way.

© Great Source

promotion (prə-mō′shən) *n.* Advancement to a higher position.

© Great Source

remote (rĭ-mōt′) *adj.* Far away; distant in time or space.

© Great Source

LESSON 25	LESSON 25	LESSON 25	LESSON 25	LESSON 25	LESSON 25
dignity	formal	hospitable	morality	suave	nicety
LESSON 26	LESSON 25	LESSON 25	LESSON 25	LESSON 25	LESSON 25
propriety	puritanical	refinement	conviction	suave	tact
LESSON 26	LESSON 26	LESSON 26	LESSON 26	LESSON 26	LESSON 26
analyze	comprehend	contemplate	conviction	engross	
LESSON 26	LESSON 26	LESSON 26	LESSON 26	LESSON 26	LESSON 26
intellect	intuition	logical	lucid	profound	
LESSON 27	LESSON 27	LESSON 27	LESSON 27	LESSON 27	LESSON 27
buttress	defensible	durable	fortify	invigorate	
LESSON 27	LESSON 27	LESSON 27	LESSON 27	LESSON 27	LESSON 27
outpost	potent	quell	resistant	valor	

dignity (dĭg'nĭ-tē) n. Pride and self-respect.	propriety (prə-prī'ĭ-tē) n. The quality of being suitable.	analyze (ăn'ə-līz') v. To separate into parts in order to understand.	intellect (ĭn'tl-ĕkt') n. The ability to think and understand.	buttress (bŭt'rĭs) n. A support or reinforcement.	outpost (out'pōst') n. A distant, isolated settlement.
© Great Source	© Great Source	© Great Source	© Great Source	© Great Source	© Great Source
formal (fôr'məl) adj. Following accepted requirements; not casual.	puritanical (pyŏŏr'ĭ-tăn'ĭ-kəl) adj. Strict in morals or behavior.	comprehend (kŏm'prĭ-hĕnd') v. To understand in depth; to grasp.	intuition (ĭn'tōō-ĭsh'ən) n. A sense or feeling; instinctive knowledge.	defensible (dĭ-fĕn'sə-bəl) adj. Capable of being proved reasonable.	potent (pōt'nt) adj. Strong; powerful.
© Great Source	© Great Source	© Great Source	© Great Source	© Great Source	© Great Source
hospitable (hŏs'pĭ-tə-bəl) adj. Treating guests graciously.	refinement (rĭ-fīn'mənt) n. Polish in manner or expression.	contemplate (kŏn'təm-plāt') v. To consider.	logical (lŏj'ĭ-kəl) adj. Clearly thought out.	durable (dŏŏr'ə-bəl) adj. Long-lasting.	quell (kwĕl) v. To quiet or pacify; to put down forcibly.
© Great Source	© Great Source	© Great Source	© Great Source	© Great Source	© Great Source
morality (mə-răl'ĭ-tē) n. Rules of right and wrong.	suave (swäv) adj. Smoothly agreeable or polite.	conviction (kən-vĭk'shən) n. Strong belief or opinion.	lucid (lōō'sĭd) adj. Clear; easy to understand.	fortify (fôr'tə-fī') v. To strengthen; make secure.	resistant (rĭ-zĭs'tənt) adj. Tending to oppose.
© Great Source	© Great Source	© Great Source	© Great Source	© Great Source	© Great Source
nicety (nī'sĭ-tē) n. A fine point or elegant feature.	tact (tăkt) n. Skill in handling difficult situations.	engross (ĕn-grōs') v. To occupy the mind fully.	profound (prə-found') adj. Deep; thorough.	invigorate (ĭn-vĭg'ə-rāt') v. To give energy to; to stimulate.	valor (văl'ər) n. Courage or boldness.
© Great Source	© Great Source	© Great Source	© Great Source	© Great Source	© Great Source

LESSON 28	LESSON 28	LESSON 28	LESSON 28	LESSON 28
belittle	envelop	exploit	facilitate	forsake
LESSON 28	LESSON 28	LESSON 28	LESSON 28	LESSON 28
impair	inflict	inhumane	rehabilitate	rejuvenate
LESSON 29	LESSON 29	LESSON 29	LESSON 29	LESSON 29
acknowledge	advocate	comply	concur	confirm
LESSON 29	LESSON 29	LESSON 29	LESSON 29	LESSON 29
conform	justify	sanction	sustain	underlie
LESSON 30	LESSON 30	LESSON 30	LESSON 30	LESSON 30
anachronism	chronic	chronicle	chronological	extemporaneous
LESSON 30	LESSON 30	LESSON 30	LESSON 30	LESSON 30
synchronize	tempo	temporal	temporary	temporize

belittle (bĭ-lĭt'l) *v.* To cause to seem small or unimportant.
© Great Source

envelop (ĕn-vĕl'əp) *v.* To surround; to enclose or wrap.
© Great Source

exploit (ĭk-sploit') *v.* To take advantage of; utilize.
© Great Source

facilitate (fə-sĭl'ĭ-tāt) *v.* To make easier.
© Great Source

forsake (fôr-sāk') *v.* To abandon.
© Great Source

impair (ĭm-pâr') *v.* To make worse; to weaken; to damage.
© Great Source

inflict (ĭn-flĭkt') *v.* To impose something unpleasant.
© Great Source

inhumane (ĭn'hyōō-mān') *adj.* Brutal; lacking compassion.
© Great Source

rehabilitate (rē'hə-bĭl'ĭ-tāt') *v.* To restore to a former state.
© Great Source

rejuvenate (rĭ-jōō'və-nāt') *v.* To restore to a youthful condition.
© Great Source

acknowledge (ăk-nŏl'ĭj) *v.* To admit as true; recognize.
© Great Source

advocate (ăd'və-kāt') *v.* To speak or write in favor of.
© Great Source

comply (kəm-plī') *v.* To obey another's command or request.
© Great Source

concur (kən-kûr') *v.* To agree.
© Great Source

confirm (kən-fûrm') *v.* To verify; to prove to be true.
© Great Source

conform (kən-fôrm') *v.* To follow an established standard.
© Great Source

justify (jŭs'tə-fī') *v.* To demonstrate to be right, fair, or useful.
© Great Source

sanction (săngk'shən) *v.* To permit, approve, or authorize.
© Great Source

sustain (sə-stān') *v.* To maintain, prolong; to endure.
© Great Source

underlie (ŭn'dər-lī') *v.* To be the support or basis of.
© Great Source

anachronism (ə-năk'rə-nĭz'əm) *n.* Something out of its proper time.
© Great Source

chronic (krŏn'ĭk) *adj.* Long-lasting; recurrent; habitual.
© Great Source

chronicle (krŏn'ĭ-kəl) *n.* A record of facts or events in order of occurrence.
© Great Source

chronological (krŏn'ə-lŏj'ĭ-kəl) *adj.* In order of occurrence.
© Great Source

extemporaneous (ĭk-stĕm'pə-rā'nē-əs) *adj.* Spoken with little preparation.
© Great Source

synchronize (sĭng'krə-nīz') *v.* To cause to agree in time or rate.
© Great Source

tempo (tĕm'pō) *n.* The rate of speed of a musical composition; rhythm.
© Great Source

temporal (tĕm'pər-əl) *adj.* Limited by time; concerning earthly things.
© Great Source

temporary (tĕm'pə-rĕr'ē) *adj.* Lasting only a short time.
© Great Source

temporize (tĕm'pə-rīz') *v.* To delay to gain time; to stall.
© Great Source